MICROLEARNING IN THE DIGITAL AGE

Microlearning in the Digital Age explores the design and implementation of bite-sized learning and training in technology-enabled environments. Grounded in research-based best practices and a robust, eight-dimensional framework, this book applies the latest developments in mobile learning, social media, and instructional/multimedia design to one of today's most innovative and accessible content delivery systems. Featuring experts from higher education, information technology, digital gaming, corporate, and other contexts, this comprehensive guide will prepare graduate students, researchers, and professionals of instructional design, e-learning, and distance education to develop engaging, cost-effective microlearning systems.

Joseph Rene Corbeil is Professor of Educational Technology at The University of Texas Rio Grande Valley, USA.

Badrul H. Khan is Founder of McWeadon Education, a professional development institution. An e-learning and instructional design consultant, he previously served as Founding Director of the Educational Technology Leadership (ETL) graduate cohort program at The George Washington University, USA.

Maria Elena Corbeil is Professor of Educational Technology at The University of Texas Rio Grande Valley, USA.

MICROLEARNING IN THE DIGITAL AGE

The Design and Delivery of Learning in Snippets

Edited by Joseph Rene Corbeil, Badrul H. Khan, and Maria Elena Corbeil

Routledge
Taylor & Francis Group

NEW YORK AND LONDON

First published 2021
by Routledge
605 Third Avenue, New York, NY 10158

and by Routledge
2 Park Square, Milton Park, Abingdon, Oxon OX14 4RN

Routledge is an imprint of the Taylor & Francis Group, an informa business

© 2021 Taylor & Francis

The right of Joseph Rene Corbeil, Badrul H. Khan, and Maria Elena Corbeil
to be identified as the authors of the editorial material, and of the authors for
their individual chapters, has been asserted in accordance with sections 77 and
78 of the Copyright, Designs and Patents Act 1988.

Library of Congress Cataloging-in-Publication Data
A catalog record for this title has been requested

ISBN: 978-0-367-42080-2 (hbk)
ISBN: 978-0-367-41051-3 (pbk)
ISBN: 978-0-367-82162-3 (ebk)

Typeset in Bembo
by Taylor & Francis Books

I dedicate this book to Dr. Maria Elena Corbeil, my wife and professional collaborator, to our children, Tina and Joseph Corbeil, and to our wonderful grandchildren, Fenton and Isaaic, and Jacob Corbeil.

Joseph Rene Corbeil

I dedicate this book to my parents, Antonio and Maria Elena Valdes for their lifelong love and support, my husband Dr. Joseph Rene Corbeil, and our nephews Nicolas, Roberto, and Antonio Suarez.

Together, we dedicate this book to learners globally.

Maria Elena Corbeil

I dedicate this book to my late parents, Mr. Lokman Khan Sherwani and Mrs. Shabnom Khanam Sherwani of Khan Manzil, Pathantooly, Chittagong, Bangladesh.

Badrul H. Khan

CONTENTS

ACKNOWLEDGEMENTS

Isaac Newton said, "If I have seen further, it is by standing on the shoulders of giants." We are grateful to have stood on the shoulders of the pioneers of microlearning, the team at Routledge, the contributing authors, the editorial review board members, and many others. The editors wish to acknowledge and express their sincere and heartfelt appreciation to everyone who participated in this project.

Thank you to Daniel Schwartz at Routledge for his commitment to this project and his, and the publishing team's, ongoing support.

We would like to offer a very special thank you to Dr. Karl M. Kapp for writing the Foreword. It was an honor to have him participate in this project.

We acknowledge our students, past and present, who motivate and challenge us every day to learn more, offer more, and do more.

We also thank Tina Corbeil for designing the cover art, and gratefully recognize the contributions of the editorial review board members for reviewing and providing thoughtful feedback for each chapter.

Lastly, we would like to recognize and thank the contributing authors for making this project possible. They invested many hours of reflection, writing, and editing to contribute their experience and expertise in e-learning, specifically in the development and application of microlearning in a variety of fields and environments.

It is our sincerest hope that this book will serve as a guide for educational policy makers, administrators, faculty, teachers, and IT personnel interested in the thoughtful and responsible implementation of microlearning in all levels of education, business, healthcare, IT, and other industries.

ABOUT THE EDITORS

Joseph Rene Corbeil is Professor of Educational Technology at The University of Texas Rio Grande Valley. He earned his doctoral degree in Education-Curriculum and Instruction with an emphasis on Instructional Technology from the University of Houston, and a Master of Education in Educational Technology from The University of Texas at Brownsville. For over 25 years, he has developed and taught fully web-based undergraduate, graduate, and doctoral courses in educational technology, and developed the first fully online undergraduate specialization in Educational Technology in Texas. He has published articles in numerous journals and contributed chapters to books on innovations in e-learning and distance education. He has earned numerous awards, including the *2019* Association for Educational Communications & Technology (AECT) *Outstanding Book Award* (Systems Thinking & Change Division), the *2019 and 2016 Online Learning Consortium (OLC) Effective Practice Award*, the *2011 Selected Papers for the International Conference on College Teaching and Learning, the 2007 EDUCAUSE Quarterly Contribution of the Year Award*. In 2012, his contributions to teaching excellence were recognized with the University of Texas System *Regents' Outstanding Teaching Award*. In 2020, his contributions to the field were recognized by the International Association of Computer Information Systems' *Computer Educator of the Year* award.

Badrul H. Khan, Ph.D. is a world-renowned speaker, author, educator, and consultant in the field of e-learning and educational technology. Professor Khan has the credit of first coining the phrase web-based instruction and popularizing the concept through his 1997 best-selling *Web-Based Instruction* book, which paved the way for the new field of e-learning. Known as the founder of modern e-learning, Dr. Khan has been honored with many awards and worldwide acclamation throughout his career. In recognition of his unique contribution to the field of e-learning coupled with his services to worldwide e-learning communities, Egyptian E-Learning University Council on August 13, 2012 appointed Dr. Badrul Khan as an honorary distinguished professor of e-learning. Professor Khan is a United States Distance Learning Association (USDLA) 2015 Hall of Fame Inductee. He is recognized as one of the Leaders in Open and Distance Education in North America. He is Founder of GyanBahan (GyanBahan.com), the Knowledge Carrier – a practical application of competency-based lifelong e-learning. He authored 12 books in e-learning and one of his managing e-learning books has been translated into 20 languages. He served as the founding Director of the Educational Technology Leadership (ETL) graduate cohort program at The George Washington University. He also served as the founding Director of the Educational Technology (ET) graduate program at the University of Texas, Brownsville. His personal Website: BadrulKhan.com

Maria Elena Corbeil, Professor of Educational Technology at The University of Texas Rio Grande Valley (UTRGV), has a doctoral degree in Education in Curriculum and Instruction from the University of Houston, a Master of Education from The University of Texas at Brownsville, and a graduate certificate in online teaching and learning from the University of Florida. For over 20 years, she has developed and taught fully online undergraduate, graduate, and doctoral Educational Technology courses. She has numerous publications on e-learning and innovations in educational technology, and has been honored with several awards, such as the *2019* Association for Educational Communications & Technology (AECT) *Outstanding Book Award* (Systems Thinking & Change Division), the *2019 and 2016 Online Learning Consortium (OLC) Effective Practice Award,* the International Association for Computer Information Systems' *Ben Bauman Teaching Excellent Award,* and in 2018, she was awarded the UTRGV *Faculty Excellence Award in Service.*

CONTRIBUTOR BIOGRAPHIES

Joseph Rene Corbeil is Professor of Educational Technology at The University of Texas Rio Grande Valley. He earned his doctoral degree in Education-Curriculum and Instruction with an emphasis on Instructional Technology from the University of Houston, and a Master of Education in Educational Technology from The University of Texas at Brownsville. For over 25 years, he has developed and taught fully web-based undergraduate, graduate, and doctoral courses in educational technology, and developed the first fully online undergraduate specialization in Educational Technology in Texas. He has published articles in numerous journals and contributed chapters to books on innovations in e-learning and distance education. He has earned numerous awards, including the *2019* Association for Educational Communications & Technology (AECT) *Outstanding Book Award* (Systems Thinking & Change Division), the *2019 and 2016 Online Learning Consortium (OLC) Effective Practice Award,* the *2011 Selected Papers for the International Conference on College Teaching and Learning, the 2007 EDUCAUSE Quarterly Contribution of the Year Award.* In 2012, his contributions to teaching excellence were recognized with the University of Texas System *Regents' Outstanding Teaching Award.* In 2020, his contributions to the field were recognized by the International Association of Computer Information Systems' *Computer Educator of the Year* award.

Maria Elena Corbeil, Professor of Educational Technology at The University of Texas Rio Grande Valley (UTRGV), has a doctoral degree in Education in Curriculum and Instruction from the University of Houston, a Master of Education from The University of Texas at Brownsville, and a graduate certificate in online teaching and learning from the University of Florida. For over 20 years, she has developed and taught fully online undergraduate, graduate, and doctoral

Educational Technology courses. She has numerous publications on e-learning and innovations in educational technology, and has been honored with several awards, such as the *2019* Association for Educational Communications & Technology (AECT) *Outstanding Book Award* (Systems Thinking & Change Division), the *2019 and 2016 Online Learning Consortium (OLC) Effective Practice Award,* the International Association for Computer Information Systems' *Ben Bauman Teaching Excellent Award,* and in 2018, she was awarded the UTRGV *Faculty Excellence Award in Service.*

Caroline M. Crawford, Ed.D., is a Professor of Instructional Design and Technology at the University of Houston-Clear Lake in Houston, Texas, U.S.A. At this point in Dr. Crawford's professional career, her main areas of interest focus upon communities of learning and practice within real world spaces, instructional design, learning theory implementation, and the appropriate and successful integration of technologies into the learning environment; the learning environment may be envisioned as face-to-face, blended, online (virtual or text-driven) environments, as well as microlearning and micro-assist supports. Dr. Crawford's contributions have been recognized with several awards, including the 2009 University of Houston-Clear Lake Outstanding Professor Award, and being named 2010 Distinguished Fellow in The Academy of Ubiquitous Communication Educators (AUCE).

Vanessa P. Dennen is a Professor of Instructional Systems & Learning Technologies at Florida State University and the Co-editor in Chief of *The Internet and Higher Education.* Her research focuses on emerging technologies for formal and informal learning, networked knowledge activities, and the development of identity and community in social media environments. Vanessa has authored more than 75 journal articles and book chapters, which have appeared in publications such as Instructional Science; Distance Education; Computers in Human Behavior; Educational Research Technology & Development, and Teachers College Record. More information can be found at http://vanessadennen.com

Renee Dyer is a librarian, professional learning designer, webmaster, and researcher in K-12, instructional technology, library sciences, and professional learning. Renee is passionate about equitable access to information and resources for all learners. She is a doctoral candidate in Instructional Systems Design and Technology at Sam Houston State University. She was named the 2020 doctoral student of the year for the College of Education. Renee delivers professional learning throughout the country and serves as the Texas Association of School Librarians Webmaster.

Rita Fennelly-Atkinson is an instructional designer, technology coach, and researcher in K-12, higher education, and the non-profit sector. She is passionate about ensuring equitable access to learning through inclusive instructional design and is currently studying accessibility issues in higher education for her dissertation. She serves as a member of the Verizon Innovative Learning Schools Advisory Council and as Sam Houston State University's student representative on the Texas Higher Education Coordinating Board's Learning Technology Advisory Committee.

Chris Gamrat, Ph.D. is an instructional designer for the College of Information Sciences and Technology at Penn State University. Chris served as the principal investigator for a seed grant that initiated the Penn State badging platform. His publications include five peer-reviewed papers, two book chapters, and numerous national conference presentations and posters. His areas of interest include lifelong learning, professional learning, and inclusive pedagogy.

Elizabeth Gross is the Assistant Director for Digital Education in Penn State's College of Agricultural Sciences. She leads the online learning development teams for the college's academic programs and also for Penn State Extension, which focuses on training, workforce development, and continuing education in agriculture. Elizabeth delivers trainings and presentations on online learning techniques and pedagogy, video-based learning, and teaching with technology. She earned her Ph.D. in English from Penn State University and also had a background in software training and technical writing. Her interests include microcredentials and alternative credentials, workforce development training, and the intersections between academic and PCO (professional, continuing, and online) education.

Darci Hall has been working in the field of Organization Development and Workforce Performance for 25 years for several Fortune 500 companies and has created over 20 programs in leadership, professional development, and technical curriculum. She is the Chief Learning Officer (CLO) of Providence St. Joseph Health where she is responsible for setting the strategic direction for the learning experiences of the 120,000+ member workforce. She ensures that the learner-centric solutions her team develops enable workforce excellence now and into the future through strategic delivery and implementation of innovative technologies and design. Previously as Senior VP (Global Learning Services) of Xerox, Darci developed, grew, and delivered high impact learning solutions for Xerox's clients and its internal workforce through expanding their learning services via strategic acquisitions and global partnerships. She has presented at several conferences on digital learning and authored columns for *Training Magazine* and *ATD*.

Johnny Hamilton is a thought leader, author, and full-stack learning designer who has led projects that have resulted in over a dozen industry awards in corporate learning innovation from Brandon Hall, BIG Innovation, eLearning Magazine, and the American Business Association. He is the Senior Design and

Innovation Consultant at Providence St. Joseph Health where he has co-launched and architected the learning experiences of multiple innovative learning platforms that incorporate cloud technologies, adaptive learning, Artificial Intelligence, Augmented Reality, and more to 120,000+ workers. He is also the co-founder and Creative Director of 2it Education Solutions LLC, where he is the Editor of the Medium publication titled, *The Future of Workplace Learning*, a podcaster of *The Future of Workplace Learning*, as well as author of six university accredited courses in technology-enabled teaching.

Theresa Hamilton has been an educator for over 20 years in many capacities including a teacher, mentor, instructional coach and trainer, content developer, and instructional designer. She is the founder and Director of Pedagogics LLC, where she promotes mindful learning through consulting, coaching, and content development. She is also a Senior Instructional Designer for Ingenuiti where she develops the learning design and core pedagogy content for international clients. During her career, she has authored multiple university accredited courses, co-developed several catalogs of courses and resources (including over 50 online courses), and written blogs.

Pamela S. Hogle owns a writing and editing business that focuses on e-learning technology and trends. Her areas of specialization include emerging technologies, microlearning, and accessible digital content. Pamela is an experienced journalist, technical writer, and e-learning content developer who has worked in Israel and the United States. She holds master's degrees in journalism and human-canine life sciences and is a former writer and editor for *Learning Solutions,* the online publication of *The Learning Guild.*

Tracy King, as Chief Learning Strategist and CEO of InspirEd, leverages her more than 20 years in workforce development consulting with organizations on education strategy and learning design. Tracy is the author of Competitive Advantage, and she advises on how to grow reliably profitable and sustainable continuing education programs that transform learners. Tracy specializes in the intersection of learning science and technology. She's a thought leader, invited speaker, master learning designer, and DELP Scholar. Her work has been featured on NBC, ABC, FOX, USA Today, The Star Tribune, and hundreds of nationally syndicated television, newspaper, and magazine outlets.

Theo Hug is Professor of Educational Sciences at the Department of Media, Society and Communication at the University of Innsbruck and coordinator of the Innsbruck Media Studies research group. His areas of interest include media education and media literacy, e-education and microlearning, theory of knowledge, methodology and philosophy of science. He is particularly interested in interfaces of medialization and knowledge dynamics as well as learning processes.

Some of his recent work focuses on instant knowledge, bricolage, and didactics of microlearning. He is the author of numerous journal articles and books, including *Didactics of Microlearning: Concepts, Discourses and Examples* (2007). Dr. Hug is credited with coining the term *microlearning* together with Mag. Gerhard Gassler. To learn more, please visit: http://hug-web.at.

Karl M. Kapp, Ed.D., is an award-winning professor of Instructional Technology at Bloomsburg University in Bloomsburg, PA. where he teaches instructional game design, gamification classes and online learning design. He is the Director of Bloomsburg's Institute for Interactive Technologies and is recognized internationally as an expert in the application of games, game-thinking and gamification to learning. Karl earned his doctoral degree from the University of Pittsburgh. Karl has authored or co-authored eight books including *The Gamification of Learning and Instruction*, it's accompanying fieldbook and the widely popular, *Play to Learn*. His latest co-authored book with Robyn Defelice is *Microlearning: Short and Sweet*. Karl is author of ten LinkedIn Learning courses including *Learning How to Increase Learner Engagement* and has been a TEDx speaker.

Badrul H. Khan, Ph.D. is a world-renowned speaker, author, educator and consultant in the field of e-learning and educational technology. Professor Khan has the credit of first coining the phrase web-based instruction and popularizing the concept through his 1997 best-selling *Web-Based Instruction* book which paved the way for the new field of e-learning. Known as the founder of modern e-learning, Dr. Khan has been honored with many awards and worldwide acclamation throughout his career. In recognition of his unique contribution to the field of e-learning coupled with his services to worldwide e-learning communities, Egyptian E-Learning University Council on August 13, 2012 appointed Dr. Badrul Khan as an honorary distinguished professor of e-learning. Professor Khan is a United States Distance Learning Association (USDLA) 2015 Hall of Fame Inductee. He is recognized as one of the Leaders in Open and Distance Education in North America. He is Founder of GyanBahan (GyanBahan.com), the Knowledge Carrier – a practical application of competency-based lifelong e-learning. He authored 12 books in e-learning and one of his managing e-learning books has been translated into 20 languages. He served as the founding Director of the Educational Technology Leadership (ETL) graduate cohort program at The George Washington University. He also served as the founding Director of the Educational Technology (ET) graduate program at the University of Texas, Brownsville. Please visit his website at: BadrulKhan.com

Megan Kohler is a learning designer with the John A. Dutton e-Education Institute at Penn State. She has served as both Conference and Program Chair for the Online Learning Consortium's Accelerate Conference. She serves as pedagogical and project lead on several impactful projects, such as the number one ranked *Epidemics: Infectious*

Disease Dynamics MOOC, the *MOOCs by Design* webinar series, and the Badges at Penn State project. Her current interests are learning experience design, micro-learning, MOOCs and collaborative design processes.

Lucas Kohnke is a Teaching Fellow in the English Language Centre at The Hong Kong Polytechnic University. Dr. Kohnke earned his Doctor of Education in Teaching English to Speakers of Other Languages from the University of Exeter. His research interests include technology-supported teaching and learning, professional development using information communication technologies (ICT), and EAP/ESP course design. Dr. Kohnke currently serves as the Chief Editor for the Linguistic Journal and is on the board of reviewers for the *TESOL Journal, Journal of Teaching English with Technology*, and the *Asian ESP Journal*.

Jako Olivier is a professor in Multimodal Learning at the North-West University (NWU), South Africa and currently holds the *UNESCO Chair on Multimodal Learning and Open Educational Resources*. He obtained his Ph.D. in 2011 during which he researched the accommodation and promotion of multilingualism in schools through blended learning. Before he joined the NWU as lecturer in 2010, he was involved in teaching information technology and languages in schools in the United Kingdom and in South Africa. From 2010 to 2015, Dr. Olivier was a lecturer in the Faculty of Arts at NWU, and in 2015, he was appointed Associate Professor in the Faculty of Education. During 2012, he was a guest lecturer at the University of Antwerp, Belgium. In 2018, he was promoted to full professor at the NWU. In 2018 and received the *Emerging Researcher Medal* from the Education Association of South Africa. Dr. Olivier's research, located within the NWU's Research Unit for Self-directed Learning, is focused on self-directed learning, multimodal learning, open educational resources, multiliteracies, individualized and contextualized blended learning, e-learning in language classrooms, online multilingualism, and macro-sociolinguistics.

Victoria Raish is the Online Learning Librarian for Penn State University. She enters the world of microlearning from a focus on micro-credentials for the past seven years. She has her Ph.D. in Learning, Design, and Technology and her master's degree in teaching. Her expertise is in qualitative research and she enjoys focusing on the student experience. She has been cited in *U.S. News & World Reports* for her work on digital badges and has published in peer-reviewed journals, book chapters, conference proceedings, and numerous presentations.

Alexander Salas is an award-winning instructional designer, eLearning expert and Chief of Awesomeness at eLearningLaunch.com. eLearning Launch is the online academy for aspiring instructional designers offering self-paced and live cohort learning experiences with personalized feedback. He specializes in the integration of instructional science with popular authoring tools, custom web design, game design, virtual and augmented realities for L&D purposes. Among his professional achievements, Alex is certified as CPTD, CompTIA CTT+, A+, Microsoft Certified Professional and Agile ScrumMaster. He was a designer of learning programs for Fortune 100 companies such as Centene Corporation, Philips, and Dell Technologies. Alex is a regular speaker and contributor at major ATD, Learning Guild, and Training Magazine conferences and publications.

Laura Sheneman has been an educator for three decades. Currently, Dr. Sheneman is a lecturer at the University of West Georgia in the Educational Technology and Foundations department. Her interests include K-12 education, educator preparation, professional development, and instructional technology. Her work primarily focuses on school librarians and other educational technology professionals. She resides in Texas and is the voice behind the internationally recognized blog and podcast called *The Librarian Influencers*.

Melissa A. Simons, M.S., is a learning and development organizational advisor and lead in the oil and gas industry and has achieved a twenty-five-year career within the realms of adult workplace learning and talent development. She has leveraged an expertise in communication design within learning and development theoretical methodologies, to deliver global instructor-led, blended hybrid learning, e-learning, and just-in-time microlearning product solutions. Her deliverables result in the application of embedded human performance principles and workforce competencies with visual literacy concepts that outline, influence, direct, or aid each project phase decision, individual or project team decision and outcome.

Carla Torgerson, M.Ed., M.B.A. has nearly 20 years of experience as an instructional designer and instructional strategist. Carla is currently a Director of Instructional Design at Bull City Learning, a specialized learning agency that consults in a variety of areas of corporate training, and develops e-learning, virtual, and live training solutions for companies in a wide range of industries, as well as non-profit organizations. She is the author of *The Microlearning Guide to Microlearning* and co-author of *Designing Microlearning*. Connect with Carla at www.linkedin.com/in/carlatorgerson

Didem Tufan earned her Bachelor of Science in Computer Education and Instructional Technology from the Middle East Technical University (METU), Ankara, Turkey in 2005. In 2008, she completed her Master of Science in Educational Sciences, Curriculum, and Instruction from the same University. Concurrently with her academic studies, she worked as a professional in corporate e-learning and software projects, as an instructional designer, project manager, and expert. Upon completing her thesis titled, *Online Knowledge Sharing and Collaboration in Networked Learning Environments in corporate context by Utilizing Social Network Analysis*, she earned her Ph.D.

degree in 2016 from METU. Currently, she is working as a manager for Cyber Security Career Learning Program in a corporate academy. She is married and the mother of two boys. Her research interests are microlearning, networked learning, social network analysis, e-learning, training in corporate context.

Kari Word is a former teacher middle school math teacher who graduated with her M.Ed. in Educational Technology from the University of Texas Rio Grande (formerly University of Texas Brownsville) in 2012. After teaching Kari transitioned into instructional design for higher ed and eventually corporate and military clients. Currently, she is a doctoral candidate in the Instructional Systems and Learning Technologies program and Florida State University.

FOREWORD

Microlearning is the topic for our times. It effectively captures the hectic and changing nature of educational content delivery. It is truly a movement forward in the design, development, and delivery of instruction.

When Robyn Defelice and I first wrote our article on microlearning "Elephant Sized Impact," we didn't realize the influence or sway that article would have on the field of learning and development but, like all evolving and moving fields, the article soon became dated. More and deeper knowledge and information was desired and necessary to advance the field. We quickly followed up that article with a book titled, *Microlearning: Short and Sweet*. The book was designed to help practitioners implement the concept of microlearning into their classrooms, training curriculum, or online learning efforts.

The book became a touchstone for microlearning design and development. But it was just a snapshot in time. It firmly grounded microlearning in the lexicon of anyone needing to understand and implement microlearning into their academic, corporate, or non-profit organizations. But, alas, time marches on and the snapshot begins to fade, representing less and less of the state-of-the-art.

Fortunately, that's where Professor Badrul H. Khan, Ph.D. and his impressive team enter the scene. I've followed Dr. Khan's pioneering work in web-based instruction since before he published his best-selling work, *Web-Based Instruction*. For as long as I can remember in my professional career, I've followed his writing, teaching, and thoughts. Many times, I've taught Badrul's concepts, ideas, and models in my graduate level classes.

Finally, having had a chance to meet him, I find he is just as energetic, entertaining, and interesting in person as he is in his writing. His passion for education and desire to help others is palatable. I am not alone as he has received multiple awards and world-wide acknowledgement of his work in e-learning.

His knowledge, passion, and wisdom for microlearning is evident in the stellar cast of microlearning experts he has assembled for this book. The collection truly captures the state-of-the-art of microlearning and provides a grounding and forward-looking platform from which you can discover all the many channels, ebbs, and flows of microlearning.

Dr. Khan and his team have assembled writings and thoughts from folks like Theo Hug who, perhaps, has dug deeper and more philosophically into the subject of microlearning than anyone else on the planet, to Carla Torgerson, who wrote one of the first practitioner-focused books related to microlearning, to Alexander Salas who takes his trademark passion and commitment for all things learning related and applies it to his writing as he explores how microlearning works with gamification (one of my favorite subjects).

The expertise in this volume starts with Professor Kahn who is not just co-editor of the collection but also serves as co-author of the first chapter along with co-editors Rene Corbeil and Maria Elena Corbeil. Together the team has created a tightly woven compendium of microlearning knowledge that should be on any academic or practitioner's shelf who even has a cursory interest in microlearning.

Joseph Rene Corbeil is a professor at The University of Texas Rio Grande Valley who has been involved in technology and distance education for over 30 years and who has developed and taught fully web-based undergraduate, graduate, and doctoral courses in educational technology. Rene Corbeil also has the distinction of having developed the first fully online undergraduate specialization in Educational Technology in Texas.

The co-editing team also includes the knowledgeable and gifted, Maria Elena Corbeil who has been working in higher education for over 20 years and who has been honored with several awards for her pioneering work in online learning. This initial chapter sets the tone and groundwork for the collection and provides a solid chapter for anyone seeking to learn more about microlearning.

Professor Khan, Joseph Rene Corbeil, and Maria Elena Corbeil have pulled together an impressive list of internationally known academics, practitioners, pioneers, and futurists that include Didem Tufan, Lucas Kohnke, Rita Fennelly-Atkinson, Renee Dyer, Megan Kohler, Chris Gamrat, Victoria Raish, Elizabeth Gross, Laura Sheneman, Pamela S. Hogle, Tracy King, Jako Olivier, Kari Knisely, Vanessa P. Dennen, Caroline M. Crawford, Melissa A. Simons, Johnny Hamilton, Theresa Hamilton, and Darci Hall.

As you read the chapters, you will begin to understand and then fully comprehend the nuances of microlearning. You'll witness microlearning examined from many facets and perspectives. You'll have a chance to ponder an instructional design model based on microlearning and consider methods of gamifying microlearning, as well as learn methods for encouraging student created microlearning. You'll have a chance to discover how to assess microlearning, how to optimize it for mobile delivery, and how to leverage the multimedia aspects of the microlearning.

Pursuing through the pages, you will discover how microlearning is implemented in K-12, higher education, and corporate settings. You'll take a deep dive into the pedagogy of microlearning and examine its origin, definition, and impact. In short, the wisdom of all the above-listed contributors will be at your fingertips. You will gain a collective of knowledge on the subject.

As you read the book, relish the knowledge, wisdom, history, and ideas that are captured in this work by this wonderful team. If you need to know about microlearning, its impact on education, academic, corporations, and even you personally, then this book will not disappoint. Investing time with this book will help you apply microlearning knowledge to your own microlearning design, development, and delivery needs.

Karl Kapp, Ed.D.
Professor of Instructional Technology, Bloomsburg University
Coauthor *Microlearning: Short and Sweet*

PREFACE

Microlearning is all the rage, but what is it exactly? What does a successful microlearning object look like? And, how sound are the pedagogical practices surrounding microlearning design and implementation? Although the term has been in use since as early as 2002, the recent proliferation of smartphones and mobile devices has brought the concept of personalized mobile learning through bite-sized learning snippets to the forefront.

Objective of the Book

This edited book examines the recent phenomenon of "microlearning" happening in online and traditional learning contexts for enhancing instruction, professional development, training, and personalized learning. Grounded in research-based best practices in instructional and multimedia design, this book provides a one-stop shop for instructional designers, e-learning professionals, content creators, trainers, and academics in K–12 and higher education interested in designing, creating, and integrating effective, bite-sized learning objects into their instructional units.

Organization of the Book

The book is divided into four sections.

- (I) Introduction
- (II) Designing Microlearning Objects
- (III) Microlearning in Academic, Corporate, and Personalized Learning Contexts
- (IV) Microlearning Today and Tomorrow

In the introductory section, the authors establish the focus and purpose of the book. They propose a multidimensional roadmap for implementing effective microlearning solutions followed by a synopsis of the origins, definitions, and applications of microlearning in educational, professional, and personalized learning contexts. Section II discusses sound pedagogical practices and multimedia design principles for designing and implementing high impact microlearning events. Suggestions for optimizing microlearning for mobile access and assessing the learning in microlearning are also addressed. Section III addresses common-sense approaches for incorporating microlearning and micro-credentials in academic, corporate, and personalized learning contexts. Section IV looks at creating self-directed multimodal learning microlearning objects, gamifying and sharing microlearning objects through Open Educational Resources (OER), and how microlearning might impact the workplace of the future.

Target Audience

This book will be of great value to designers, developers, instructors, and instructional facilitators of online, blended, and mobile learning education and training content. This book can be used as a textbook or supplementary resource in Educational/Instructional Technology programs and courses focusing on instructional design for e-learning, distance education, and web-based multimedia. This book can also serve as a handbook to guide administrators, IT professionals, human resource managers, instructional designers, mobile app developers, trainers, and faculty in the planning, development, and implementation of successful microlearning content.

PART I
Introduction

1

A MULTIDIMENSIONAL ROADMAP FOR IMPLEMENTING EFFECTIVE MICROLEARNING SOLUTIONS

Maria Elena Corbeil, Joseph Rene Corbeil, and Badrul H. Khan

Microlearning in the Digital Age

According to a recent report by the Association for Talent Development (ATD), "microlearning is one of the most widely discussed and debated trends in the learning industry" (2018, p. 1). Recent research results substantiate the impact that microlearning has, and will have, on personalized, professional learning. For example, the authors of Axonify's *2018 Microlearning Global Benchmark Report* observed, "microlearning is used across dozens of industries to support a multitude of training applications" (p. 4). Their report revealed increased development and implementation of microlearning in a variety of fields, ranging from sales, communications, and healthcare, to telemarketing, investing, and others (Axonify, 2018). This is due in part to strengths microlearning brings to corporate training, which according to Hogle in Chapter 9 of this book are:

1. preparation for training through *preparatory* exposure to content prior to the first day of formal learning
2. review and reinforcement of prior learning though subscription delivery of follow-up activities and quick reference job aids
3. teaching dense, fact-based content through *spaced repetition* and *spaced practice*
4. supporting workers in applying training through post-training support or job aids available on demand (p. 142–143).

It is not surprising then that the benefits of microlearning in training and performance development contexts are well documented as workers need to be able to learn new skills and knowledge quickly to apply them to specific tasks or situations on the job.

Microlearning is also starting to take its place in K-12 and higher education. The NMC/CoSN *Horizon Report: 2017 K–12 Edition* lists microlearning as one of the learning technologies that their K-12 Expert Panel noted as *up and coming* in education, observing that "these include technologies that are changing the landscape of learning, whether formal or informal, by making it more accessible and personalized" (p. 39). In educational contexts, microlearning strategies can assist in delivering just-in-time informational and instructional content in short, manageable bursts, matching the way learners of all ages are accessing information that interests them in and outside of class. Microlearning also allows learners to not only be consumers of content, but also producers of it, as new technologies, readily available on mobile devices, allow learners to create apps, movies, games, podcasts, and more. Olivier, in Chapter 11, presents an illustrative case study and proposes practical steps to create opportunities conducive to effective student self-directed multimodal learning through microlearning object creation.

As such, the benefits of microlearning can be harnessed to increase the transfer from short-term to long-term memory by helping to reduce cognitive load (Nelson & Elison-Bowers, 2007; Perry, 2017; Major & Calandrino, 2018). In addition, educational researchers are beginning to explore the impact of microlearning on heutagogy – learning how to learn through self-direction and creation of learning goals (Hase & Kenyon, 2007). According to Semingson, Crosslin, and Dellinger (2015), "microcontent could provide a scaffolded way for learners to step into self-determination by creating smaller, focused assignments" (p. 475). Agrawal (2017) agrees, noting that "while Microlearning is often associated with eLearning and corporates, it can easily be adopted for K12 as well" (para. 8). Sheneman, in Chapter 8 proposes:

> Through a spiraling microlearning curriculum that repeats and gets more complex as time passes, microlearning objects can be used throughout the lesson cycle to pre-assess students' knowledge of a concept, during instruction to introduce new concepts and lay a foundation that future lessons are built on, and to reinforce concepts post-instruction.
>
> *(p. 136)*

Microlearning has also found its way into higher education, being implemented and researched in several specializations such as healthcare, management, education, business, and others. A Pass Educational Group, LLC (2019) published *Higher Education Learning Trends in 2019*, in which microlearning was the number one trend they predicted for higher education, noting "[h]igher ed institutions are jumping on this type of learning, too" (para. 3), bringing with it two changes in the way the curriculum is developed and implemented, mainly by "breaking up blocks of learning into bite-sized pieces, and including application steps to reinforce and extend learning" (para. 4). Similarly, Pandey (2020) listed microlearning as one of the top eLearning trends for 2020, for delivering "high impact and immersive learning experiences" (para. 5). This makes it ideal for specializations such as teacher preparation. Crawford and Semeiuk (2017) observed, "[m]icro-learning efforts address the inherent needs of a teacher educator, through short, focused cognitive microlearning events that are shared through a teacher education program's mobile application environment," while focusing on "pedagogies that incorporate active learning within mobile technologies that are most likely to enhance meaningful learning" (Abstract, para. 1). Similarly, Elwood, Johnson, and Perales (2018), used microlearning to share examples of successful applications of flipped instruction with future teachers and mentors. The potential for micro-learning in higher education can be extended even further, as Kohler, et. al., in Chapter 7 proposes, to provide learners opportunities to earn micro-credentials in their college and university courses that can help them build their skills and resumes in preparation for the workforce.

Likewise, in Chapter 13, Word and Dennen assert that one of the benefits of microlearning content is the ability to share it. They observe, "[t]he developing market for small scope, Internet-distributed, just-in-time learning experiences potentially changes the locus and economics of learning design, development, and distribution activities from larger institutions to smaller ones, or even individuals" (p. 200). It is in this way, that teachers and learning professionals are able to develop and share what they create globally and contribute to the library of Open Educational Resources. In their chapter, Word and Dennen describe ways in which creators of microlearning objects can maximize the benefits of Open Educational Resources, while taking into consideration copyright and other important aspects of microlearning development and sharing.

Despite the growing consensus on the use of microlearning and its benefits for performance development and education, experts agree that microlearning is not achieved by merely cutting up existing content into small pieces. According to Berkowitz (2017), "true microlearning is built on purpose" (para. 3). Consequently, Theo Hug, in Chapter 3, when referring to sound pedagogy for microlearning, emphasizes, "[t]oday, being able to successfully design, organize, and evaluate meaningful learning processes is one of the most critical challenges faced by educators and trainers" (p. 50). To address this challenge, this chapter promotes a unifying framework for identifying and analyzing the major issues surrounding the thoughtful and purposeful implementation of microlearning in educational, training, performance, and talent development contexts.

A Framework for Designing, Implementing, and Assessing Microlearning

In 2007, Badrul Khan introduced the concept of learning *snippets* for delivering quick, cost-effective, and meaningful training solutions to organizations for performance improvement (Khan, 2007). He categorized learning snippets into two kinds: (1) *informational snippets*, learning objects used to deliver quick information to a target audience, and (2) *instructional snippets*, learning objects used to teach a single concept or skill (Khan, 2019, p. 278). Although he originally envisioned both types of snippets as reinforcing agents for the training world, his thoughts about microlearning have evolved to include various forms of informal and formal learning, including self-directed learning and learning in K–12 and higher education contexts. Khan (2020) developed the following definition for microlearning:[1]

> Microlearning can be viewed as a single objective-focused, outcome-based, stand-alone, meaningful, and interactive learning unit delivered in bite-sized snippets (i.e., a short modular format) either digitally (i.e., via computer, tablet, or mobile phone) or non-digitally (i.e., as via a flashcard or booklet).

Khan (2001) proposed the use of the *E-Learning Framework* to analyze the eight dimensions of an organization's training/learning culture (pedagogical, technological, interface design, evaluation, management, resource support, ethical, and institutional). The framework allows stakeholders to review an organization's existing learning environment from the perspective of what works, what doesn't, and recommend various cost-effective, efficient, and meaningful training/instructional solutions based on the organizational mission and strategy. In this context, the framework serves as a refining filter for identifying training/instructional solutions.

Guided by the framework, organizations can design, develop, evaluate, and implement effective learning snippets with appropriate instructional strategies and delivery methods. By integrating instructional strategies with appropriate delivery mechanisms, organizations can achieve better results and a higher return on investment. Figure 1.1 (see p. 7) presents Khan's *E-Learning Framework* visualized through the lens of microlearning. The outer octagon represents the eight dimensions of the framework while the inner octagon lists qualities of microlearning representative of each dimension. The droplets in the center of the octagon represent bite-sized, single-objective, learning objects that can stand-alone or contribute to a larger learning enterprise.

Khan's framework consists of eight dimensions. Each dimension represents a category of issues that need to be considered prior to implementation in order to create a successful learning experience:

- the **pedagogical** dimension addresses issues pertaining to teaching and learning, in particular, how instructional content is designed, delivered, and implemented, with an emphasis on the identification of learners' needs and how the learning objectives will be achieved. The pedagogical dimension addresses issues related to practices involving microlearning design, development, implementation, and evaluation.
- the **technological** dimension is concerned with the learning environment, its creation, and the tools required to create and deliver the learning. This dimension also addresses hardware and software requirements, as well as

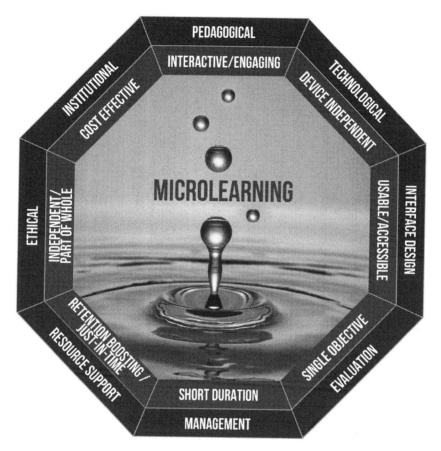

FIGURE 1.1 Khan's e-learning framework perceived through the lens of microlearning

infrastructure planning, including the selection of the most suitable delivery system for achieving the institution's learning goals. Technical requirements such as the server capacities, bandwidth, security, backups, and other infrastructure issues are also addressed. In the context of microlearning, the technological dimension addresses issues related to learners' or workers' access to the tools (hardware, software, infrastructure) needed to connect to the microlearning resources.

- the **interface design** dimension is concerned with factors related to the overall look and feel of the learning environment. With regard to microlearning, the interface design dimension addresses issues related to user interface design, ease-of-use, usability, navigability, and adaptiveness of learning objects for mobile learning.
- the **evaluation** dimension addresses the assessment of learners; evaluation of the instruction and learning environment; assessment of content development

processes and of the persons involved in the design process (i.e., the planning, design, production, and evaluation teams); review of instructional design processes (i.e., planning, design, development, and evaluation); and evaluation of e-learning at the program and institutional levels. In Chapter 6, Fennelly-Atkinson and Dyer provides a guide for the design of effective microlearning assessments that are inventive, targeted, specific, and yield useful and informative data.

• the **management** dimension deals with issues related to the management of the learning program, such as the continuation, updating, and upkeep of the learning environment. The management dimension can address issues related to quality control, budgeting, staffing, security, and scheduling of microlearning.

• the **resource support** dimension considers all of the technical and human resource support systems required to create and support meaningful online learning experiences. Examples include web-based and telephone technical support, as well as access to digital libraries, online tutorials, podcasts, glossaries, and Frequently Asked Questions (FAQs).

• the **ethical** dimension identifies the ethical issues that need to be addressed in the design, development, and implementation of e-learning resources. Issues pertaining to social and political influence, diversity, geographical diversity, bias, the digital divide, information accessibility, and etiquette are addressed. Legal issues address privacy, plagiarism, and copyright.

• the **institutional** dimension addresses issues pertaining to administrative, academic, and learner support services. This dimension focuses on how the organization can disseminate knowledge and learning resources to workers that is timeline and cost effective.

Identifying Potential Issues in Designing, Implementing, and Assessing Microlearning

Before a new microlearning initiative is implemented, each of the aforementioned dimensions should be analyzed to ensure a smooth implementation. When evaluating potential issues, Khan (2005) recommends presenting them in the form of questions to help stakeholders think through new and existing initiatives thoroughly. Table 1.1 presents potential questions associated with the adoption of microlearning for educational and professional development initiatives. The issues below are representative of concerns stakeholders may hold about microlearning and are by no means exhaustive (Khan, 2005). As institutions gain experience with the use of microlearning for teaching and professional development, more factors may emerge.

In summary, Khan's (2005) *E-learning Framework* provides a structure and guiding methodology to meaningfully utilize microlearning to promote learning and professional development. While several microlearning issues may cut across

TABLE 1.1 Potential issues of microlearning in educational, training, performance, and talent development contexts

Dimension	Issues or Questions
Pedagogical	• How sound are the pedagogical practices surrounding micro-learning design and implementation?
	• What are the pedagogical limits of microlearning?
	• How long is microlearning?
Technological	• Do all learners/workers have access to the tools (hardware, software, infrastructure) needed to access the microlearning resources?
	• Are the microlearning resources available 24/7, just-in-time, and on-demand?
	• Is the delivery system suitable for distributing microlearning content across multiple device platforms and operating systems?
	• Does the organization possess the server capacity, bandwidth, security, backups, and other infrastructure resources to support microlearning?
Interface Design	• Is the user interface friendly, easy to navigate, and usable?
	• Are the microlearning resources mobile-friendly?
	• Are the microlearning resources visual and delivered in media-rich formats?
	• Are the microlearning resources Americans with Disabilities Act (ADA) compliant?
Evaluation	• How do we assess the learning in microlearning?
	• What are the elements that make up a successful microlearning event?
	• For informal learning, what data are available to assess the learning and/or mastery of the objectives?
Management	• How much will it cost to implement a microlearning initiative?
	• Who will manage the continuation, updating, and upkeep of the microlearning resources?
	• Who will be responsible for managing security?
	• How do we address issues of quality control?
Resource Support	• How can microlearning assist in providing just-in-time and on-demand technical and human resource support?
	• How can microlearning be used to address Frequently Asked Questions (FAQs) and learner support?
Ethical	• Do the microlearning resources address issues related to diversity, bias, and the digital divide?
Institutional	• How can organizations disseminate knowledge and learning resources to workers that is timely and cost-effective?

multiple disciplines and professions, each organization is different and faces its own unique challenges (Khan, 2005). Only after thoughtful consideration of the benefits and risks of microlearning across all affected dimensions can an organization make informed decisions on how to proceed.

Summary

What is the future of microlearning? According to the 2019 *Microlearning Market by Component* Report, microlearning investments are expected to grow from $1.5 billion in 2019 to $2.7 billion over the next five years (Research and Markets, 2019). The growth is attributed to "the increasing demand for training of deskless and mobile workers across industries and a growing need for skills-based and result-oriented training among enterprises" (para. 1). Accordingly, "[b]usinesses are keen on adopting training methods that are directly inclined toward a learning objective, which focuses on particular skills …" (Research and Markets, 2019, para. 5). Hamilton, Hall, and Hamilton (see Chapter 15) predict that microlearning will evolve in the following ways to meet the changing needs of workplace skills and learning:

- change from earning degrees to developing skills
- shift from Push Paradigm for learning (content is assigned) to Pull Paradigm (workers seek content when needed)
- use of Internet of Things for time and place independent learning
- learning adapts to me (instead of me adapting to the learning)
- nano-learning less than a minute to complete, occurs over a period of weeks.

As Khan (2020) noted in a keynote presentation at the *2020 NATO Training Technology Conference (NTTC)*, "microlearning is perfectly suited for today's fast-moving world. From the instructors' perspective, it is quick to develop, and from the learners' perspective, it is easily accessible whenever they need it." Similarly, in Chapter 7, Kohler, et. al., observe that microlearning has the capacity to significantly transform traditional learning experiences both in the classroom and in the workplace. They note,

> With digital technologies so thoroughly transforming the limitations of learning by time and space through the rise of online learning and ease of multimedia authoring technologies, it makes sense that the systems for delivering, tracking, and storing this learning also evolve.
>
> *(p. 126)*

As the learning landscape continues to rapidly change, the eight dimensions of the *E-Learning Framework* can help guide the design, development, implementation, and evaluation of sound microlearning in fields ranging from business, healthcare, education, technology, and more.

Discussion Questions

1. Describe three ways in which microlearning can be implemented in your organization or field for professional development? Please provide examples.
2. List the top five questions or issues from the *E-Learning Framework* dimensions that would need to be addressed in your organization for the implementation of an effective microlearning initiative?
3. Which of the dimensions of the *E-Learning Framework* would be the **most challenging** for you or your organization to address for the implementation of microlearning? Why?
4. Which of the dimensions of the *E-Learning Framework* would be **the easiest** for you or your organization to address for the implementation of microlearning? Why?

Note

1 Khan acknowledges the contribution of Rene Corbeil and Karl Kapp for providing constructive feedback for improving the microlearning definition.

References

A Pass Educational Group, LLC (2019). Higher education learning trends in 2019. https://apasseducation.com/education-blog/higher-education-learning-trends-in-2019.

Agrawal, H. (2017). Microlearning: The next big thing in education? www.getmagicbox.com/blog/microlearning-next-big-thing-education.

ATD Research. (2017). Microlearning: Delivering bite-sized knowledge. www.td.org/research-reports/microlearning-delivering-bite-sized-knowledge.

Axonify (2018). 2018 Microlearning global benchmark report. https://axonify.com/wp-content/uploads/2018/07/2018-axonify-microlearning-global-benchmark-report.pdf.

Berkowitz, M. (2017). How to create engaging microlearning content. https://blog.grovo.com/create-engaging-microlearning-content.

Crawford, C. M. & Semeniuk, M. (2017). Recognizing Design-Based Research as Coursework and Experiential Support: Micro-Learning as Integrated Teacher Candidate Coursework and Field-Based Understandings. In P. Resta & S. Smith (Eds.), Proceedings of Society for Information Technology & Teacher Education International Conference (pp. 827–832). Austin, TX, United States: Association for the Advancement of Computing in Education (AACE). www.learntechlib.org/primary/p/177359.

Elwood, S., Johnson, R. D., & Perales, C. (2018). The Vignette TaBLE: Team-based Blended Learning Experiences with Classroom Mentors and Teacher Candidates. In J. Keengwe (Ed.), *Handbook of Research on Mobile Technology, Constructivism, and Meaningful Learning* (pp. 259–279). Hershey, PA: IGI Global. doi:10.4018/978-1-5225-3949-0.ch014.

Fennelly-Atkinson, R. & Dyer, R. (2021). Assessing the Learning in Microlearning. In J. R. Corbeil, B. H. Khan, & M. E. Corbeil (Eds.). *Microlearning in the Digital Age: The Design and Delivery of Learning in Snippets*. New York: Routledge.

Hamilton, J., Hall, D., & Hamilton, T. (2021). Microlearning in the Workplace of the Future. In J. R. Corbeil, B. H. Khan, & M. E. Corbeil (Eds.). *Microlearning in the Digital Age: The Design and Delivery of Learning in Snippets*. New York: Routledge.

Hase, S. & Kenyon, C. (2007). Heutagogy: A child of complexity theory. *Complicity: An International Journal of Complexity and Education*, 4(1), 111–117.

Hogle, P. (2021). Microlearning in Corporate Settings. In J. R. Corbeil, B. H. Khan, & M. E. Corbeil (Eds.). *Microlearning in the Digital Age: The Design and Delivery of Learning in Snippets*. New York: Routledge.

Hug, T. (2021). Sound Pedagogy Practices for Designing and Implementing Microlearning Objects. In J. R. Corbeil, B. H. Khan, & M. E. Corbeil (Eds.). *Microlearning in the Digital Age: The Design and Delivery of Learning in Snippets*. New York: Routledge.

Kapp, K.M. & Defelice. R.A. (2019). *Microlearning: Short and Sweet*. Alexandria, VA: Association for Talent Development. ATD Press.

Khan, B. H. (2001). A Framework for Web-Based Learning. In Khan, B. H., (Ed.), *Web-Based Training*, Englewood Cliffs, NJ: Educational Technology Publications, 75–98.

Khan, B. H. (2005). *Managing E-learning: Design, Delivery, Implementation, and Evaluation*. Hershey, PS: IGI Global.

Khan, B. (2019). Microlearning: Quick and meaningful snippets for training solutions. *International Journal of Research in Educational Sciences. (IJRES)*, 2(2), 275–284. http://iafh. net/index.php/IJRES/article/view/107.

Khan, B. H. (2020, June 2–4). Microlearning: Snippets of e-learning [Keynote presentation]. NATO Training Technology Conference (NTTC), Virtual Conference. www. youtube.com/watch?v=7BkN44j9oVU.

Khan, B. (2020, July). What and why microlearning?www.linkedin.com/posts/dista ncelearning_microlearning-definition-e-learning-framework-activity-66848874438099 39456-AvsV.

Khan, B. H. & Granato, L. A. (2007). Snippets: Quick and meaningful training solutions. http://asianvu.com/digital-library/elearning/Training_Snippets_by_Khan_Granato.pdf.

Kohler, M., Gamrat, C., Raish, V., & Gross, E. (2021). Microlearning and Microcredentials in Higher Education. In J. R. Corbeil, B. H. Khan, & M. E. Corbeil (Eds.). *Microlearning in the Digital Age: The Design and Delivery of Learning in Snippets*. New York: Routledge.

Major, A. & Calandrino, T. (2018). Beyond chunking: Micro-learning secrets for effective online design. NSUWorks. https://nsuworks.nova.edu/cgi/viewcontent.cgi?article= 1013&context=fdla-journal.

Nelson, C. & Elison-Bowers, P. (2007). Micro-level design for multimedia-enhanced online courses. *MERLOT Journal of Online Learning and Teaching*, 3(4). 383–394.

NMC/CoSN Horizon Report: 2017 K–12 Edition. (2017). https://cdn.nmc.org/media/ 2017-nmc-cosn-horizon-report-k12-EN.pdf.

Olivier, J. (2021). Creating Microlearning Objects Within Self-Directed Multimodal Learning Contexts. In J. R. Corbeil, B. H. Khan, & M. E. Corbeil (Eds.). *Microlearning in the Digital Age: The Design and Delivery of Learning in Snippets*. New York: Routledge.

Pandey, A. (2020). E-learning trends in 2020. https://elearningindustry.com/elearning-trends-in-2020.

Perry, M. (2017). Learning trend: Microlearning. *Canadian Journal of Medical Laboratory Science*, 79(2).

Research and Markets (2019, July). Microlearning market by component (solution and services), organization size, deployment type, industry (retail, manufacturing and logistics, BFSI, Telecom and IT, Healthcare and Life Sciences), and Region – Global Forecast to 2024. https://cutt.ly/stwexC5.

Semingson, P., Crosslin, M., & Dellinger, J. (2015). Microlearning as a Tool to Engage Students in Online and Blended Learning. In D. Rutledge & D. Slykhuis (Eds.),

Proceedings of Society for Information Technology & Teacher Education International Conference 2015 (pp. 474–479). Chesapeake, VA: Association for the Advancement of Computing in Education (AACE).

Sheneman, L. (2021). Microlearning in K-12 Settings. In J. R. Corbeil, B. H. Khan, & M. E. Corbeil (Eds.). *Microlearning in the Digital Age: The Design and Delivery of Learning in Snippets*. New York: Routledge.

Word, K. & Dennen, V. (2021). Sharing Microlearning Materials as Open Educational Resources (OER). In J. R. Corbeil, B. H. Khan, & M. E. Corbeil (Eds.). *Microlearning in the Digital Age: The Design and Delivery of Learning in Snippets*. New York: Routledge.

2

WHAT IS MICROLEARNING? ORIGIN, DEFINITIONS, AND APPLICATIONS

Carla Torgerson

Introduction

According to a recent report by the Association for Talent Development (ATD), "microlearning is one of the most widely discussed and debated trends in the learning industry" (2018, p. 1). In many ways, microlearning is not new. It is something effective educators have been doing for decades. But in many other ways, it is the latest trend causing instructional professionals to think differently about everything they do.

With this much excitement about a *new* idea, vague definitions and differing approaches proliferate the landscape. Many people say they are using microlearning, but they are doing different things. Because microlearning has been poorly defined, there is a lot of hype but no follow-through – no common definitions, no widely accepted best-practices, no guidelines to follow.

This leaves most practitioners struggling to sort through the noise. Due to the hype surrounding microlearning, there is the risk that practitioners will blindly follow a trend without purpose or success, and the opposite risk of avoiding microlearning because they do not want to follow a trend they do not understand. Somewhere in the middle is a place where we can make sense of microlearning, what it is, the value it brings to our learners, and how to do it well. With that common understanding practitioners can more confidently use these approaches where they make the most sense, and with the best results.

In this chapter, we will discuss the microlearning phenomenon, where it all began and what factors are driving this hype cycle. Then, we will compare definitions proposed across the industry and form an operational definition that can be discussed (and even debated!). Finally, we will look at the many uses of microlearning, how it is used in a myriad of personal settings, and then consider how those personal experiences can transcend into workplace training and development, as well as formal educational settings in PreK-12 and higher education, including graduate and professional education.

The Microlearning Phenomenon

Where It All Began

Educational researcher Theo Hug is credited with being one of the founders of current thinking about microlearning. Hug suggests the term was first used as early as 2002 (McGovern, 2017). However, Hug also points out that the term *microteaching* was used by scholars at Stanford University in the 1960s as they conceived an approach of teach – *critique* – *re-teach* – *critique*, which broke classroom teaching into smaller portions of content (Hug, 2005).

The bottom line here is that even if we did not call it *microlearning*, we have all been using the ideas and ideals of microlearning for a very, very long time, long before this hype began. Effective teachers have always been aware of avoiding cognitive overload, of breaking content into manageable chunks that made it easier for learners to process and absorb.

However, the recent proliferation of smartphones and tablets has brought the concept of learning through bite-sized chunks to the forefront. Ideas like consuming content just-in-time, and at precisely the learners' moment of need can be accomplished more easily now than ever before. Although researchers have been considering ideas like microteaching, microlearning, and micro=knowledge for a long time (EduTech Wiki, 2016), I believe that current concepts surrounding microlearning, particularly in workplace education, are being driven by the learners themselves.

Having smartphones with access to the Internet in our pockets is so commonplace that we do not think about it anymore. However, those small devices we carry every day provide countless opportunities for us to look up information or to learn something new whenever we want it, at our precise moment of need or moment of curiosity. This power cannot be overstated, even if we take it for granted.

We all do this kind of just-in-time learning in our personal lives, and now we are looking to capitalize on similar approaches to make ourselves more efficient at work. As a practitioner in workplace education, I have observed over many years how microlearning is very much a bottom-up phenomenon: employees see the value of microlearning in their personal lives, and then ask their employers to provide bite-sized content for their workplace learning. Over time, microlearning has become formalized and entrenched in workplace education, and is now pushing into the spaces of higher education, including graduate and professional education, and PreK-12 education as well.

The movement of microlearning from personal learning to corporate learning is similar to how mobile technologies entered the workplace. Prior to smartphones and tablets, all major technology (computers, printers, fax machines, etc.) were in use in corporate environments for a long time before they made their way into our homes. There was a top-down approach to technology where businesses researched equipment, made major financial investments, and then provided the technology to employees. The advent of smartphones and tablets changed all that; individuals had mobile phones at home before their employers provided them at work. This is why BYOD (bring your own device) policies became so ubiquitous in recent years as corporations dealt with employees who wanted to use their personal phones for business purposes. Today, even if employers provide employees smartphones for work, the origins of mobile technology in the workplace began bottom-up, rather than top-down (C. Udell, personal communication, January 2014). This shift is incredibly important because the forces driving the use of mobile technologies at work, and now microlearning too, are not coming from the organization, they are coming from the employee.

Factors Driving Microlearning

I have long talked about a flywheel of factors driving the use of microlearning for workplace training. I believe there are three major societal factors that are coming together right now, and this confluence of factors is creating a situation where the value of microlearning is being recognized more than ever before. The factors driving microlearning are bottom-up and learner driven, and as such, have significant implications for learning and talent development professionals.

Mobile Devices

As illustrated in Figure 2.1 (see p. 000), mobile devices are one of the three major factors driving microlearning. As discussed earlier, smart phones and tablets are ubiquitous and have a strong influence in our daily lives. Although we do many things on our mobile devices, an important one is getting small pieces of support, knowledge, or learning on whatever topic we need at the moment we need it. For example, let's say you are on your way to meet a friend at a new restaurant and you get lost. Most likely you will use a map on your phone to get directions. In educational terms, you are using *performance support*. You are trying to perform a task (get to the restaurant) and you are getting support to help you perform that task more effectively.

Similarly, let's say you are having a conversation with a group of colleagues and you say, "that's familiar, let me look that up," you will most likely open a web browser and search for that piece of information on the Internet. In educational terms, you are consuming *micro-knowledge*. Finally, if you are at home and want to learn how to fix your leaky faucet, you may read some blogs or watch

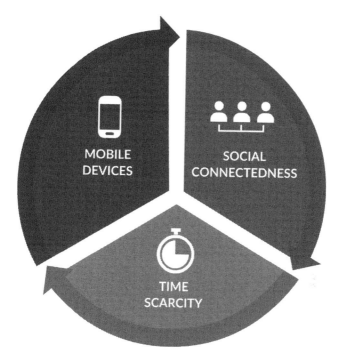

FIGURE 2.1 Flywheel of factors driving microlearning
Source: Torgerson (2016); Torgerson & Iannone (2020)

some short videos about how to do it. In educational terms, you are engaging in *microlearning*.

It does not matter if the content is provided as performance support, micro-knowledge, or microlearning, it is helping you do something more effectively. This is the crux of what average people may not recognize: educationally they are using slightly different kinds of self-directed learning. That does not matter to them; the learners just know that the materials are helping them do what they want to do.

As a result, workers are now pressuring their employers to provide similar instructional approaches for their workplace training. In addition, training and development professionals are also recognizing these ways of learning in their personal lives and are asking how they can capitalize on mobile and desktop technology to help workers learn and perform better. For all of us, the ubiquity of Internet-connected devices and our constant use of them is improving performance in our daily lives and now we want to incorporate those same techniques into our formal education as well.

Social Connectedness

The second factor driving microlearning is social connectedness. Human beings, who are highly social, learn a lot from each other. We have always learned from each other, but with the advent of technology, we have super-charged our social learning. For example, instead of asking the colleagues sitting next to me how to solve a problem, I now have access to a much wider array of experts. I can search the Internet for blogs. I can go to online social communities and post my specific question. I can also send an email or text message to someone that I know has likely faced a similar situation or problem. In all cases I am accessing people from a very wide social network, enabled by the technology that surrounds me.

This ability to connect socially to such a wide network of friends, colleagues, and even strangers has super-charged our ability to learn from each other. Distance and time zones no longer matter. We can find and connect with other people who have solved the same types of problems, and who are eager to share their wisdom and expertise with us. Professional networking sites like LinkedIn and countless professional blogs are empowering us to think about learning from each other in new ways in the workplace too.

Time Scarcity

The third factor driving microlearning is time scarcity. Here is a question for you … If you were not reading this book right now, what would you be doing? I bet it would only take a matter of seconds for you to identify another task – something else you would be doing with your time. You certainly would not be bored or wondering how to fill your day.

That is because in our current society, adults have no shortage of things to do, commitments and priorities to fill their time. In fact, right now Amazon has over 70,000 titles on the topic of *time management*, showing the popularity of trying to find ways to use one of our most precious commodities most wisely. This is true in both our personal lives and at work.

When people need help with a task in their personal lives, they expect to find the knowledge they need right away. They will leave blogs and YouTube videos quickly if they do not find what they are looking for. The same is true at work where they are constantly looking to get their learning and performance support most efficiently, so they can get on with their work duties.

Research from Bersin tells us that employees spend less than 1 percent of a typical workweek on training (Bersin by Deloitte, 2014). And of course, that time is highly distributed – you do not get to the end of the week and have 24 minutes left over – and frankly, if you did, you would just go home early, happy to start the weekend. Because our time for workplace learning is very short and fragmented it is natural for employees to ask, "Can I learn that faster?" or "Can I just look it up?" Adults are always self-assessing how their time is being used and always looking for ways to use their time more effectively. For these reasons, I believe time scarcity is the biggest driver of workplace microlearning from both our learners and their operational leaders, and it is not about being short, it is about being *efficient*.

If we put all three of these together – ubiquitous mobile device usage, access to powerful and broad social networks, and a need to use time as efficiently as possible – we have a perfect combination of factors that drives people's interest in using microlearning.

Defining Microlearning

To date, the term *microlearning* has not been adequately defined. While practitioners may agree that microlearning is short, how short and in what modalities it can best be delivered is up for debate. There are some people who say microlearning should only be delivered electronically, others will say it is only appropriate for informal learning (such as when someone googles for an answer to a problem), and others will say it is only video based.

Let's look at a few definitions leading thought leaders and researchers have proposed:

- educational researcher Theo Hug considers three different levels of education, the micro, meso, and macro levels, where the micro level is the smallest unit of instruction. He says the instruction can last from "less than a second up to more than one hour" (Hug, 2005, p. 3) and that it can be delivered via any modality, including face-to-face and any kind of multimedia, and that it includes instruction designed from any educational approach, including behaviorist, constructivist, problem-oriented, and many others (Hug, 2005).
- workplace learning researcher Will Thalheimer defines microlearning as "[r] elatively short engagements in learning-related activities—typically ranging from a few seconds up to 20 minutes (or up to an hour in some cases)—that may provide any combination of content presentation, review, practice, reflection, behavioral prompting, performance support, goal reminding, persuasive messaging, task assignments, social interaction, diagnosis, coaching, management interaction, or other learning-related methodologies" (Thalheimer, 2017, para. 3). For Thalheimer (2017), microlearning can be used to replace courses, augment courses, provide practice and repetition, provide just-in-time learning, or provide performance support or nudges to support behavior.
- another well-respected researcher, Patti Shank, does not provide a formal definition, but she reminds us that "microlearning must be primarily about learning, not content" (2018, para. 11) and "microlearning is not mostly about technology" (2018, para. 12).
- in their book, *Microlearning: Short and Sweet*, Kapp and Defelice (2019) define microlearning as "an instructional unit that provides a short engagement in an activity intentionally designed to elicit a specific outcome from the participant" (p. 11). As with others, they say the learning must be a discrete instructional unit that can stand on its own and they further suggest it be an "engaging but brief experience to achieve a focused outcome" (p. 13) and

they purposely avoid a specific timeframe because different performance needs will need more or less seat time.

- in my first book (Torgerson, 2016), I took a far less academic approach. I defined microlearning as content that could be consumed in five minutes or less, but said the best guidance for length and format was to self-reference: "Would you give up your time in a busy day for this learning?" (Torgerson, 2016, p. 8). As I have explored and used microlearning more, I have evolved my definition but continue to keep a strong focus on the learner. In my latest book, microlearning is defined as, "short-form content that is just long enough to give learners what they need at that moment and get on with their work" (Torgerson & Iannone, 2020, p. 9). We describe that microlearning can be used in four primary ways: 1) preparation before a longer learning event, 2) follow-up to support a longer learning event, 3) stand-alone training, and 4) performance support (Torgerson & Iannone, 2020). While we believe seat times in a definition about microlearning are limiting, we think such guidelines are incredibly helpful to practitioners, so we recommend that depending on your use, the seat time for microlearning in workplace settings will generally range from less than 30 seconds to up to 10 minutes (Torgerson & Iannone, 2020).

For the purposes of this chapter, which transcends different educational environments, PreK-12, higher education, and workforce training, and which includes both formal and informal learning, I propose we be as broad and all-encompassing as possible. So, for our purposes here, let's define microlearning as **an educational experience that is focused, short, and effective** (see Figure 2.2 below):

- **focused**: the hallmark of microlearning is a focus on the smallest discrete unit of learning, generally a single learning objective or a single reinforcement activity. This enables us to focus the learner's attention, avoid cognitive overload, and provide an environment where we can more easily assess the learner's proficiency.
- **short**: because it is focused on a single learning objective, the learning activity will naturally be short in duration. How short exactly will depend on the learning objective and the performance outcome you are seeking. Also, the learner's time should be used well; the length of the lesson is enough to properly address the learning objective while using the learner's time efficiently.
- **effective**: focus and brevity still require sound instructional practice. Consider your use of educational theories, your modalities, and any use of instructional technology to ensure that the learning objectives are achieved, whether the microlearning is teaching a new concept, reinforcing an existing concept, or something else.

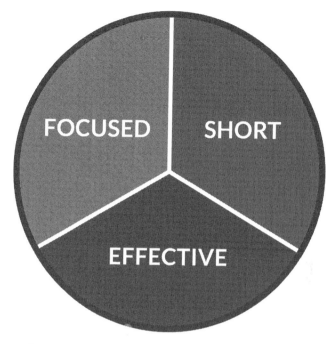

FIGURE 2.2 Definition of microlearning

The Many Uses of Microlearning

Personalized Learning

Some would start this discussion by looking at how microlearning is used in educational institutions or workplace settings, but as I have said, I believe this trend really started from people just like you and me recognizing how they were learning in their personal lives. This became a grass-roots movement that moved into workplace training and development and is now moving into other educational settings. With that in mind, let's first start by thinking about how *you* use microlearning in your daily life.

If you are reading this book, you will likely fall into one of two groups. If you are in the first group, you are a college student studying some branch of education such as educational technology, instructional design, K-12 education, post-secondary education, or workplace education. If you are in the second group, you are a practitioner in one of those fields, or even others. Either way you are an adult learner, and that means you have a personal life!

That personal life is filled with things you want to learn more about – maybe how to fix something in your home, how to better raise your children, how to better understand your physical ailments, or how to make a more delicious supper tonight. In all these examples, there is something you want to learn more about, but because the learning is self-directed and optional, you are in complete control of determining what learning assets meet your needs and when you are *done* with any resource or all learning on the topic.

To be sure, this is informal learning. The late Jay Cross, a leader in this space, said that informal learning is the "unofficial, unscheduled, impromptu way people learn to do their jobs. ... [it] is like riding a bike: the rider chooses the destination, the speed, and the route." (Malamed, n.d., para. 3–4). Cross further wrote that "[f]ormal learning—classes and workshops—is the source of only 10 to 20 percent of what people learn at work" (Cross, 2007, p. iii).

Of course, when your *work* is achieving things in your personal life, you use even more informal learning, and taking formal classes becomes even more rare. Let's make this real with a quick example. Recently, I was having dinner with my family when someone noticed that the rather large container of sour cream was about to expire. Not wanting to throw food away I immediately thought of making a sour cream cake. However, I had never made a sour cream cake before. So, I did the same thing you would probably do ... I pulled out my phone and searched the Internet for how to make a sour cream cake. I found a recipe with clear instructions and tips for how to do the task well, and I am pleased to report that a few days later we had a very delicious sour cream cake.

My needs were simple, but as a learner I was very exacting – the instruction had to be clear, it had to meet my very specific need, and it had to use my time effectively. If it did not meet those three criteria extremely well, I went on to the next resource in search of materials that met my needs better.

This behavior is not unusual; in fact, it is so commonplace that you may not even realize all the times you use your phone, tablet, or laptop to learn something. You look up information, read *how to* guides or blogs, and watch short videos about topics you need answers for or that you are just curious about.

Human beings have always been curious and have always been learning from the world around them. The difference now is that we have technology, the Internet, and all our mobile connections to it, that enable us to learn whatever we want whenever we want. And now that we have realized how often we do that and how much it helps us we are asking how that kind of learning can also be used at work and school to enable us to learn more efficiently and effectively.

Workplace Training and Development

Workplace learning is focused on helping employees to improve specific skills and abilities so they can perform better in their jobs. Best practices include wrapping that learning in the real context of how the employee does that specific job, using specific situations and scenarios that learners are likely to experience on the job. So, for example, if I want to teach the tax accountants at a *Fortune 500* company about the latest tax law changes, I will focus on those things that are relevant to that business size and their specific industry. I will not be teaching the accountants things that are not relevant to the work they do, like changes for the not-for-profit sector or the impacts to filing personal taxes.

We always want to teach people effectively, but in workplace training there is an additional goal (sometimes pressure) to be as efficient as possible. Our employees have jobs to do. Those are the duties they were hired to do. It is what the organization pays them to do, and it will always be their top priority. Learning and getting better at that job will always be a second priority (or lower!). This is not only true for the learner, but also the organizational leaders who approve how much of the employee's time can be used for training.

Consider for a moment this conversation between an employee and his/her manager:

> **Manager**: "You haven't met any of your KPIs for this quarter."
> (KPIs are key performance indicators, or an employee's specific operational goals.)
> **Employee**: "That's because I've gone to a two-day training class every week for the past two months. I'm learning so much!"

We all want to have employees who are engaged with getting better and smarter, but it cannot come at the expense of not getting their work done. In fact, that is so obvious that a conversation like the one above seems absurd. It would only happen with employees who are not doing their jobs properly.

So, as workplace learning and development professionals, we are always facing a balance in figuring out the amount of time needed to effectively teach necessary skills well, but also get people back to their operational duties so they can get their work done.

Given those circumstances you can see how operational leaders, learners, and even progressive training and development professionals would look at how they are learning in short snippets in their personal lives and try to apply that to workplace learning and development. Sometimes workplace learning requires dedicated time in a classroom, but sometimes we can give employees access to short bits of learning and be equally or more effective at helping them to perform better.

Workplace learning professionals use microlearning in a variety of ways to teach new content, reinforce that content, or expand existing skills. In my latest book (Torgerson & Iannone, 2020), I recommend that microlearning in workplace settings be used in four main ways:

- preparation before a learning event
- follow-up to support a learning event
- stand-alone training
- performance support

Figure 2.3 presents these four primary uses of microlearning in the workplace. Let's take a look at examples of each.

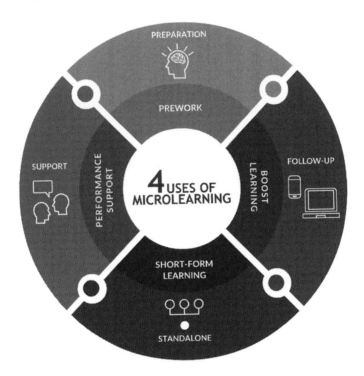

FIGURE 2.3 Four uses of microlearning
Source: Torgerson & Iannone (2020)

Preparation Before a Learning Event

In a former role, I designed leadership development training in a large healthcare organization. Our classes were attended by employees throughout the organization, from clinicians to finance staff to facilities maintenance staff. Some of these employees had enough control over their work that it was reasonable to expect them to complete some pre-work before coming to a class. But for others it was not so simple. Let's say a nurse manager came to class and said, "I'm sorry I didn't get my pre-work done; we had a code on the floor yesterday." Of course, that was acceptable. Not only was the nurse putting operational duties first, but in this case the nurse was ensuring a patient did not die. In our highly clinical environment, there were a myriad of really good reasons for not completing pre-work, but that also made it challenging for us to use pre-work to support classroom instruction to the extent we desired.

Thinking about pre-work in small, bite-sized chunks can help in situations where it is challenging to get people to complete their pre-work. Instead of having an article or e-learning module that will take 30 minutes or an hour to complete, if you can tell learners it will take just five or 10 minutes, you have a greater chance they will be able to fit it in between their operational duties. Even if they do not complete the pre-work, you can encourage them to take a quick look at the article or activity in the few minutes before the class starts or during a break.

Follow-Up to Support a Learning Event

After any training is over, whether live or virtual, synchronous or asynchronous, best educational practices prescribe having some sort of follow-up. We all know that repetition and reinforcement are critical to good learning, but classes and e-learning modules are not often designed with a strong follow-up component. Researchers like Art Kohn and B. Price Kerfoot, as well as companies like *Qstream* and *Axonify* are doing really interesting work focused on follow-up, reinforcement, and repetition. Some even call this *boost learning* because the reinforcement is boosting what was learned in the classroom.

There are many ways microlearning can be used to provide follow-up to longer forms of instruction. For example, the instructor can send learners follow-up emails or text messages after a learning event to remind learners of the key concepts that were covered. These messages can be spaced over days, weeks, and even months. Some systems like *Mobile Coach* can also add chatbot functionality to text messages; learners are presented with a question in a text message, the learners respond, and then they receive feedback. Research from Art Kohn (2014) shows that follow-up repetition and reinforcement does not need to take a lot of time to be effective. He found that follow-up content that takes five seconds to consume is just as effective as content that takes 30 seconds or five minutes to consume (Kohn, 2014).

Another form of follow-up is to have a system like *Axonify* or *Qstream* that pushes questions to employees on their computers or mobile devices. Employees answer a question or two every few days, receiving feedback and additional content when they get a question wrong. Gamification and leaderboards can further enhance the follow-up activities and make it fun for employees to participate, and it takes just a few minutes at the start of the workday for an employee to engage with the content.

Stand-Alone Training

Systems like *Qstream* and *Axonify* can also be used for stand-alone training. There are many concepts that our employees probably know something about, even if they have not been formally trained on them. A lot of compliance topics and soft skills fit in this area, such as what to do if you see someone shoplifting in your store, or how to deliver excellent customer service; you already have an idea what to do whether you have had training on the topic or not.

So, rather than having formal training, progressive organizations use systems like *Axonify* and *Qstream* to present questions about content that the learner probably knows something about, but may not know the specific approaches, policies, or procedures at that organization. These systems generally have an adaptive testing algorithm so if learners answer a question incorrectly, they will see additional questions about similar topics more frequently than if they answered the question correctly. Some organizations are even considering how these few minutes every week spent answering questions and receiving feedback can fulfil state and federal mandates, such as those requiring compliance training on a particular topic for 60 minutes every year.

In addition, e-learning modules and videos can be purposely designed to teach a concept in a short amount of time. For example, I recently developed a course for a medical device manufacturer who needed its sales representatives to know how the organization was changing certain approaches to the technical security and cyberse-curity of their devices. When we assessed what the representatives really needed to know and how it would impact their job, we were able to streamline the course to about seven minutes, including practice activities with a customer. If we had pro-vided more information that was not relevant to the sales representatives' specific need, the learners may have responded negatively to the training. Adult learners are always self-assessing if their time is being used well, and learning professionals are embracing the notion that courses can, and sometimes should, be short.

Performance Support

When our employees are doing their job tasks, they sometimes need support to perform more effectively. For example, have you ever been in the middle of working on something in Microsoft Word or Excel, maybe adding footnotes or creating a pivot table, and you cannot remember exactly how to perform the task? Most likely you quickly looked in the Help menu or searched the Internet for how to do it. In educational terms, this form of self-help is called *performance support* – just-in-time content accessed at the moment you are performing the task and need some assistance. Job aids and checklists are other examples of per-formance support.

Oftentimes, we have classes where we teach people how to do something new, but we do not provide optimal support for them as they apply these new skills on the job. We often provide practice activities during the class, but the real practice happens on the job, when the employee applies the new skills. Research from Gottfredson and Mosher (2012), pioneers in workplace performance sup-port, found that if they provided performance support after a class, they could not only reduce classroom time by half, but in addition, the employee would achieve competency in using those skills on the job twice as fast. So not only do the employees spend less time in training, but when those employees are back on the job their performance also improves at a faster rate.

Performance support is rarely used to its fullest extent, and this is certainly an area where microlearning has an important role. Any time you create just-in-time training in a PDF, a short video, or a short e-learning module, you are creating microlearning for use as performance support. This also gets us into the latest trend in workplace learning and development: *workflow learning*. This is the idea of teaching workers how to perform a task while they are doing it on the job. Instead of stopping work to watch a five-minute video and then returning to the task, the support is integrated into the job task such that the employee does not even stop work. One example of workflow learning is receiving pop-up notifications with tips and techniques when it is detected that the learner is not performing optimally. Advances in technology, including artificial intelligence and personalized content, will increase the possibilities for workflow learning in the future.

K-12 and Higher Education

Compared to workplace education, K-12 and higher education differ in one major way – how we perceive the use of time. In workplace education, we are always looking for how to get people trained and competent as quickly and efficiently as possible so they can get back to their operational duties. In K-12 and higher education, however, learning does not end when the learners have mastered all the competencies, it ends after a predetermined period of time. For example, if my son's first grade teacher told me she had a marvelous new way to teach and she could get all of her students to achieve the state standards by the end of February, I certainly would not expect the school year to end three months early. I would expect her to use the rest of the school year to provide additional educational experiences. The same is true in higher education. In both cases, students and other stakeholders expect the entire time to be used, and the teachers are generally paid based on an assumption that they are working with students for the entire duration. So, the notion of microlearning in these formal learning environments is different – efficiency is not as critical as efficacy, and the primary role of microlearning in K-12 and higher education is focused entirely on improving learning effectiveness using approaches such as chunking, scaffolding, and performance support.

K-12 Education

In many ways, we have used the ideals of microlearning in K-12 education for decades because they are just sound educational practice. When I taught elementary and middle school more than 20 years ago, we were always breaking content down to its smallest unit of measure and teaching that well before moving on to the next concept, and this is still true today. For example, I recently got a text message from my son's first grade teacher that said, "This week we balanced equations with expressions on both sides of the equals sign and learned 'ng' blends." I was reminded at that moment that K-12 educators have always been working with micro-content, focusing on small, discrete pieces of content because it is critical that teachers ensure understanding of key foundational concepts before building other, more advanced ideas on top of them.

While we did not use the term *microlearning* when I was a classroom teacher, you can find the term being discussed in K-12 circles today. For example, the *Professional Learning Board* (n.d.), an organization that helps Minnesota teachers meet continuing education mandates has a blog post about the value of microlearning in the classroom. In it they promote the value of microlearning, but the things they write about are those same things that elementary teachers have been doing for decades: short activities catered to children's short attention spans, using small chunks of content to improve comprehension and retention, and using a variety of media to engage students in different ways (Professional Learning Board, n.d.).

Although the ideas of microlearning really are not new in K-12 education, this space (like all other branches of education) continues to evolve in its use of technology to provide content in ways that are personalized to students' needs and provide repetition or reference in ways that engage students. When I was teaching in the elementary classroom, we were using paper-based materials and large desktop computers; now my son uses a variety of apps on his classroom iPad, and of course this use of technology will continue to evolve, making microlearning increasingly accessible and popular.

Higher Education

Similar to K-12, skilled faculty members in higher education, including graduate and professional education, have been using the ideals of microlearning for a very long time. Despite this, excitement about *new* approaches of microlearning are becoming more common in the academy. As Bogardus Cortez writes in her discussion of microlearning in higher education environments, "[e]ducators have been doing it for years without labeling it as such" (2018, para. 4). The goal is to break content down into smaller pieces to prevent cognitive overload and provide smaller concepts for students to discuss and apply. It also facilitates repetition and reinforcement that enable the learning to stick (Bogardus Cortez, 2018).

Trowbridge, Waterbury, and Sudbury remind us that for college students, "[i]nformal microlearning occurs on multiple levels every day … [and] students have become accustomed to gathering and consuming information in bursts" (2017, para. 5). As a result, this is causing some faculty members to think about how they can capitalize on short-form learning, particularly through social channels to support their classroom teaching – in just the same way their students are learning in their daily lives on *Instagram*, *Facebook*, and *Twitter*. Trowbridge, Waterbury, and Sudbury advocate for this sort of interaction in and out of the classroom because "encouraging contributions … on the social environment gives students the opportunity to synthesize information and use higher order thinking skills" (para. 85) as they practice, discuss, and apply those concepts they are learning in class.

Educators in higher education environments, including professional and graduate education, are always looking to make their teaching more effective, and microlearning may be the latest word people use to describe a variety of things that they are doing; but other than using the latest technology in that instruction, the teaching approaches are not all that new. They are still using the same effective educational practices they have used for a long time.

However, in higher education, we see some very interesting movements around micro-credentialing – that is, how these educational institutions think about the curriculum and structure of certificate and degree programs. As Gallagher writes, "colleges and universities that seek to meet corporate needs must move beyond monolithic programs and think in terms of competencies, unbundling curriculum, modularizing and 'microlearning'" (2017, para. 14).

Many institutions of higher education, especially those in career and technical education are starting to take their degree programs and break them into multiple shorter programs of study. They offer badges or certificates to those students who complete a small number of related courses, and multiple badges or certificates can lead to a degree. There are several advantages to this approach. First, students can earn just the certificate(s) that are targeted to the work they want to do, and second, they can complete their studies and start their career more quickly. Alternately, students with certificates can obtain work in their chosen fields while working on other certificates and/or earning a degree. Some students might pursue a more individualized educational path that includes earning a badge or certificate, working for a while, then coming back to school for more education as they complete their degree as more experienced (and probably more engaged) students. This movement toward micro-credentialing is particularly strong in technical fields where it is easier to assess and certify students on specific skills. This is because you can chunk those skills into certificates rather than requiring the student to complete an entire degree before being able to enter the workforce in their chosen field.

Summary and Next Steps

In many ways, microlearning is not new – it is something effective educators have been doing for decades. But in many other ways it is the latest trend causing instructional professionals to think differently about everything they do. The microlearning phenomenon is really a grass-roots movement driven by people recognizing how they are learning in their daily lives, especially using their mobile devices and the Internet, to become more effective in a multitude of ways. So now, those people are asking how we can use these same ideas in their workplace learning, enabling them to learn more efficiently and effectively at work. The broad embrace of these principles in workplace learning is now causing microlearning to be considered in higher education and K-12 environments as well.

For this book, we define microlearning as **an educational experience that is focused, short, and effective**. Microlearning is based on foundational concepts of learning that have been in practice for decades. These include avoiding cognitive overload, breaking content into its smallest pieces to enable effective learning of complex objectives over time and using repetition and reinforcement to support long-term retention. The microlearning trend is helping to remind us of those practices and to use them more regularly. It is also causing new technologies to be developed that support delivering personalized and short-form content to learners of all ages.

As microlearning evolves, I am most interested in seeing how workplace learning and performance support evolves. How will we be supporting employees just-in-time, providing content and support while they are in the flow of work? I am eager to see how artificial intelligence and access to bigger datasets about our learners will drive our ability to support employees with personalized just-in-time content that will help them to do their jobs most effectively.

Discussion Questions

1. In this chapter, we defined microlearning as an educational experience that is focused, short, and effective. Do you agree with this definition? Why or why not?

2. In this chapter, we discussed three factors driving interest in microlearning: mobile device usage, social connectedness, and time scarcity. Do you agree that these factors are driving the push to use microlearning? Are there other factors you would add to this list?

3. What are some ways you used microlearning to learn something in your personal life in the past week? What was most effective? What was least effective?

4. What are some of the best ways educators and instructional designers can use microlearning in workplace education? In higher education? In K-12 education?

5. In this chapter, we discussed the use of time as a fundamental difference between using microlearning in workplaces compared to K-12 and post-secondary settings. Do you agree with this? Why or why not?

References

ATD. (2018). Microlearning: Bite-sized content. https://d22bbllmj4tvv8.cloudfront.net/a 4/b2/97956b4245e0940bd9388fde54b0/tk-microlearning-ebook-as-v3.pdf.
Bersin by Deloitte. (2014). Meet the modern learner. Infographic.

Bogardus Cortez, M. (2018, January). What is microlearning: The education tactic stopping student burnout syndrome. EdTech Focus on Higher Education. https://edtechmagazine. com/higher/k12/article/2018/01/what-microlearning-education-tactic-stopping-student-burnout-syndrome.

Cross, J. (2007). *Informal Learning: Rediscovering the Natural Pathways That Inspire Innovation and Performance*. San Francisco: Pfeiffer.

EduTech Wiki. (2016). Microlearning. http://edutechwiki.unige.ch/en/Microlearning.

Gallagher, S. (2017, November). As corporate world moves toward curated 'microlearning,' higher ed must adapt. EdSurge. www.edsurge.com/news/2017-11-06-as-corporate-world-moves-toward-curated-microlearning-higher-ed-must-adapt.

Gottfredson, C. & Mosher, B. (2012, May). "We're lost, but we're making good time": Performance support to the rescue. *Learning Solutions*. https://learningsolutionsmag.com/articles/934/were-lost-but-were-making-good-time-performance-support-to-the-rescue.

Hug, T. (2005). *Micro learning and narration: Exploring possibilities of utilization of narrations and storytelling for the designing of "micro units" and didactical micro-learning arrangements*. Paper presented at the fourth Media in Transition conference, May 6–8, 2005, MIT, Cambridge (MA), USA. https://pdfs.semanticscholar.org/3687/48054120bdb5448dd70dcc59fe7208 f20eb6.pdf.

Kapp, K. & Defelice, R. (2019). *Microlearning: Short and Sweet*. Alexandria, VA: ATD Press.

Kohn, A. (2014, May). Brain science: Enable your brain to remember almost everything. *Learning Solutions*. https://learningsolutionsmag.com/articles/1423/brain-science-enable-your-brain-to-remember-almost-everything.

Malamed, C. (n.d.). Informal learning: An interview with Jay Cross. http://theelearningcoach. com/elearning2-0/informal-learning-an-interview-with-jay-cross/.

McGovern, M. (2017). Who coined the term microlearning?https://www.quora.com/ Who-coined-the-term-microlearning.

Professional Learning Board. (n.d.). Microlearning in the classroom. https://k12teachersta ffdevelopment.com/tlb/microlearning-in-the-classroom/.

Shank, P. (2018, February). Microlearning, macrolearning. What does research tell us? eLearning Industry. https://elearningindustry.com/microlearning-macrolearning-research-tell-us.

Thalheimer, W. (2017). Definition of microLearning. www.worklearning.com/2017/01/ 13/definition-of-microlearning/.

Torgerson, C. (2016). The microlearning guide to microlearning. Torgerson Consulting.

Torgerson, C. & Iannone, S. (2020). *What Works in Talent Development: Designing Micro-learning*. Alexandria, VA: ATD Press.

Trowbridge, S., Waterbury C., & Sudbury, L. (2017, April). Learning in bursts: Micro-learning with social media. EDUCAUSE Review. https://er.educause.edu/articles/ 2017/4/learning-in-bursts-microlearning-with-social-media.

PART II

Designing Microlearning Objects

3

SOUND PEDAGOGY PRACTICES FOR DESIGNING AND IMPLEMENTING MICROLEARNING OBJECTS

Theo Hug

Introduction

While pedagogy is a widely used concept in education policy, research, and practice, the terms "sound pedagogy" and "microlearning" appear rather rarely in these arenas. This is not surprising since the term "pedagogy" can be traced back to Plato's political philosophy and his concept of paideia (Cooper, 1997; Jaeger, 1986; Lichtenstein, 1970), whereas the term "microlearning" has been in use for less than 20 years (Hug, 2005). Denotations and connotations of pedagogy and pedagogical practices refer to a wide field of historic and contemporary phenomena including learning, teaching, educating, instructing, leading, guiding, consulting, helping, upbringing, and enabling personal or social development. Also, with the case of microlearning, there are numerous characterizations and definitions currently circulating the Internet. These commonly refer to specific forms of micro-content and learning tools, bite-sized learning in training contexts or short engagements in teaching or learning-related activities.

Even though pedagogy and microlearning refer to a great diversity of educational, cultural, and socio-technical phenomena, they have a few things in common. Firstly, they can refer to phenomena *avant la lettre* (Hierdeis, 2007). Long before the documentation of systematic thinking of content, goals, forms, and methods of pedagogy, the survival of the next generation had to be secured. Similarly, before educational research and social theory were established as academic endeavors, knowledge of how to steer clear of cultural and nature-related difficulties had to be imparted. Secondly, both fields are struggling with enormous complexities and issues of simplicity, especially when it comes to practical applications in ever changing mediated environments. Thirdly, the work of metaphors in these fields is often underestimated, be it in the context of everyday practices or in the context of examination of pedagogy, learning, and teaching as art, science, or profession. Fourthly, both fields can be characterized by paradoxical structures, not least regarding terminological issues. Communicating concepts and practices of pedagogy, education, and learning is related to phenomena that can be found around the globe although we usually do not have simple translations from one language to another for any one of these terms. This also applies to the term communication. Fifthly, pedagogy, education, and learning are contested concepts. Corresponding characterizations and definitions are always situated in a field of tension between conceptual clarification and politics of concepts (*Begriffspolitik*) – a field of tension that is quite rarely reflected upon explicitly.

These introductory considerations already demonstrate that in an era of ongoing digitization, globalization and medialization, hopes for a *really* sound pedagogy serving as *the* or at least the most important starting point for all kinds of microlearning applications are questionable. The dream of an all-embracing pedagogy that could function as a solid and proven framework for designing microlearning objects and practices is over, whether or not we emphatically plead for placing the highest emphasis on pedagogical expertise in educational contexts. This does not mean we should leave the sensitive issues of learning and education to the administrative units dealing with day-to-day practical considerations, or to pedagogically unskilled IT technicians or even to the greedy, out-of-control global education industry with numerous financial interests. It is rather a reminder that we cannot avoid navigating through unexplored territory between continuities of thinking within pedagogical traditions and challenges of digital, media-cultural, and social transformation. In this situation, it can be useful to recall Otto Neurath's metaphor of the ship-at-sea rebuild, which was originally aimed at a critique of the basic role of protocol sentences as the central starting point of the sciences: "We are like sailors who must rebuild their ship on the open sea, never able to dismantle it in dry-dock and to reconstruct it there out of the best materials" (Neurath, 1959, p. 201).

This should not be taken as a plea for an uncritical pedagogical practicality (*Praktizismus*), an educational technicism without requiring ethical considerations or an empiricism which lacks serious theoretical underpinning. I would rather question the argument that sound pedagogical practices are conceivable only on the basis of a specific learning theory, a general educational theory (*Bildungstheorie*) or a critical theory of society, culture, or technology. There is a multitude of possible microlearning applications as related to more or less "sound" pedagogy practices. However, an over-hasty reduction of this complexity to a set of pedagogies and web-based tools for microlearning is only available at the cost of pedagogical relevance, theoretical solidity, and sustainable development of education systems.

If we are interested in trustworthy forms of educational designs, we need to be aware of the wider contexts of changing media-historical constellations, educational, and learning cultural developments, as well as evolving socio-technical systems. For that purpose, the concept of the simultaneity of the non-simultaneous can be fruitfully applied. This figure of thought has been and still is important in the context of discourses in the historical self-understanding of postmodernity (Schmieder, 2017). It can also contribute to a better understanding of various languages related to

- different ways of describing and designing microlearning concepts, objects, and applications
- different forms of dealing with time and conflicting time regimes
- rhetoric of innovation and pressure to change on educational institutions and training facilities, and not least, to
- power asymmetries between the administrative, economic, pedagogical, political, and technological actors involved in shaping the future of education.

In the following sections of this paper, I will elaborate on the abovementioned points with the goal to discuss important aspects of sound pedagogy with regards to microlearning. Finally, the chapter reflects on contemporary challenges for education and learning. In doing so, it highlights the relevance of combining micro-, meso-, and macro-perspectives of learning and the need to develop new pedagogical paradoxes and innovative design principles for educational transformation.

Defining Sound Pedagogy Practices and Exemplifying Micro-Perspectives

First of all, what does sound pedagogy mean and what are sound pedagogical practices? How can sound pedagogy be used as a framework for microlearning and dealing with micro-content? While some educationalists, trainers, and instructional designers use these expressions quite commonly, I am not at ease with them. Correspondingly, I want to pause for a moment and consider horizons of their meaning.

Certainly, there are literal and non-literal uses of speech, also in the case of our topic. Expressions like "sound pedagogy" can be used in both verbatim and figurative, non-literal ways. As metaphors they can contribute to *common sense* production and community building among educationalists or even in societies. But their common use should not hide the fact that creative potentials, tendencies of familiarization, and mediating functions across various discursive contexts are not the only relevant aspects here. Apart from functions of bridge building and visualization of the invisible, there are also issues of oversimplification, misleading ambiguity, and concealment of problematic dimensions. Typically, the clarification of specific meanings requires a mutual reference between literal and non-literal concepts as well as a consideration of their contextual use. Since the expression "sound pedagogy" plays a key role in this chapter, a closer look at basic interpretations is worthwhile.

Sound Pedagogy – Literal Interpretations

Sound pedagogies, in a literal sense, refer to educational approaches exploring the world of music and cultures of listening, supporting learning processes by acoustic means, or creating sonic media artifacts. As in other pedagogical approaches, theoretical analysis, empirical study, and practical applications may be developed rather separately or in intertwined forms. Droumeva and Murphy (2016), for example, aim at synergies between theory and practice through further development of pedagogies of listening (Hua, 2012; Schafer, 1992) and combinations of applied audiovisual media work as well as theoretical analysis of critical cultural texts. Another approach to production pedagogies has been presented by Tinkle (2015). He argues, that "sonic artists since Cage have critiqued music's normalizing and hierarchical pedagogies, but simultaneously offered their own strikingly ambitious counter-pedagogies, often addressing listening not only within an aesthetic frame, but in the very life of the subject" (Tinkle, 2015, p. 222). In his framework, he goes beyond didactic approaches and techniques for listening to music widely used in music education. Instead, he is focusing on techniques for listening in general and opening up corresponding emancipatory potentials, democratic interaction, and possibilities for more immediate forms of participation than conventional Western musical training allows for. In conclusion, he states that just

> as traditional music education aims primarily to make a person 'literate' in the sign system of Western art music, sound pedagogy embeds us in practices of listening that, like language, are culturally contingent and constrain what can be heard or understood.
>
> *(Tinkle, 2015, p. 230)*

Practices related to sound pedagogies or pedagogies of listening may refer to affirmative or critical understandings of educational work and research. In any case, practices, learning topics, and media productions can be designed and analyzed by considering micro-, meso-, and macro-perspectives of learning. For example, creating audio-based narratives in classrooms considering individual interests related to a topic usually involve a bundle of didactic elements. These may correspond with suggestions, invitations, guidance, support, and briefing as regards to specific technical skills, aspects of sound design, relevant cultural codes, proposed messages, elements of storytelling, etc. – all of this is always dependent on previous knowledge, existing abilities, levels of instruction and learning cultural contexts.

Focusing on specific elements may be part of a rigorously structured teaching concept, a semi-structured project-oriented approach, or an action learning approach without any preconceived views of the outcomes. However, the didactic arrangement is conceptualized, practices such as training activities by repeated exercises, as frequent modes of performance or as professional pedagogical engagement – can always be taken into account on micro-, meso-, and macro-levels. Practices – as jointly performed procedures in specific contexts, based on mutual orientations of the actors involved – can always be connected, for example, with

- specific relationships between concrete learners, teachers, subjects, interventions, and things (micro-level)
- institutional contexts of meaning-making and issues of organizational learning (meso-level)
- cultural traditions, media-historic constellations and societal structures (macro-level).

In doing so, it can be illustrated how micro-dimensions of pedagogical practices are relevant for individual learning as well as for institutional development and the societal organization of educational issues. Depending on *how* the three levels are distinguished and conceptualized, and *how* specific aspects are contextualized and interrelated, this can be done in manifold ways with reference to various theoretical approaches including social or media-cultural systems theory (Luhmann, 2012; Schmidt, 2005), human ecology theory (Bronfenbrenner, 1979; Bubolz & Sontag, 1993), and practice theory (*Praxistheorie*) (Schatzki, 2001; Schäfer, 2016).

It is important to be aware that practices of microlearning and microteaching are a matter of *perspectivation* of processes and process results rather than of a generally accepted and reliably surveyed microcosm of the world of education. Depending on the specific pedagogical tasks and contexts, it makes sense to refer to the quality of a tone, a single design element, a sound snippet, a sound map, or a course unit as micro-unit, for example. In all probability, there is no theoretical limit to how small a unit of instruction can be. The minuteness of a micro-unit of instruction is always relative to the standards accepted in a specific context as well as to practical plausibility and viability. Moreover, if a practical example of a soundscape as a result of a media production assignment is uploaded onto You-Tube, this can serve as a starting point for reflections on action and the relevance of "global microstructures" (Knorr Cetina & Bruegger, 2002) in everyday life as well as contexts of amateur and professional production of sonic representations.

The benefits of such an approach to microlearning are not only flexible options for educational design and enhanced options for reflecting on educational tasks and their relevance in individual, organizational, and societal contexts. The benefits also refer to

- overcoming still widespread myths of taking learning results as direct effects of teaching practices
- enhancing perspectives for critical thinking and reflecting interrelations of individual, organizational, and societal relevance structures
- relating intended functions and factual educational dynamics and outcomes.

From a pragmatic perspective, endeavors of dealing with complexity and contingency can be frustrating and demanding, especially in situations in which workplace-specific and practical everyday challenges are already over-demanding. Accordingly, it can be helpful to link moments of microlearning with concrete time frames, such as five or fifteen minutes. Of course, such time frames are arbitrary, and depending on the context of practice there may be good reasons to define "micro" as a few seconds, a few minutes, or in some cases even an hour, particularly as the subjective perception of time may be more important than electronically measured time.

Similarly, microdosing has become relevant in medical research and attempts to increase physical or mental performance or improve creativity and emotional balance. In the same way, educational forms of "microdosing" can create opportunities for experiential learning and joint reflection and promote a culture of curiosity in sound pedagogy. A good example is the project *Minute of Listening* (Welch, 2019),[1] promoted by Sound and Music, the national charity for new music in the UK. It supports pupils in the development of listening skills, language usage, creative work, and interpersonal skills. The project aims to

- Enable every primary school child to experience the richness and diversity the world of music and sound has to offer;
- Promote a culture of curious, active and reflective listening in schools;
- Introduce music and sound as a stimulus for analytical thinking and imaginative enquiry;
- Create a daily opportunity for experiential learning, group discussion and conceptual exploration;
- Make an impact on the social cohesion of classes/group;
- Make an impact on individual pupils' concentration, listening and collaboration skills; and
- Provide all teachers, whether confident musicians or not, with a resource through which they can develop their repertoire of creative learning, with the act of listening to music and sound becoming a window to other creative opportunities (both musical and non-musical).

(Welch, 2019)

Possibilities to experience the diversity of the world of music and sound can be particularly relevant in education, not only with regards to a variety of codes underlying art music from all over the world but also from the perspective of different modes of meaning-making and frameworks of pedagogy in general.

A good example of an approach dealing with the relationship between visuals and sound is *Biophilia*, a studio album by the Icelandic singer Björk (2011), and the corresponding *Biophilia* App.[2] This approach aims at rethinking the relationship between nature and technology and opening up creative modes of intuitive and embodied forms of music making (Dibben, 2014). Using touchscreens as an intuitive tool for making music and exploring aspects of musical structures through natural-world phenomena for reasonably short periods of time (approx. 15 minutes) can be characterized as a multimodal form of microlearning. Moreover, both in institutional education, as well as in the context of extracurricular activities, the approach can serve as a "corrective to ocularcentric banking pedagogies where knowledge is fixed and progress is unidirectionally measured" (Abramo, 2014, p. 78).

In contrast, there are also microlearning approaches for sound pedagogies that aim at making use of music cultures and listening habits for educational purposes. A successful example is *Flocabulary*, [3] an approach that features engaging ways to teach and to learn by means of hip-hop videos. The key point about the project, which connects a wide range of applications in support of efficient vocabulary building, memorizing standardized content of K-12 curricula and developing 21st-century skills, is utilization of rhythm and rhyme. The short sequences can be flexibly embedded in curricular structures and various didactic designs. However, it would be short-sighted to only recognize aspects of increasing memory performance here. No less important are questions of motivation as well as the development of learning cultures in educational institutions and connecting formal and informal learning contexts. In addition, ethical and practical limitations of the utilization of genuine musical cultures as related to hip-hop movements and the musical genre for educational purposes should be considered, too.

To summarize the above sections, two things can be highlighted: first of all, there are multifaceted options for the integration of short aural microlearning activities both in music education and in formal and non-formal educational contexts. Even though the term "microlearning" is rarely used in the context of sound pedagogies, it makes sense to differentiate micro-, meso-, and macro-perspectives of learning as regards pedagogical concepts and corresponding practices. Secondly, sound pedagogies, in a literal sense, point beyond themselves and cultures of listening or educational approaches exploring the world of music. They remind us of the relative relevance of analytic, cognitive, acoustic, or visual ways of understanding and worldmaking. They also remind us of the importance of multimodal and multicodal forms of meaning-making as well as the potentials of multisensory approaches and different modes of resonance. Finally, they contribute to understanding why sound pedagogies in a non-literal sense require integrative forms of the development of creative, critical, and computational thinking, especially in times of digitization and globalization.

Sound Pedagogy – Non-Literal Interpretations

Non-literal interpretations of sound pedagogies are different from literal interpretations in a number of respects. While literal interpretations aim at more or less thoughtful clarifications of the subject and corresponding theoretical, empirical, or application-oriented dimensions, non-literal interpretations of sound pedagogies commonly refer to a wide range of metaphorical descriptions. Although the goal of most metaphorical uses is some kind of "profound pedagogy" in contrast to shallow forms, typically, meanings as well as issues of enlightening and obscuring aspects of metaphorical expressions are not explicitly reflected. For example, Agostinho et al. (2005) describe the basic features of a Smart Learning Design Framework (SLDF) and "tools to support academics to design pedagogically sound learning environments" (p. 77). In contrast to older repositories of learning objects, the framework offers support for academic teachers to integrate selected learning objects with learning designs and to enable high-quality learning experiences for students. While the paper does not provide a detailed explanation of the pedagogical "soundness" of learning environments, the project website translates the expression as "proven learning designs."[4] Here, it is up to the reader to interpret characteristics of proof in a weaker or stronger sense as: useful, tried and tested, established, reliable, or proven in a strict or truth-oriented sense.

Similarly, the objective of the work described in Miao et al. (2009) is "to support practitioners in developing pedagogically sound and technically executable learning designs" (p. 260). They argue "that a pedagogy-specific modeling language may be a promising approach to help teachers to develop, communicate, understand, adopt, and adapt learning designs and enable computers to interpret, instantiate, and automate learning designs in practice as well" (p. 260). Moreover, they state that "a technically executable learning design can support teachers and students to focus on their substantive teaching and learning activities, minimizing concerns about coordination and logistical activities" (p. 259f). Like Agostinho et al. (2005), Miao et al. (2009) do not provide a comprehensive definition of "sound pedagogies." Although they are aware that generic notations and a flexible modeling language are needed in order to support a wide range of pedagogical strategies, they do not reflect on limitations of dealing with demands of machine-interpretable forms, of the formalization of pedagogical principles, and of the formal educational process modeling languages. Here, "soundness" of pedagogy practices refers to technical executability of formal descriptions of a selection of typical teaching and learning activities – mostly for the purposes of distance learning – rather than, for example, the practical viability of meaningful pedagogies based on educational theories, rich in both content and sense of orientation. Paradoxically, such metaphorical uses of "sound pedagogies" leave the exact meaning of this expression open-ended, claims of a solid pedagogical basis and flexible educational processes that are important for teachers and learners are suggested.

Two things are important at this point. Firstly, metaphorical uses of expressions like sound pedagogy may be intended as a way to distinguish contemporary "smart" forms of learning design from 20th century forms of instructional design for web-based training and distant learning focusing on repositories of learning objects while at the same time lacking didactic considerations and flexible tools for pedagogical activities. Secondly, as far as such kinds of metaphorical uses aim at reasonable argumentation and references in respect of research-based pedagogy, they tend to show characteristics of vague and *pars pro toto* arguments. Even without an in-depth analysis of the sound metaphor, a wide range of meanings can be demonstrated.

If we take metaphors as "linguistic vehicles through which something new is constructed" (Krippendorff, 2009, p. 51), we find a variety of options for framing qualities of pedagogies and pedagogical practices by means and meanings of sound. It makes a difference which of the meanings is at the heart of the argument and how it is used as a source for framing the target: solid or stable, prudent or senseful, stable or secure, reliable or reasonable, sober-minded or based on good judgment, logically or legally valid, agreeing with accepted views or free from misapprehension or fallacy, scientifically proven or based on thorough knowledge and experience, and other similar meanings. Regardless whether a special meaning, a bundle of meanings, or the whole semantic field is used for characterizing "sound pedagogies" in a concrete case, there are always perspectives that are highlighted or opened up while others are concealed or obscured. Moreover, there are always corresponding tendencies of the implicit or explicit inclusion or exclusion of pedagogies and pedagogy practices.

For example, if "sound pedagogy" refers to a pedagogy based on thorough experience and the learning environment, it allows for various practical choices and modes of orchestrating micro-didactic elements as related to different learning designs. This could apply to Montessori methods as well as a set of learning methods as provided in a digital environment based on the Smart Learning Design Framework (SLDF). However, modes of concentrating on the needs, talents, and abilities of each individual learner, the significance of personal development, and enhancement of scopes of action as well as ways of pedagogical reasoning for microlearning might differ substantially – occasionally to the point of mutually denying "soundness," for example, in terms of allegations of short-sighted educational technicism on the one hand, and technophobic pedagogical tenet on the other.

This brings us to the second point I would like to make here. Let us put the various meanings of the sound-metaphor aside for a moment. Even if we agree on research-based and theoretically justified pedagogy as a synonym for sound pedagogy, and even if we focus on the academic research and not on the administrative or commercial applications research that is oriented towards very specific practical requirements, we are not facing easy solutions that allow for doubtlessly clear attributions of sound pedagogy practices to generally accepted pedagogies based on empirical evidence or theoretical reasoning. First of all, pedagogical practices are rather seldom connected to one teaching method or learning theory, or to a specific set of results from educational research only. Secondly, even if a microlearning pedagogy is research-based, the corresponding pedagogical practices may be anything but sound translations of a profound background. Last but not least, the question of what counts as high-quality research and excellent scholarship is controversially discussed in academia. The role of "soundness" and "rigor" in educational research and its relation to research funding policies, or to political, economic or other ideologies, is a matter of academic communities and educational research cultures in different countries rather than of a standardized and globally accepted set of criteria for "normal science" (Bridges, 2019; Keiner, 2019; Smeyers, 2019). Relationships between empirical research, systematic theory formation, education as discipline, and contexts of pedagogical application have been characterized in many ways. Especially, if we look beyond various research communities and academic cultures in different regions of the world, there is no consensus in sight as regards to modes of disciplining thought, designing learning research, as well as designing and evaluating pedagogical practices.

If we want to avoid hasty judgments by riding on the wave of mainstreamed research trends and going with the flow of questionable microlearning hypes, we have to carefully navigate between Scylla and Charybdis, between pragmatic short-term solutions in view of limited resources and sustainable solutions based on prudent approaches, and, between differentiated reasoning and innovative thinking concerning relations of micro-, meso-, and macro-perspectives of learning. This involves an awareness of diverse discursive contexts of framing micro-content and microlearning practices.

The importance of paradigmatic differences for designing microlearning practices and dealing with micro-units can be illustrated by prototypical examples referring to learning theories on the one hand and educational theories on the other. Often, talk of designing and implementing microlearning objects is associated with instructional design or types of learning design that put a strong emphasis on technical feasibility of controlled learning processes and outcomes.

In *Microlearning: Short and Sweet* (2019), Karl M. Kapp and Robyn A. Defelice take an all-encompassing approach in order to "demystify what microlearning really is, to offer all the learning theories and research that supports it, and to present an actionable road map for planning, implementing, designing, and evaluating it" (2019, p. v). The authors define microlearning as "an instructional unit that provides a short engagement in an activity intentionally designed to elicit a specific outcome from the participant" (2019, p. 11). In their understanding, microlearning units are deliberately designed small didactic arrangements as part of larger learning ecosystems aiming at highly probable and desired outcomes at calculable expenditures. This kind of educational calculation places the instructional units – including tools, resources, and "everything the participant needs" (2019, p. 11) – at the disposal of instructors, microlearning providers, and key decision-makers. The role of participants – the authors avoid the terms learner and student (2019, p. 13) – is to be committed to the intentionally designed microlearning events and to contribute actively and at best to the production of the intended outcomes. The short and effective units thus aim at performance and behavior changes, typically of employees, managers, or all staff members of companies.

Kapp and Defelice (2019, pp. 41–54) illustrate their approach to microlearning by a sample of use cases referring to a typology of pensive-based, performance-based, persuasive-based, post-instruction-based, practice-based, and preparation-based microlearning. It is obvious that there are some paradoxes at work here. On the one hand, the whole approach is goal- and performance-oriented; on the other hand, performance-based microlearning is characterized as an immediate or near-term type of performance that can "supplement, reinforce, and augment training" (p. 45). In the case of "pensive microlearning," learners are asked "to reflect upon an idea, situation, or learning task" (p. 43). This type is based on Roger Schank's idea of a "sounding board,"[5] a digital environment that leads the learner through a brainstorm session. Pensive microlearning is meant to "hone critical thinking and creative problem-solving" (p. 44). However, further details concerning an understanding of critical thinking, corresponding theoretical foundations, and their relevance for the "soundness" of the described microlearning practices are not available in this volume.

As for suggestions of "following sound design principles" (p. 113) in order to make microlearning engaging, effective, and successful, Kapp and Defelice (2019, pp. 114–135) present an outline of practical suggestions regarding the following fields: writing style, questions, podcasting, graphics and visuals, gamification, short sims, and storyboarding, with "short and sweet" acting as the meta-principle. However, the authors provide some practical hints for the production of small and appealing instructional units, but no well-considered design principles related to design theory, learning theory, or educational research. Although their links to developments in learning theory are rather loose, trainers, IT professionals, and human resource managers may find some useful instructions concerning micro-formats, especially in workplace learning and on-the-job training.

For critical thinkers and educationalists who are interested in theoretical backgrounds, such an understanding of "sound pedagogy," "sound design principles," and "sound pedagogy principles," is problematic, not simply because of a strong orientation towards common-sense thinking and optimization on micro-levels of learning without questioning the goals. It is also problematic for other reasons, especially related to multiple reductionisms. Firstly, there is the notion of learners as "participants" to be led through ready-made micro-programs aiming at unchallenged goals of behavioral shaping. In this conception of output-driven streamlining, learners are taken as objects to be handled rather than as subjects capable of differentiated meaning-making, reflexive decision-taking, and meaningful action. A second reductionist tendency concerns the predominantly strategic and technical understanding of "implementation" (Kapp & Defelice 2019, pp. 89–108). If microlearning is related to new media practices and learning cultures, too, then it does not make much sense to focus primarily on rational enforcement, instrumental execution, or top-down unrolling of the programs. Implementation should rather be considered as the thoughtful introduction of innovative learning practices, context-sensitive actualization of educational concepts fostering open-mindedness, fruition of creative ideas, or transformative translation of abstract concepts in concrete situations.

A third reductionism is related to instrumental perspectives on learning as "tool" and to learning discourses generally. For practicing educationalists and trainers, focusing on a selection of learning theories and repeating the mantra of a threefold classification of the world of learning – behaviorism, cognitivism, and constructivism, supplementing connectivism as the latest highlight in the evolution of learning theories – may seem helpful. It may also seem sufficient for practitioners, although important aspects concerning forms of learning how to learn, unconscious dimensions of learning, living or alienated learning, as well as modes of learning of organizations, generations, and societies are being ignored (Hug, 2010). However, a major dimension of reductionism is the mode of exclusively focusing on learning and learning research itself. It is one thing to acknowledge learning sciences (Sawyer, 2014) and its achievements as widely discussed in Anglo-American research contexts. It is another thing to consider such perspectives as the most important areas of responsibility in the context of education and pedagogy. For one thing, there are many research fields – including philosophy, psychology, sociology, pedagogy, history, computer science, neuroscience, sustainability studies, organization studies, media studies, and gender studies – contributing to a better understanding of processes and phenomena of learning. Then again, pedagogy as educational research dealing with pedagogical practices is a research field on its own, even if we are mindful of its fuzzy boundaries (Glaser & Keiner, 2014) and even if we value reference disciplines as Johann Friedrich Herbart (1776–1841) already did in his introduction to *Umriss pädagogischer Vorlesungen* (1841) with a view to philosophy and psychology as early as 180 years ago (Hug, 2013, p. 44f).

While Herbart (1841, p. 1) focused on the educationability (*Bildsamkeit*) of humans as the basic concept of pedagogy, he also emphasized the relevance of focusing on "native" concepts of pedagogy – concepts that are original or endemic to the discipline.[6] He argues as follows:

> It would arguably be better if pedagogy remembered its endemic [*einheimisch*] concepts as accurately as possible and made an effort to cultivate independent thinking, whereby it would become the center of a research sphere and avoid the risk of being governed by a stranger as a distant, conquered province.
>
> *(Herbart, 1806, p. 8)*

More than 200 years later, issues of assigning content-related competence and functional responsibility have become more complex but not less relevant. Various aspirations to do research from neuroscientific, psychological, sociological, historical, or philosophical perspectives asking questions *about* aspects of education (Biesta, 2011, p. 190; Friesen, 2019) go hand in hand with claims of a primary responsibility for educational practices coming from state, economic, or ecclesiastic powers, and also from media institutions and the global education industry (Verger et al., 2016). However, mainstream developments are oriented towards instrumentalism and technological perspectives while educational questions from pedagogical perspectives play a minor role, not only in the Anglo-American world but increasingly all over the world, not least in continental Europe.

Web-didactics as developed by Meder (2006) and Swertz (2004) is an example of a sound pedagogy, which aims at further developing pedagogical traditions of the integration of synthetic and analytical micro-steps as formerly suggested by Herbart (1806). In this approach, the didactic transformation and organization of knowledge is designed on the basis of didactical micro-models as applicable to different forms of knowledge, like orientational knowledge (*Orientierungswissen*), explanational knowledge (*Erklärungswissen*), know-how (*Handlungswissen*), or source-knowledge (*Quellenwissen*). Depending on specific contexts of education, condition, and decision, micro-models describing the didactic succession of micro-steps can be effectuated. Swertz (2004, pp. 86–90) distinguishes five basic micro-didactic models: task-oriented model, overview-oriented model, role-based model, theory-driven model, and test-oriented model. In contrast to the Smart Learning Design Framework (Agostinho et al., 2005) or Khan's (2007, 2019) often-cited Flexible Learning Framework for training delivery, high educational aspirations with reference to educational theory (*Bildungstheorie*) play an important role here.

Another example of a non-literal interpretation of sound pedagogies is "vignette research" as developed by Schratz et al. (2014). In contrast to "sound science" based on assumptions of calculability, countability, and measurability of learning experiences, this phenomenological approach focuses on the micro-level of the classroom and experiences of learners (Agostini et al., 2018). If the attention is consistently directed to the side of the learner, this opens up possibilities for the analysis of learner experiences "beyond the reach of teaching and measurement" (Schratz et al., 2014). Although the authors admit that crafting vignettes as short descriptions of pedagogically relevant moments is a creative process that cannot be standardized, the "vignettes do, however, undergo critical processes for assessing their quality according to vividness, wholeness, and authenticity" (Schratz et al., 2014, p. 129). Here, pedagogy is not a "conquered province" but an approach to lived experience research that emphasizes the primacy of pedagogy in order to contribute to (1) school research and (2) to foundational research into learning. Moreover, analysis of vignettes has so far enabled the distinction of over 100 verbal expressions dealing with micro-activities (Schratz et al., 2014, p. 131). This establishes new perspectives for a better understanding of pedagogical teaching and learning practices and also for further developments in micro-didactics as related to the successful management of micro-content and contingencies between microteaching and microlearning.

Another increasingly relevant aspect of designing microlearning in education refers to media-cultural developments and informal learning contexts. As we have seen, "learning by small units in small steps has a tradition, which reaches beyond the documented development of civilization" (Hierdeis, 2007, p. 48). Multi-faceted didactic concepts connecting micro-steps for pedagogical purposes have been developed, some of them aiming at bridging formal and informal learning contexts. This should remind us of the fact that it was not only micro-content especially designed for educational purposes that played a role in the history of learning but also other micro-formats like anecdotes, aphorisms, cues, jokes, graffiti, wisdom sayings, short stories, or short films. In today's algorithmic cultures, new forms have been emerging such as GIFs, memes, micro-movies, micro-games, podcasts, digital storytelling, flash fiction, and all sorts of "learning snippets," data-driven learning fragments, or content chips fueled by artificial intelligence (AI), often in contexts of Internet-based everyday practices. For some years now, these cultural practices at the crossroads of physical and digital technologies, spaces and time, and activities and relational ecologies, have been described in terms of post-digital practices (Cramer, 2015; Bishop et al., 2017).

While the preference for issues of digital technologies, technical infrastructures, and technology use proves to be problematic in educational contexts, there are promising options for the integration of various micro-formats in formal education. A good example is the cultural ecological approach to mobile learning developed by Pachler, Bachmair, and Cook (2010). In contrast to widespread forms of implementing microlearning objects in monitoring and surveillance systems for learning and education ("eduveillance"), which are based on principles of output-oriented knowledge production, the authors focus on mobile cultural resources that emerge in the ever-changing interplay of structures, agency, and cultural practices they call the "mobile complex." Correspondingly, considering these cultural resources for learning as appropriation, or *Bildung,* is crucial here. Inasmuch as cultural objects – *"as symbolic material integral to users' personal lifeworlds"* (Bachmair & Pachler, 2014, p. 53; italics in org.) – can be taken as microlearning objects, they can serve as mediators of formal and informal learning cultures and contexts. As for connecting micro-content, learning activities, and discursive practices in educational settings, Pachler et al. (2010) identify four didactic parameters – learning sets, relationship to the object of learning, institutional emphasis on expertise, and modes of representation (see Table 3.1) – which offer purchase on

- the features of media and of mobile devices
- conversations teachers and students engage in inside and outside the school
- the overall educational and didactic discourse about learning.

(Pachler et al., 2010, p. 297)

The parameters span the poles "static" and "flexible" and provide multifarious opportunities for embedding and organizing micro-steps in concrete educational settings and situations (Bachmair & Pachler, 2014, pp. 65–66). Conversely, they also represent modes of operationalization of the socio-cultural ecological approach. Regarding guidelines for planning mobile learning, the authors point out six basic strategies that allow for a specification of educational and didactic potentials within the four parameters:

TABLE 3.1 Didactic parameters for analyzing and planning within the mobile space of convergence and learning

Parameter A: Learning sets
Pole: Practice of the school – Pole: Practices of mobile media
Parameter B: Relationship to the object of learning
Pole: Mimetic reproduction – Pole: Personal reconstruction
Parameter C: Institutional emphasis on expertise
Pole: School curriculum – Pole: Personal expertise
Parameter D: Modes of representation
Pole: Discrete (mono media, mono modal) – Pole: Convergent

(Pachler et al., 2010, p. 298)

a   to integrate informal learning in formal learning contexts […]
b   setting up episodes of situated learning […]
c   generating learning and media contexts […]
d   mobile devices serve as conversational threads […]
e   supporting students as naïve experts, e. g. of media use in everyday life within the school […]
f   setting up responsive contexts for personal development and learning.
(Bachmair & Pachler, 2014, p. 67)

Examples of this approach to microlearning as mobile learning (Hug, 2015) show that there are diverse applications (Friedrich et al., 2011), not least for the empowerment of at-risk learners.

One interesting finding in this section is that non-literal interpretations of sound pedagogy or "soundness" of pedagogical research and practices are serving as strong claims waiving a critical analysis of methodological alternatives and precise descriptions of research strategies or pedagogical approaches to microlearning. A closer examination shows a wide range of understandings of the sound metaphor as related to being useful, senseful, tested, established, research-based, theoretically justified, reliable, or proven. If learning sciences oriented towards methodologies of natural sciences are taken as the pinnacle, or most important understanding of sound scientific investigation of contemporary learning and education, this would be a serious misunderstanding of educational endeavors and a problematic form of ignoring the limitations of quantitative empirical research. Moreover, if sound pedagogy practices of microlearning are identified mainly with education as calculable output, deliverable commodity and output-driven streamlining of learners as "learning objects," problematic reductionisms of pedagogical potentials are at work. Then again, the examples discussed in this section have shown that there are many options for designing and implementing microlearning in terms of education as relation, transgression, or transformative processes of *Bildung* (Siljander et al., 2012).

Summary and Future Perspectives

This chapter has set out to describe and clarify notions of sound pedagogy and corresponding practices for designing and implementing microlearning. It has been shown that organizing learning as organizing small units and small learning steps has a long tradition that reaches back far beyond the documented history of pedagogy and civilization. Today, being able to successfully design, organize, and evaluate meaningful learning processes is one of the most critical challenges faced by educators and trainers. Understandingly, a feverish search for appropriate methods and good practices is going on. While microteaching concepts and practices have been developed for more than half a century, terms like micro-content, micromedia, and microlearning have been used for less than 20 years, not entirely coincidental with the emergence of various micro-formats in diverse media-cultural contexts.

On the one hand, introducing new vocabulary like microlearning and probing corresponding practices can open up innovative perspectives as well as fruitful options for rethinking and redesigning education and training. On the other hand, new terminology can also trigger semantic confusion and contribute to the dissemination of misleading statements and problematic developments. As for designing and implementing microlearning objects, we have seen that there are contrasting, and also contradictory pedagogies and practices. Moreover, there are claims referring to sound pedagogies that are loosely connected to psychological learning theories but not at all to pedagogies as related to educational theory (Bildungstheorie), long-standing traditions of pedagogy, or transformative learning (Taylor & Cranton, 2012; Laros et al., 2017).

Much of the discourses dealing with microlearning are conducted in commercial weblogs and training magazines, dedicated to branding products and selling services, and not to theoretical foundation or profound empirical research. Microlearning is a good example of a blurring concept that is used more often for purposes of marketing or conceptual politics (*Begriffspolitik*) than for differentiated analysis or thoughtful reasoning. As in other cases of pedagogical issues, there is a certain risk here that scientific views and theoretical or empirical work are hastily narrowed down by processes of mechanization, digitization, datafication, commercialization, politicization, and popularization. Hence, some kinds of "Ed-Tech" discourse on microlearning can be seen as part of the problem rather than part of a sustainable solution for the future of learning, education, and training.

Furthermore, the study has also shown that both literal and non-literal interpretations of sound pedagogy offer multiple perspectives for designing and evaluating micro-didactic arrangements. In both cases, prototypical examples of promising concepts and practices, as well as reductionist tendencies were identified as results. In doing so, the important role of enlightening and obscuring aspects of metaphorical uses of terms like "sound pedagogy" or "sound pedagogical practices" has been revealed. An in-depth analysis of these metaphors remains a task for future research.

The same applies to metaphorical uses of snippets, crumbs, bites, bytes, chips, pinches, granules, patches, fragments, facets, episodes, or nuggets as conceptual elements of different forms of knowledge, skills, or competencies and also as elements of educational practices, cultures, and discourses.

It is important to consider that it is not enough to say that microlearning and dealing with micro-content are always related to a larger topic, a wider scope of themes, a discursive context, and an ensemble of media-cultural practices. The question is *how* these relations are conceptualized and brought to practice and *how* purposes of education and learning are reasoned, not least also in relation to education as an end itself. For example, if the goals of microlearning, as well as means-end reasoning, are taken for granted, then talking of "sound pedagogy" is likely to be part of a language of instrumentalism and an orientation towards technological feasibility or enforcement of learner behavior and enhanced productivity. If the goals and modes of microlearning are subject to reflection and discussion, it is more likely that a discussion on "sound pedagogy" would refer to a language of emancipation, empowerment, self-determination, transgression, or educational transformation beyond technically executable learning.

As for future perspectives for sound pedagogy practices for microlearning, there are diverse challenges ranging from digital capitalism and global education industry, through artificial intelligence (AI), educational robotics and machine learning, to developments of synthetic biology and digital climate change. All these developments share common elements including the following:

- all of them deal with designing and implementing micro- or nano-structures that have enormous potential for the transformation of social, cultural, and societal meso- and macro-structures. At the same time, deep structures, subtle dynamics of change, and modes of transformation remain largely misunderstood. Learning cultures and educational institutions constitute just one of many contexts of application here.
- big industries and their change agents tend to suggest one innovation pathway without considering alternatives or attaching much importance to the clarification of issues of accountability (Mansell, 2018). Efforts to visualize contingencies, to make transformation processes comprehensible, and to point out and test alternative development paths take place in niches but not as part of well-funded research programs or mainstream politics.
- all of them call for reflections on the educational relevance of post-humanist and post-anthropocentric dimensions (Bayley, 2018; Braidotti, 2019) and for further development of trajectories of artificiality (Krippendorff, 2011; Capurro, 1995).
- they also call for enhancements of contextual thinking beyond meaning contexts, personal contexts, and discourse contexts (van Goor et al., 2004, p. 176) towards considering user-generated, data-driven, and computational contexts.

- all of them depend on enormous investments, constellations of hegemonic or leadership interests, and complex interplays of both technological and cultural developments, as well as mathematical constructions, scientific achievements, and high-tech developments.
- they continue a long history of imagination of automated technological applications, and to a large extent, they are living on imagined futures and all sorts of tech-pledges including Ed-Tech promises.

Of course, the challenges for designing and implementing microlearning objects vary depending on direct or indirect dimensions and temporal horizons. Thinking of ongoing and near-term developments, guiding principles of co-creation in the context of collective media practices that involve humans and non-human systems are already helpful now. Here is an example of how such a principle can be relevant in institutional education as well as in public realms: "Create projects that don't originate from the single-author vision. Rather, ideas originate from relationships" (Cizek et al., 2019). Then again, the bio-fabrication of nano-bots for microlearning to be implemented in human bodies is more a part of speculative futures for the time being. No matter, if we consider such a development as deliverance and decolonization of oppressive learning systems, or as a dystopic horror scenario of total control, then, ethical deliberations, regulations, and optional design principles should be discussed publicly before facts are established without any communication or negotiation of the interests of various groups and world regions.

As this chapter shows, reflecting on how micro-perspectives of learning and education are related to meso- and macro-perspectives remains an ongoing task in view of pedagogical, ethical, cultural, technological, political, and economic dimensions of micro-didactics and datafication in education (Williamson, 2020). Considering merely the practical aspects of the implementation of microlearning objects into learning environments would not only mean that wider contexts and the political, socio-economic, and media-cultural significance of microlearning practices in formal and informal contexts are neglected, it would also mean completely underestimating the relevance of differentiated analyses of new paradoxical structures and design principles.

This is not to say that well-known pedagogical antinomies and paradoxes – such as freedom and coercion, foreign and self-determination, uniformity and diversity, mobilization and stabilization, adaptation and resistance, or proximity and distance – have become irrelevant. New paradoxes have emerged that are significant for the analysis and design of sound pedagogies, for example medial dynamics of inclusion and exclusion, initiatives claiming open educational resources (OER) and media colonialization of learning environments, digital capitalism and knowledge commons, or declarations of open forms of learning and non-transparent forms of learning analytics (Hug, 2018). As regards the need of contemporary design principles for sound pedagogies for microlearning, future research can build on innovative design principles, for example for mobile learning (Kukulska-Hulme & Traxler, 2020, p. 193) and for processes of co-creation involving human and non-human actors (Cizek et al., 2019). Furthermore, it can also build on design theory (Krippendorff, 2011) aiming at overcoming overly narrow techno-pedagogical perspectives.

Discussion Questions

1. Search online for a microlearning example as related to sound pedagogy in a literal sense or choose one from the examples mentioned in this chapter:
2. a) How do its characteristics on a micro-level correspond with institutional contexts of meaning-making and issues of organizational learning (meso-level) and with cultural traditions, media-historic constellations, and societal structures (macro-level)?
3. b) How can it contribute to integrative forms of the individual and the institutional development of creative, critical, and computational thinking?
4. Search online for a non-literal interpretation of "sound pedagogy" in the context of microlearning or choose one from the examples mentioned in this chapter:

   a How do its basic features on a micro-level correspond with institutional contexts of meaning-making and issues of organizational learning (meso-level) and with cultural traditions, media-historic constellations and societal structures (macro-level)?

   b Which perspectives for microlearning are highlighted or opened up by the metaphorical use of "soundness" or "sound pedagogy" and which perspectives are concealed or obscured?

5. Which are the most relevant kinds of reductionism mentioned in this chapter and why are they important in your view?
6. Think of future perspectives for microlearning practices based on sound pedagogies and the challenges mentioned in this chapter: What would be a viable guiding principle for designing microlearning content and environments that involve humans and non-human systems?
7. Consider the notion of a "digital climate change": how can micro-steps in learning and communication contribute to structural changes on meso- and macro-levels in educational and societal contexts?
8. Note: The expression "digital climate change" refers to a wide range of phenomena including changes in digital media, changes that digital media bring about as well as climate changes (in a literal sense) co-determined by energy consumption of IT systems.

Notes

1 For examples of applications, see www.minuteoflistening.org/ and http://hoerminute.at/.
2 For download options of the *Biophilia* app, see https://bjork-biophilia-ios.soft112.com/.

3 For examples of the hip-hop approach, see www.flocabulary.com/.
4 For a description of the project and a collection of designs, see www.learningdesigns. uow.edu.au.
5 The *Engines for Education* hyperbook, written by Roger Schank and Chip Cleary, is available at www.engines4ed.org/hyperbook/nodes/educator-outline.html.
6 In the German speaking world, the following concepts are widely accepted as pedagogy: education (*Bildung*), education as upbringing (*Erziehung*), school, teaching (*Unterricht*), more recently also learning as a pedagogical concept (Göhlich & Zirfas, 2007).

References

Abramo, J. (2014). Music education that resonates: An epistemology and pedagogy of sound. *Philosophy of Music Education Review*, 22(1), 78–95.

Agostinho, S., Bennett, S. J., Lockyer, L., Harper, B., & Lukasiak, J. (2005). *Supporting the development of pedagogically sound learning environments using learning designs and learning objects*. In J. Gutierrez, F. Santaro & P. Isaias (Eds.), IADIS International Conference WWW/Internet 2005 (pp. 77–80). Lisbon, Portugal: International Association for the Development of the Information Society.

Agostini, E., Schratz, M., & Risse, E. (2018). *Lernseits denken - erfolgreich unterrichten. Personalisiertes Lehren und Lernen in der Schule*. Hamburg: AOL-Verlag.

Bachmair, B. & Pachler, N. (2014). A cultural ecological frame for mobility and learning. *MedienPädagogik*, 24, 53–74. https://doi.org/10.21240/mpaed/24/2014.09.04.X.

Bayley, A. (2018). *Posthuman Pedagogies in Practice. Arts based Approaches for Developing Participatory Futures*. Cham: Palgrave Macmillan.

Biesta, G. (2011). Disciplines and theory in the academic study of education: A comparative analysis of the Anglo-American and Continental construction of the field. *Pedagogy, Culture & Society*, 19(2), 175–192, doi:10.1080/14681366.2011.582255.

Bishop, R., Gansing, K., Parikka, J., & Wilk, E. (Eds.). (2017). *Across & Beyond: A Transmediale Reader on Post-digital Practices, Concepts, and Institutions*. Berlin: Sternberg Press.

Björk (2011). *Biophilia*. [LP, CD, digital]. One Little Indian Records/Well Hart.

Braidotti, R. (2019). *Posthuman Knowledge*. Cambridge, UK: Polity Press.

Bridges, D. (2019). 'Rigour', 'discipline' and the 'systematic' in educational research – and why they matter. *European Educational Research Journal*, 18(5), 499–512. https://doi.org/10.1177/1474904119868558.

Bronfenbrenner, U. (1979). *The Ecology of Human Development: Experiments by Nature and Design*. Cambridge, MA: Harvard University Press.

Bubolz, M. M., & Sontag, M. S. (1993). Human Ecology Theory. In P. G. Boss, W. J. Doherty, R. LaRossa, W. R. Schumm, & S. K. Steinmetz (Eds.), *Sourcebook of Family Theories and Methods: A Contextual Approach* (pp. 419–450). Plenum Press. https://doi.org/10.1007/978-0-387-85764-0_17.

Capurro, R. (1995). On artificiality. Working paper published by IMES (Istituto Metodologico Economico Statistico) Laboratory for the Culture of the Artificial, Università di Urbino, Dir. Massimo Negrotti (IMES-LCA WP-15 November1995). www.capurro.de/artif.htm.

Cizek, K., Uricchio, W., Anderson, J., Agui Carter, M., Harris, T. A., Holmes, M., & Stephenson, M. (2019). Part 1: 'We are here': Starting points in co-creation. https://wip.mitpress.mit.edu/pub/collective-wisdom-part-1.

Cooper, J. M. (Ed.) (1997). *Plato: Complete Works*. Indianapolis: Hackett.

Cramer, F. (2015). What is 'Post-Digital'? In D. M. Berry & M. Dieter (Eds.), *Postdigital Aesthetics: Art, Computation and Design* (pp. 12–26). New York, NY: Palgrave Macmillan.

Dibben, N. (2014). Visualizing the App Album with Björk's *Biophilia*. In C. Vernallis, A. Herzog, & J. Richardson (Eds.), *The Oxford Handbook of Sound and Image in Digital Media* (pp. 682–706). Oxford: Oxford University Press. doi:10.1093/oxfordhb/9780199757640.013.012.

Droumeva, M. & Murphy, D. (2016). *A Sound Pedagogy: Active Learning Through Media Production*. EDULEARN16 Proceedings from the 8th International Conference on Education and New Learning Technologies, 3974–3982. http://10.0.82.133/edulearn.2016.1949.

Friedrich, K., Bachmair, B., & Risch, M. (2011). *Mobiles Lernen mit dem Handy: Herausforderung und Chance für den Unterricht*. Weinheim: Beltz.

Friesen, N. (2019). Educational research in America today: Relentless instrumentalism and scholarly backlash. *Erziehungswissenschaft*, 59(30), 77–83. https://doi.org/10.3224/ezw.v30i2.09 [https://www.budrich-journals.de/index.php/ew/article/view/34590/29606].

Glaser, E. & Keiner, E. (Eds.) (2014). *Unscharfe Grenzen – eine Disziplin im Dialog. Pädagogik, Erziehungswissenschaft, Bildungswissenschaft, Empirische Bildungsforschung*. Bad Heilbrunn: Klinkhardt.

Göhlich, M. & Zirfas, J. (2007). *Lernen: Ein pädagogischer Grundbegriff*. Stuttgart: Kohlhammer.

Herbart, J. F. (1806). *Allgemeine Pädagogik aus dem Zweck der Erziehung abgeleitet*. Göttingen: J. F. Röwer.

Herbart, J. F. (1841). *Umriss pädagogischer Vorlesungen* (2nd ed.). Göttingen: Verlag der Dieterichschen Buchhandlung.

Hierdeis, H. (2007). From Meno to Microlearning: A Historical Survey. In T. Hug (Ed.), *Didactics of Microlearning: Concepts, Discourses and Examples* (pp. 35–52). Münster: Waxmann.

Hua, Z. (2012). Turning to the pedagogy of "listening." *Complicity: An International Journal of Complexity and Education*, 9(1), 57–74.

Hug, T. (2005). *Micro learning and narration: Exploring possibilities of utilization of narrations and storytelling for the designing of "micro units" and didactical micro-learning arrangements*. Paper presented at the International Conference Media in Transition 4 The Work of Stories at the MIT in Cambridge (MA), USA, May 6–8, 2005. http://web.mit.edu/comm-forum/legacy/mit4/papers/hug.pdf.

Hug, T. (2010). Radical constructivism mainstreaming: A desirable endeavor? Critical considerations using examples from educational studies and learning theory. In *Constructivist Foundations*, Special Issue Dedicated to the Work and Memory of Ernst von Glasersfeld: Can Radical Constructivism become a Mainstream Endeavor? (A. Quale & A. Riegler, Eds.), 6(1), 58–64. http://constructivist.info/6/1/058.

Hug, T. (2013). Key concepts in education: Critical issues beyond definition and discursive practices. *Seminar.net – International Journal of Media, Technology and Lifelong Learning*, 9(2), 43–58. http://seminar.net/images/stories/vol9-issue2/Theo_Hug_-_Key_Concepts_in_Education.pdf.

Hug, T. (2015). Microlearning and Mobile Learning. In Y. Zheng (Ed.), *Encyclopedia of Mobile Phone Behavior* (pp. 490–505). (Vols 1–3). Hershey, PA: IGI Global. doi:10.4018/978-1-4666-8239-9.

Hug, T. (2018). Herausforderungen für Lernen und Bildung im Medienzeitalter – Zur Einführung. In T. Hug (Ed.): *Medienpädagogik – Herausforderungen für Lernen und Bildung im Medienzeitalter* (pp. 7–17). Innsbruck: Innsbruck University Press.

Jaeger, W. (1986). *Paideia: The Ideals of Greek Culture: Volume III: The Conflict of Cultural Ideals in the Age of Plato*. Oxford: Oxford University Press. (Original work published 1939).

Kapp, K. M. & Defelice, R. A. (2019). *Microlearning: Short and Sweet.* Alexandria, VA: ATD Press.

Keiner, E. (2019). 'Rigour', 'discipline' and the 'systematic': The cultural construction of educational research identities? *European Educational Research Journal,* 18(5), 527–545. https://doi.org/10.1177/1474904118824935.

Khan, B. H. (2007). Flexible Learning in an Open and Distributed Environment. In B. H. Khan (Ed.), *Flexible Learning in an Information Society* (pp. 1–17). Hershey, PA: Information Science Publishing.

Khan, B. (2019). Microlearning: Quick and meaningful snippets for training solutions. *International Journal of Research in Educational Sciences (IJRES),* 2(2), 275–284. http://iafh.net/index.php/IJRES/article/view/107.

Knorr Cetina, K. & Bruegger, U. (2002). Global microstructures: The virtual societies of financial markets. *American Journal of Sociology,* 107(4), 905–950.

Krippendorff, K. (2009). *On Communicating: Otherness, Meaning, and Information.* F. Bermejo (Ed.). New York: Routledge.

Krippendorff, K. (2011). Principles of design and a trajectory of artificiality. *Journal of Product Innovation Management,* 28(3), 411–418. https://onlinelibrary.wiley.com/doi/epdf/10.1111/j.1540-5885.2011.00814.x.

Kukulska-Hulme, A. & Traxler, J. (2020). Design Principles for Learning with Mobile Devices. In H. Beetham & R. Sharpe (Eds.) (2020). *Rethinking Pedagogy for a Digital Age* (pp. 181–196) (3rd ed.). New York: Routledge. https://doi.org/10.4324/9781351252805.

Laros, A., Fuhr, T., & Taylor, E. W. (Eds.). (2017). *Transformative Learning Meets Bildung: An International Exchange.* Rotterdam: Sense Publishers. www.sensepublishers.com/media/3021-transformative-learning-meets-bildung.pdf.

Lichtenstein, E. (1970). *Der Ursprung der Pädagogik im griechischen Denken (Paideia I).* Hannover: Hermann Schroedel.

Luhmann, N. (2012). *Theory of Society* (Vols. 1–2, R. Barrett, Trans.). Stanford, CA: Stanford University Press.

Mansell, R. (2018). Transformative communication technologies: The accountability challenge. 36th Boehm-Bawerk lecture – Inauguration of the Department of Media, Society and Communication. *Kleine Medienreihe* (Vol. 2). Innsbruck: Innsbruck University Press.

Meder, N. (2006). *Web-Didaktik: Eine neue Didaktik webbasierten, vernetzten Lernens.* Bielefeld: Bertelsmann.

Miao, Y., van der Klink, M., Boon, J., Sloep, P., & Koper, R. (2009). Enabling teachers to develop pedagogically sound and technically executable learning designs. *Distance Education,* 30(2), 259–276. doi:10.1080/01587910903023223.

MiCA – Music Austria (Ed.) (2019). Hörminute für Volksschulklassen [Listening Minute for Elementary School Classes]. http://hoerminute.at/Hoerminute_Konzept.pdf.

Neurath, O. (1959). Protocol Sentences. In A. J. Ayer (Ed.), *Logical Positivism* (pp. 199–208). Glencoe, IL: Free Press.

Pachler, N., Bachmair, B., & Cook, J. (2010). *Mobile Learning: Structures, Agency, Practices.* New York: Springer.

Sawyer, R. K. (Ed.) (2014). *The Cambridge Handbook of the Learning Sciences.* Cambridge: Cambridge University Press.

Schafer, R. M. (1992). *A Sound Education.* Ontario, Canada: Arcana. https://monoskop.org/images/7/7b/Schafer_R_Murray_A_Sound_Education_100_Exercises_in_Listening_and_Soundmaking.pdf.

Schäfer, H. (2016). *Praxistheorie: Ein soziologisches Forschungsprogramm.* Bielefeld: Transcript.

Schatzki, T. R. (2001). Practice Theory. In T. Schatzki, K. Knorr Cetina & E. von Savigny (Eds.), *The Practice Turn in Contemporary Theory* (pp. 1–14). London/New York: Routledge.

Schmieder, F. (2017). Gleichzeitigkeit des Ungleichzeitigen. Zur Kritik und Aktualität einer Denkfigur. *Zeitschrift für Kritische Sozialtheorie und Philosophie*, 4(1–2), 325–363. https://doi.org/10.1515/zksp-2017-0017.

Schmidt, S. J. (2005). *Lernen, Wissen, Kompetenz, Kultur. Vorschläge zur Bestimmung von vier Unbekannten.* Heidelberg: C. Auer.

Schratz, M., Westfall-Greiter, T., & Schwarz, J. F. (2014). Beyond the reach of teaching and measurement: Methodology and initial findings of the Innsbruck vignette research. *Pensamiento Educativo Revista de Investigación Educacional Latinoamericana*, 51(1), 123–134. http://pensamientoeducativo.uc.cl/files/journals/2/articles/573/public/573-1733-1-PB.pdf.

Siljander, P., Kivelä, A., & Sutinen, A. (Eds.) (2012). *Theories of Bildung and Growth. Connections and Controversies Between Continental Educational Thinking and American Pragmatism.* Rotterdam: Sense Publishers.

Smeyers, P. (2019). How to characterize research and scholarship that matters for the educational field? *European Educational Research Journal*, 18(5), 622–635. https://doi.org/10.1177/1474904119865857.

Swertz, C. (2004). *Didaktisches Design: Ein Leitfaden für den Aufbau hypermedialer Lernsysteme mit der Web-Didaktik.* Bielefeld: Bertelsmann.

Taylor, E. W. & Cranton, P. (2012). *The Handbook of Transformative Learning. Theory, Research, and Practice.* San Francisco, CA: Jossey-Bass.

Tinkle, A. (2015). Sound pedagogy: Teaching listening since Cage. *Organised Sound*, 20 [Special Issue 02: Sound Art and Music, Historical Continuum and Mimetic Fissures], 222–230. doi:10.1017/S1355771815000102.

van Goor, R., Heyting, F. G., & Vreeke, G. (2004). Beyond foundations: Signs of a new normativity in philosophy of education. *Educational Theory*, 54(2), 173–192. doi:10.1111/j.1741-5446.2004.00013.x.

Verger, A.; Steiner-Khamsi, G., & Lubienski, C. (2016). *World Yearbook of Education 2016: The Global Education Industry.* New York: Routledge.

Welch, G.*et al.* (2019). Case studies: Minute of listening. www.inspire-music.org/case-studies/50-minute-of-listening.

Williamson, B. (2020). Datafication of Education. A Critical Approach to Emerging Analytics Technologies and Practices. In H. Beetham & R. Sharpe (Eds.) (2020). *Rethinking Pedagogy for a Digital Age* (pp. 212–226) (3rd ed.). New York: Routledge. https://doi.org/10.4324/9781351252805.

4

MULTIMEDIA DESIGN PRINCIPLES FOR MICROLEARNING

Didem Tufan

Introduction

Despite the variety of ways microlearning is defined, generally, it refers to relatively short forms of learning materials, which are brief, compact, complementary, and connected flexibly to each other (Schmidt, 2007). As underlined by Simon (1974), the benefit of microlearning is based on the view that people can learn better and more effectively when the content is broken down into digestible parts and thus, learning can be achieved in small steps. The question, How can we design microlearning materials so they can be processed more effectively? can be answered by Baumgartner (2013), who introduces the idea of Action Levels for Learning Settings, through which he presents a hierarchy of interaction levels for learning. According to the proposed hierarchy, interactions can be designed in three levels: (1) micro-level, (2) meso-level and (3) macro-level. This hierarchy defines interactions in terms of time sequences ranging from seconds, minutes, hours, and years. In other words, interactions may range from seconds (e.g., the learner clicking on an object), to a curriculum made up of several modules, to even including educational policies at the far end of the interaction hierarchy. Baumgartner underlines the significance of having an awareness of this layered perspective in planning and designing educational interactions. Due to the nature of microlearning, this chapter focuses on the micro-level layers of instructional design, which represent the briefest interaction level.

In addition, Mayer's Principles of Multimedia Learning are based on cognitive learning theory. Figure 4.1 below provides a visual representation of the cognitive theory of multimedia learning, representing the flow of information from the senses towards the form of knowledge.

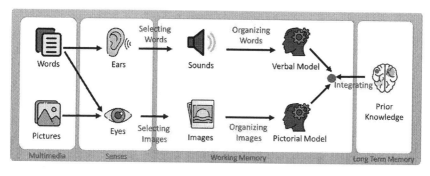

FIGURE 4.1 Cognitive theory of multimedia learning (adapted from Clark & Mayer, 2016)

According to cognitive theory, the limited capacity of humans' working memory results in three different kinds of kinds of demands on their cognitive processing capacity (Mayer, 2009; Sweller, Ayres, & Kalyuga, 2011; Clark & Mayer, 2016). See Table 4.1 below.

As a result of learners' limited cognitive potential for processing, managing extraneous processing, essential processing, and generative processing becomes the challenge for learning professionals (Sweller, Ayres, & Kalyuga, 2011; Mayer, 2014b; Clark & Mayer 2016), especially when designing or selecting microlearning content. In fact, the ways in which to avoid or manage these challenges, constitutes the basis for many of the principles set forth by Mayer and his colleagues.

TABLE 4.1 Kinds of demands on cognitive processing capacity (Clark & Mayer, 2016)

Main Assumption	Description
Extraneous processing	The type of cognitive processing which is not directly related with the main instructional aim and caused by poor instructional design, such as having too much inessential visual and graphical elements.
Essential processing	The type of cognitive processing used to portray the fundamental aspects of the learning material. It is generated as a result of the difficulty of the material. For example, learning a process with 10 steps requires more essential processing than learning a process with 5 steps.
Generative processing	The type of cognitive processing intended for a more profound internalization of the fundamental material. It covers the organization and integration of the knowledge. It is generated by the willingness of the learner to understand the subject. Instructional methods which promote learner engagement in the subject can support this type of processing.

The section that follows provides a summary of Mayer's Principles of Multimedia Learning with microlearning examples and design tips to serve as a guide for the design decisions required for developing effective microlearning content.

Multimedia Design Principles for Microlearning

The Multimedia Principle

Mayer and Clark's (2016) Multimedia Principle is one of the most recognized principles in instructional design. It is grounded in the cognitive theory of learning, which posits that deeper learning takes place more effectively if learners can establish connections between words and graphics in their mind. Therefore, using meaningful images and related text can be an effective tool to activate deeper learning (Mayer, 2009). As a result, as seen exemplified in Figure 4.2 (see p. 000), Clark and Mayer (2016) recommend the use of both visual elements, such as drawings, charts, graphs, maps, or photos, and dynamic animation or video, rather than using only printed or spoken text. As Mayer (2009) notes, "people learn better from words and pictures than from pictures alone" (p. 223). In addition, since the extensive use of technological devices, such as computers, mobile phones, tablets, is now standard operations for learners accessing instructional content, how to effectively use graphics and text when designing microlearning is an important consideration for the instructional designers, educators, and human development professionals who are selecting and/or creating microlearning content.

Multimedia Principle

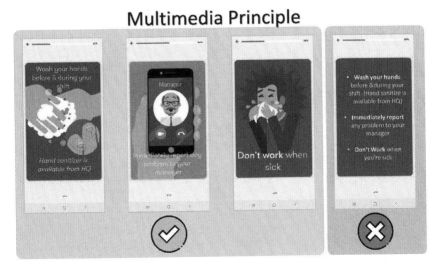

FIGURE 4.2 Multimedia principle (talentcards, n.d.)

Clark and Mayer (2016) categorize the usage of graphics according to their functions. This categorization can help instructional designers and instructors select appropriate graphics when designing microlearning. It can also help learning professionals select microlearning content that effectively uses graphics according to the functions. See Table 4.2 below.

The unified structure of microlearning, which includes one objective or competency, makes the lesson structure more complex, and therefore, requires additions to the core uses of graphics listed in Table 4.2 (see p. 000). For example, a topic tree or subject list is insufficient when learners determine their own learning paths. As Hug (2010) notes, the learning chunks themselves need to be graphically represented for learners. As such, competency maps, learner competency dashboards, or learning pathways, can be added to the list above, as additional graphical uses specific for microlearning experiences (Zhang & West, 2020). Figure 4.3 (see p. 000) shows an example of a visual learning pathway. Figure 4.4 (see p. 000) provides an example of a learner dashboard.

Key Microlearning Design Tips

- Include relevant visual elements to convey the instructional message, rather than having only verbal representations of it.
- Select images that adhere to Mayer's Multimedia Principle.
- Keep in mind that images should add to or help explain the information presented, not detract from it.
- Use more representational, organizational, relational, transformational, or interpretive visuals, rather than decorative ones.

TABLE 4.2 Usage of graphics according to their functions (adapted from Clark & Mayer, 2016, p. 73)

Type of graphic	Explanation of use
Decorative	Graphics used for artistic reasons or just for fun
Representational	Graphics showing the form or look of an object
Organizational	Graphics that reflect the connections among content, such as a mind map
Relational	Graphics that reflect the quantitative properties of the content, such as a pie chart or a color map
Transformational	Graphics reflecting the change over time or space, such as the life cycle of a frog
Interpretive	Graphics that makes a phenomenon visible, concrete, or tangible, such as a water cycle graph or visual that shows how a modem works

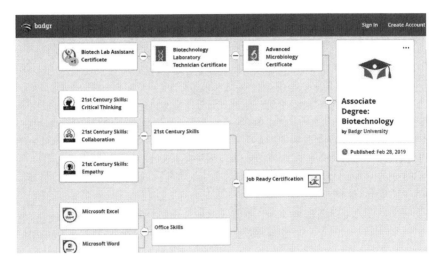

FIGURE 4.3 An example of visual learning pathways (Badgr.com, n.d.)

- Find ways to graphically represent the learning progress of learners' micro-learning experiences, such as using competency maps, dashboards, or visual pathways (see Figures 4.3 and 4.4 on p. 000).

The Contiguity Principle

Another principle asserted by Mayer (2009) is the Contiguity Principle. This principle suggests aligning words and related graphics. It targets minimizing the extraneous processing needed to coordinate the words with their related visuals (Mayer, 2016). Mayer presents two types of contiguity: Spatial Contiguity and Temporal Contiguity, described below.

Spatial Contiguity Principle

The Spatial Contiguity Principle deals with the space between text and related visuals on the screen. According to the principle, people learn better when text and corresponding graphics are physically placed near to each other (Clark & Mayer, 2016). The concern is that learners may experience cognitive load when the Spatial Contiguity Principle is violated. According to MindTools (n.d.) "'Cognitive load' relates to the amount of information that working memory can hold at one time … since working memory has a limited capacity, instructional methods should avoid overloading it with additional activities that don't directly contribute to learning" (What is Cognitive Load Theory, para. 2). For instance, examine the two diagrams showing the parts of a sewing machine in Figure 4.5 (see p. 000). As is evident on the left side of the figure, when the names are not

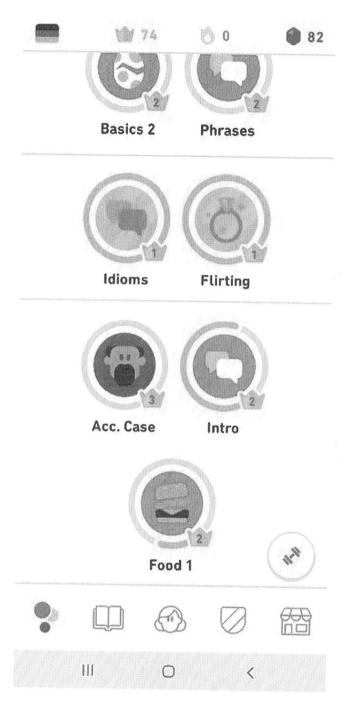

FIGURE 4.4 An example of a learner dashboard from Duolingo (Duolingo.com, n.d.)

Spatial Contiguity Principle

placed near the images of the corresponding parts, it becomes more challenging
to match the name with the part of the object.

Temporal Contiguity Principle

In the Temporal Contiguity Principle, Clark and Mayer recommend that corresponding words and pictures be presented at the same time (Clark & Mayer,
2016). When related parts of narration and animation are presented simultaneously, the learner is more likely to keep the information in their working
memory simultaneously. Consequently, learners will be able to form mental
relations between verbal and visual representations (Mayer, 2009).

Key Microlearning Design Tips

- Keep text and related graphics physically close together depending on your
  screen size.
- In order to adhere to the Spatial Contiguity Principle, regardless of the
  device size, consider applying adaptive user interface design.
- Ensure that your design is modest enough, so the audience knows where to
  look for information.
- Ensure that there is no latency between the voiceover audio and visuals/
  animations.
- If a new process is being introduced, the animation (or visual) should be
  occurring at the same time as the voiceover audio. This is preferred over

having the voiceover audio play first, and then watching a visual after. It can be achieved by ensuring the voiceover audio is always timed well with visuals or animations.

The Modality Principle

The Modality Principle states that humans learn better from visuals and narrated text than from visuals and printed words (Mayer & Pilegard, 2014). This principle underlines that using too much text, in addition to visuals, can affect learners' working memory, which in turn, affects learning negatively. The Modality Principle does not imply avoiding on-screen text, rather, it notes that too much text, in addition to graphical elements, can result in cognitive overload (Mayer, 2016).

Overall, there continues to be strong support for using narration rather than on-screen text to describe graphics, especially when the presentation is complex or fast-paced and when the verbal material is familiar and in short segments. In particular, audio narrations must be brief and clear to be effective (Clark & Mayer, 2016).

Key Microlearning Design Tips

- When using voiceover, limit the use of on-screen text.
- Consider the use of visual elements. Use text for only key ideas, lists, or instructions that need to be written.

The Redundancy Principle

The Redundancy Principle asserts that learning is more effectively accomplished when there is narration and graphics instead of narration, graphics, and on-screen text. In this principle, when there is narration of the graphics, the text on-screen is perceived as redundant (Mayer, 2009). See Figure 4.6 below for a graphical summary for The Redundancy Principle.

If there is redundancy in a microlearning object, the learner may experience extraneous processing. The visual channel of the learner becomes overwhelmed while trying to browse both the visuals and on-screen text, in addition to spending mental effort in trying to match the narration and on-screen text.

Figure 4.7 above presents a screenshot from an educational TED-Ed (n.d.) video, which is an example of appropriate adherence to the Redundancy Principle. It includes narration in addition to some graphical elements/animations. On-screen text is only visible when there is an important point to underline. In the screenshot in Figure 4.7 above, only key words are written on the screen. The longer explanations are presented by the narrator.

According to Clark and Mayer (2016), however, there is a condition to the Redundancy Principle, which they call boundary conditions. Clark and Mayer

Redundancy Principle

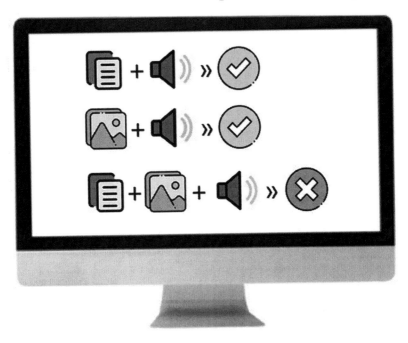

FIGURE 4.6 A visual summary for the Redundancy Principle

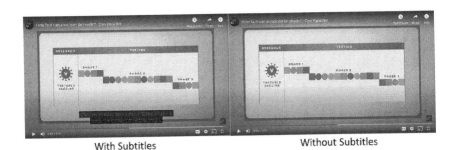

With Subtitles   Without Subtitles

FIGURE 4.7 Sample screenshot from an educational Ted-Ed video with and without
subtitles (TEDEd.com, n.d.)

define boundary conditions as exceptions that occur to the Redundancy Principle, "when there is limited or no graphic information on the screen, the lesson is
slow-paced or learner-paced, there are 'hard-to-hear' technical or unfamiliar
words, or there are only a few unobtrusive printed words" (p. 144). Under these

circumstances, the researchers suggest adding on-screen text. For instance, learners with less advanced language skills may decide to use the closed caption (CC) feature while watching the video in Figure 4.6 (see p. 000). In such a case, the text acts as a support for the learner to reduce cognitive load.

Key Microlearning Design Tips

- When using graphics, limit the use of on-screen text.
- If there is video narration, provide on/off option for both narration and closed captioning (CC).
- Take into consideration the target learners. If the microlearning content is being designed for language learners or learners of varying abilities, include closed captioning with on/off option.

The Coherence Principle

The Coherence Principle suggests that people learn best when extraneous, distracting material is not included in learning content. Mayer and Moreno (2003) suggest eliminating any kind of material, such as text, and audio, that does not support the central instructional goal. The authors name this elimination process as "weeding" (p. 48).

Microlearning is designed as a small instructional unit to prompt a specific learning outcome from the learner (Kapp & Defelice, 2019). Furthermore, the small size and fast consumable structure is perceived as the "essence" of microlearning (Zhang & West, 2020, p. 316). This is why adhering to the Coherence Principle becomes significantly important for the design of microlearning content. In parallel to the weeding suggestion made by Mayer and Moreno (2003), for the design of microlearning, Zhang and West (2020) suggest revising each learning unit numerous times to eliminate the information that is not necessary for answering fundamental questions or performing the main skill.

The cognitive theory of multimedia learning assumes that working memory capacity is limited. Because of this reason, adding extra materials to a lesson can restrain learning (Mayer, 2016).

Key Microlearning Design Tips

- Use concise narration and on-screen text by omitting extraneous words added for interest, technical depth, or expansion of key ideas. Always ask, "Is this necessary?"
- Use contextual graphics, animation, and video.
- When editing a material, think about simplicity. Do not hesitate to weed out the unnecessary parts.

The Personalization Principle

The Personalization Principle asserts that humans learn better from a more informal, conversational voice than a formal, direct, mechanical style voice (Clark & Mayer, 2016). The Personalization Principle guides learning designers to consider factors such as the style of text used in learning materials. According to Mayer (2009) people learn better from multimedia presentations when words are presented in a conversational style, rather than in a formal style (Moreno & Mayer, 2004). For example, Figure 4.8 (see p. 000) provides a part of a course outline from Udemy, a well-known online learning platform. The lesson headings represent an example for personalized text in the form of course outline. Note that even the course headings are written in the first person to address the

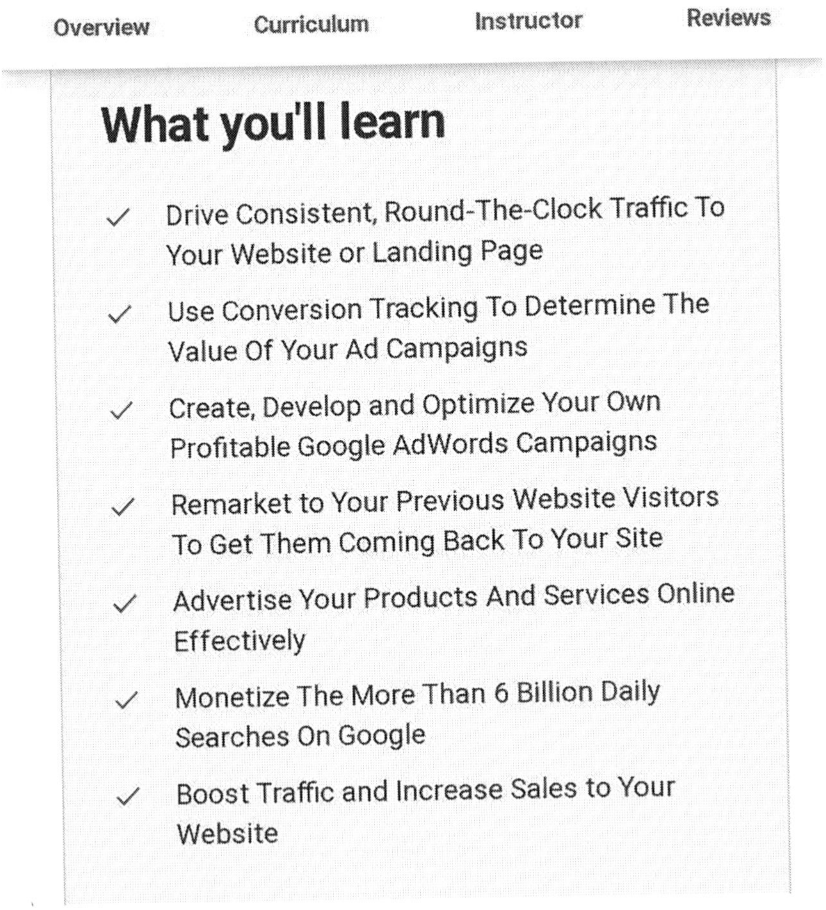

| Overview | Curriculum | Instructor | Reviews |

What you'll learn

✓ Drive Consistent, Round-The-Clock Traffic To Your Website or Landing Page

✓ Use Conversion Tracking To Determine The Value Of Your Ad Campaigns

✓ Create, Develop and Optimize Your Own Profitable Google AdWords Campaigns

✓ Remarket to Your Previous Website Visitors To Get Them Coming Back To Your Site

✓ Advertise Your Products And Services Online Effectively

✓ Monetize The More Than 6 Billion Daily Searches On Google

✓ Boost Traffic and Increase Sales to Your Website

FIGURE 4.8 Example screenshot from a Udemy course outline

learner directly (example: Drive consistent, round-the-clock traffic to your website or landing page).

The second focus of the Personalization Principle is the use of polite wording. The principle asserts that on-screen agents should be polite (Clark & Mayer, 2016). For example, Figure 4.9 (see p. 000) shows a screenshot of Duolingo (Duo), the screen agent for a well-known microlearning language app. In this example, Duo provides feedback by directly addressing the learner using a conversational style. For example, in frame three below, Duo says, "This challenge is no match for you."

The theory behind the Personalization Principle is directly linked to the psychology of the learner. Clark and Mayer (2016) state that personalization of learning materials stands as an "instructional technique" that stimulates related mental espousal. Keeping this in mind, the Personalization Principle suggests communicating in a conversational style (p. 184).

Clark and Mayer (2016) refer to cognitive theory stating, "instruction should not only present information but also prime the appropriate cognitive processing in the learner as people try all their best to understand the material" (p. 184). When the material is presented in a conversational style, learners feel as if they are in a conversation, which prompts them to try harder to understand the content more effectively.

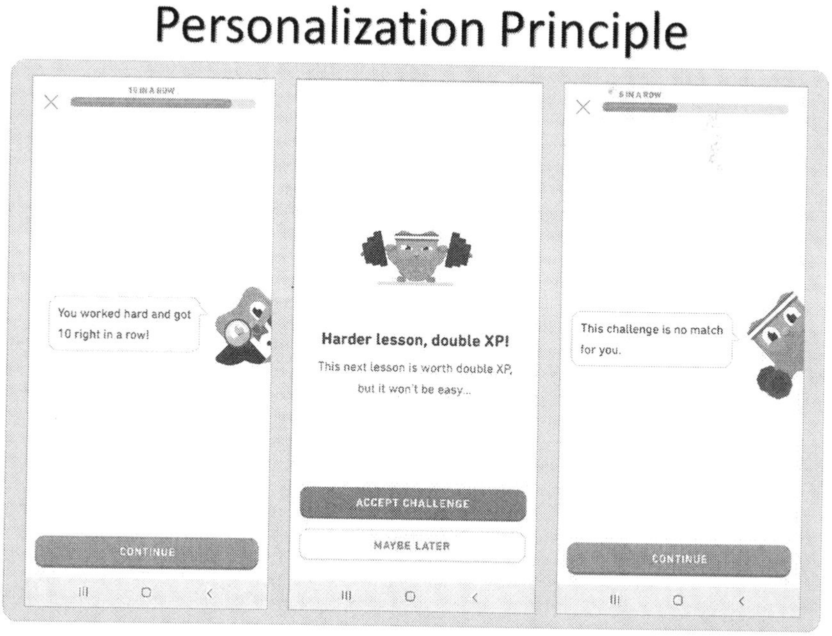

Personalization Principle

FIGURE 4.9 Sample screenshots from Duolingo's on-screen agent (Duolingo.com, n.d.)

Key Microlearning Design Tips

- Keep the language simple and casual.
- Avoid using too formal a voice. Avoid use of long and complex text.

The Voice Principle

The Personalization Principle includes focusing on the voice of the learning materials. Experimental studies (Mayer & DaPra, 2012; Mayer, Sobko, & Mautone, 2003; Atkinson, Mayer, & Merrill, 2005; Nass & Brave, 2007) revealed more positive results when the learning materials were presented with a human voice rather than a machine-generated voice. As a result, when developing or selecting microlearning content, consider using, or looking for, those with content delivered by a human voice. Fortunately, technological improvements have reached a point where a computer-generated voice is becoming harder to discriminate from a human voice.

Key Microlearning Design Tips

- Avoid use of a computer-generated voice that does not sound natural.
- When possible, select narrations created by professionals, or ask the narrator to practice the script to ensure a natural tone of voice when recording microlearning content.

The Segmenting Principle

As has been addressed in the chapter, the Principles of Multimedia Learning aim at reducing learners' cognitive load to enable them to grasp the learning materials. But what if the material itself is too complex? To address this, Clark and Mayer (2016) present the Segmenting Principle, which recommends dividing a multimedia message in "user-paced segments" (p. 175). If learning materials are self-paced and distributed as manageable units, the learner will have the mental capacity to organize the words into a "verbal model," and the pictures into a "pictorial model" (Clark & Mayer, 2016, p. 179). In this way, adhering to the Segmenting Principle allows learners to manage their own essential cognitive processing.

The Segmenting Principle has been researched extensively in the literature. For example, Mayer and Chandler (2001) compared the transfer test results of learners who receive the continuous form of a narrated animation versus the segmented/self-paced version of the same presentation. According to the results, learners who received the segmented presentation, performed better on transfer tests. Similar results are reported by other studies in favor of segmenting the learning materials to increase learning, such as: Moreno (2007), who used continuous video versus a segmented single topic video; Mayer, Dow, and Mayer (2003) who studied the use of continuous narrated animation versus click-and-see type segmented animation; and Schar and Zimmermann (2007), who studied an animated continuous lesson versus the same lesson with a pause button. The studies present interesting findings with implications for the design of microlearning content. For example, from their study results, Schar and Zimmermann recommend using a continue button for segmenting, rather than a pause button.

Microlearning, by definition, shows parallelisms with the idea of segmenting. For instance, in his book titled, Didactics of Microlearning: Concepts, Discourses and Examples, Hug (2007) defines microlearning as "an expression of a specific perspective which, in contrast to meso and macro aspects, is directed towards relatively small and time-restricted learning units and activities" (p. 12–13). As Zhang and West (2020) note, "[m]erely dividing a traditional training lesson into smaller chunks is not sufficient to promise effective microlearning" (p. 315). Jahnke et al. (2019) conducted a study to reveal the Inherent Design Principles of Mobile Microlearning. They first reviewed the literature, then conducted interviews with industry professionals of mobile- and micro-learning systems. They report "chunked courses" as a part of inherent design principles, which includes "short time, bite-sized lessons" focusing on a "single learning objective/topic/concept/idea and helps users do just one thing optimally; it has low complexity" (p. 607).

Figure 4.10 (see p. 000) shows examples of bite-sized microlearning design from two different microlearning applications: (1) Duolingo (on the left) and (2) Talentcards (on the right). In Duolingo, the information is downsized into very small, digestible units and they are arranged in accordance with the learners' level of pre-knowledge. In Talentcards, each card set is organized in a way that presents one aim for each instructional objective.

Key Microlearning Design Tips

- Provide learners with control over the pace of learning by adding next/stop/continue buttons.
- Build in ways for learners to control the speed of videos.
- Allow learners to control the speed of the voice.
- Divide the learning material into smaller, bite-sized, easily consumable chunks.
- Assign a single learning objective/topic/concept/idea to each bite-sized chunk of learning material.

The Pre-Training Principle

The Pre-Training Principle states that humans learn better if they know the names and characteristics of key concepts beforehand (Clark & Mayer, 2016).

Segmenting Principle

FIGURE 4.10 Examples of bite-sized, segmented microlearning design (Duolingo, n.d. and Talentcards.com, n.d.)

Clark and Mayer (2016) note that providing the basic definitions, terms, or concepts before the start of the learning activity enhances the learning experience. The theoretical rationale behind the Pre-Training Principle is mainly reducing cognitive processing. It is appropriate to adhere to the Pre-Training Principle when the learning material is likely to overload learners' cognitive systems. Under these circumstances, when complex learning material is required, pre-training is helpful to facilitate the learners' cognitive processes (Mayer, R. E. & Pilegard, C., 2014).

Like the other principles, the Pre-Training Principle has been studied by researchers such as Mayer, Mathias, and Wetzell (2002), whose study revealed that pre-training groups performed better on transfer tests than groups that did not receive pre-training. Following this early study, other studies reported similar results in favor of pre-training. Also, Mayer & Pilegard's (2014) meta-analysis revealed positive results in favor of pre-training across different multimedia learning contexts (Eitel, Scheiter, & Schüler, 2013; Clarke, Ayres, & Sweller, 2005; Mayer, Mautone, & Prothero, 2002).

Clark and Mayer (2016) also suggest "a quick orientation session at the start of a virtual classroom session that applies the pre-training principle" (p. 209). This suggestion is not only applicable for the virtual classroom, but also important for different delivery methods, such as mobile applications, learning managements systems, or other online environments. Figure 4.11 (see p. 000) shows samples from microlearning applications that offer an orientation at the beginning of the learning experience.

Key Microlearning Design Tips

- Evaluate the material being designed for microlearning and identify key concepts that could be presented prior to the microlearning moment.
- Provide an introductory orientation, course aid, tour, or user guide for the learning environment.
- Create an *understanding the basics* component, which remains accessible at all times.
- If the content is complex, include a *key concepts* section.

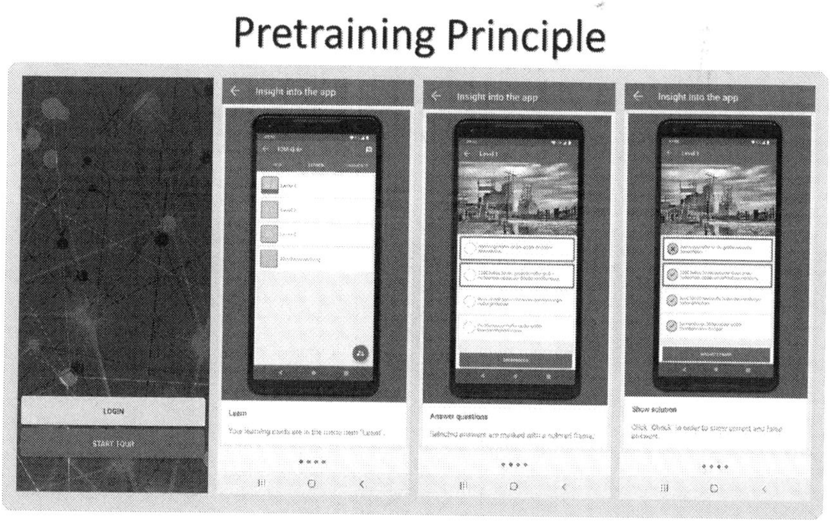

FIGURE 4.11 Examples of orientation screen from a microlearning app

Multimedia Design Principles for Effective Instructional Videos

The research on the Multimedia Principle dates back to 30 years ago. Since then, technology used to create media has changed significantly. Video has become a prominent medium for delivering content and learning materials. As a result, recently, Mayer and his colleagues published research focusing on "increasing the effectiveness of instructional video" (Mayer, Fiorella & Stull, 2020). In this work, they introduce additional principles specifically focusing on video production, which will be discussed in this section of the chapter.

The Dynamic Drawing Principle

This principle suggests that learning is improved if, in the video, the instructor draws visuals on a board, rather than pointing to the already driven visuals on the screen. This principle is based on two theories: (1) Social Agency Theory (Mayer, 2014), and (2) Embodiment Theory (Robbins & Aydele, 2009). Social Agency Theory (Mayer, 2014) underlines the significance of facilitators' drawing movements during the delivery of a learning object as a social cue, which promotes the feeling of social partnership, resulting in better learning. Correspondingly, learners might feel as if they are doing the drawing themselves if they see the instructor drawing in the video. This is defined as the sense of self-reference according to embodiment theory suggested by Robbins and Aydede (2009). Figure 4.12 below shows screenshots of a video from of a microlearning app, Math Tutor. In the screen shot on the left, the instructor is pointing to already drawn illustrations, while the instructor on the right is writing and drawing as he presents.

The Gaze Guidance Principle

The Gaze Guidance Principle deals with the onscreen instructor's gaze in a video. It states that humans learn best when the instructor shifts gaze between the learners and

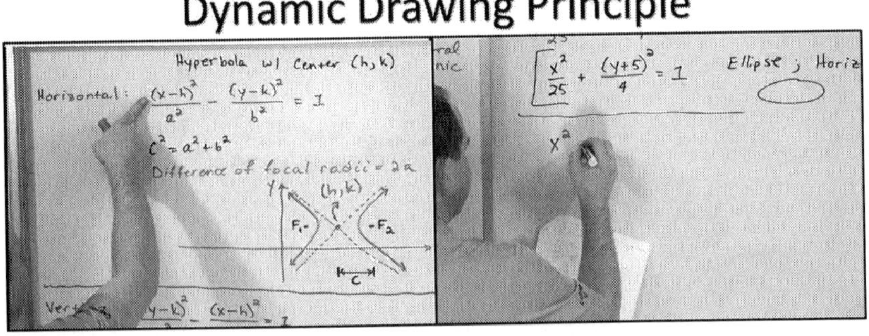

FIGURE 4.12 Representation of the Dynamic Drawing Principle

the board, rather than focusing on only the learner or the board. Mayer et al. (2020) explain that the Gaze Guidance Principle is founded on the Mayer's (2014) Social Agency Theory. For example, the eye gaze of the instructor in the video seen in Figure 4.13 below, creates the feeling of working in partnership, which in turn results in better learning from the instructional video (Mayer et al., 2020).

The Generative Activity Principle

The Generative Activity Principle states that humans learn best from video lectures when they are required to participate in activities such as summarizing, writing explanations, or physically mimicking the instructor's actions (Mayer et al., 2020). Studies show that learners perform better when they take notes during a computer programming or statistics video lecture (Peper & Mayer, 1978); a 23-min. video lecture on how car engines work (Peper & Mayer, 1986); or an 11-min. video lecture on taking photos with a 35 mm camera (Shrager & Mayer, 1989). In a more recent study conducted by Fiorella et al. (2016), college learners performed better when they engaged in a generative activity by imitating the instructor's actions while watching the video about constructing a complex circuit board. Although microlearning videos are suggested to be shorter (e.g., 5–6 minutes) than the videos used in these reported experiments, learners can be instructed to participate in generative activities like summarizing, writing explanations, or repeating what is being demonstrated in microlearning videos.

The Perspective Principle

The Perspective Principle states that humans learn best from manual demonstration videos when they are shown in the form of the first-person perspective, instead of the third-person perspective (Mayer et al., 2020). Fiorella et al. (2016) reported on two studies in which learners who received the first-person video format performed significantly better on posttests than learners who viewed the third-person video.

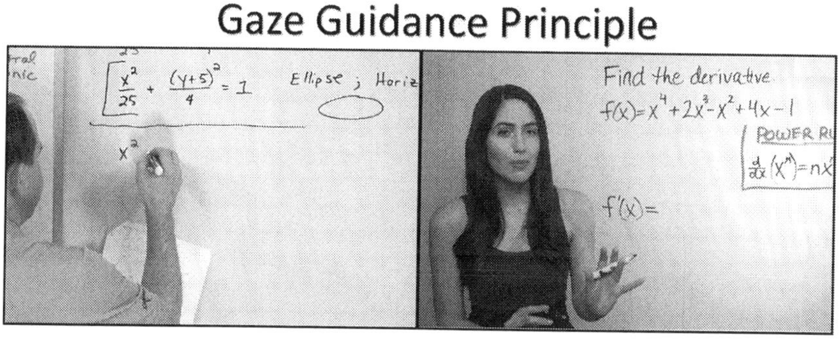

FIGURE 4.13 Representation of the Gaze Guidance Principle

Perspective Principle

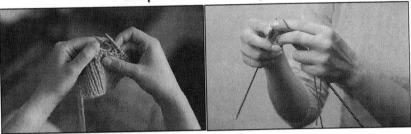

FIGURE 4.14 Knitting from a first-person perspective (left panel) and a third-person perspective (right panel) (Pixabay.com, n.d.)

The Subtitle Principle

The use of closed captions was addressed in the discussion of the Redundancy Principle earlier in the chapter. In 2020, Mayer et al. named this strategy the Subtitle Principle for learning videos. It states, "[p]eople learn better from videos recorded in the learners' second language when printed subtitles are added or used to replace spoken words" (p. 841). The Subtitle Principle suggests if learners are watching a learning video in their second language, subtitles at the bottom of the screen should duplicate the narrator in this second language, or the narration should be replaced by the subtitles. Also, Mayer et al. suggest that the pace of the video should be slow enough to help learners' working memory manage the printed text being presented.

Summary

The future of the design and applications of microlearning are unlimited as the technology and research advance rapidly in this area. However, as the technology available for the creation of microlearning content improves and becomes more readily available, questions arise regarding best design practices for the creation of those multimedia. This chapter presented Mayer's (2009) Principles of Multimedia Learning, and the more recent Multimedia Design Principles for Effective Instructional Videos (Mayer, Fiorella, & Stull, 2020) to provide a guide for instructional designers' and learning professionals' creation and selection of microlearning content. It is hoped that this chapter serves as guide for the design of improved microlearning events and increased learning for the learners who participate in it.

Discussion Questions

1. For microlearning, which is the most significant principle among those described in this chapter and why?

2. Think about microlearning examples or applications you have implemented or experienced. Select two principles and explain how each is met in your microlearning example. Discuss compatible and incompatible aspects according to the principles you selected.

3. When you think about all the principles, which of the principles is the hardest to implement in microlearning? Please explain why?

4. As you know, today, most learners use different tools to access learning content, such as mobile phones, tablets, or computers. Considering microlearning applications and/or implementation you have experienced, which principle is affected most from this variety of content sources?

References

Atkinson, R. K., Mayer, R. E., & Merrill, M. M. (2005). Fostering social agency in multimedia learning: Examining the impact of an animated agent's voice. *Contemporary Educational Psychology*, 30(1), 117–139. https://doi.org/10.1016/j.cedpsych.2004.07.001.

Badgr.com (n.d.). Example of visual for learning pathways. https://badgr.com/public/pathway/5ad8eee4c9494851f4893554.

Baumgartner, P. (2013). Educational Dimensions of Microlearning – Towards a Taxonomy for Microlearning. In Roth, M., Bruck, P., & Sedlaczek, M. (Eds.) *Designing Microlearning Experiences – Building Up Knowledge in Organisations and Companies*. Innsbruck: Innsbruck University Press.

Schär, S., & Zimmermann, P. G. (2007). Investigating means to reduce cognitive load from animations: Applying differentiated measures of knowledge representation. *Journal of Research on Technology in Education*, 40(1), 64–78. https://doi.org/10.1080/15391523.2007.10782497.

Clark, R. C., & Mayer, R. E. (2016). *e-Learning and the Science of Instruction: Proven Guidelines for Consumers and Designers of Multimedia Learning*. Hoboken, NJ: Wiley.

Clarke, T., Ayres, P., & Sweller, J. (2005). The impact of sequencing and prior knowledge on learning mathematics through spreadsheet applications. *Educational Technology Research and Development*, 53(3), 15–24. https://doi.org/10.1007/BF02504794.

Clothingindustry.blogspot.com (n.d.). Sewing-machine-parts and related functions. https://clothingindustry.blogspot.com/2018/01/sewing-machine-parts-functions.html.

Duolingo.com. (n.d.). Duolingo. www.duolingo.com.

Eitel, A., Scheiter, K., & Schüler, A. (2013). How inspecting a picture affects processing of text in multimedia learning. *Applied Cognitive Psychology*, 27(4), 451–461. https://doi.org/10.1002/acp.2922.

Fiorella, L., & Mayer, R. E. (2016). Effects of observing the instructor draw diagrams on learning from multimedia messages. *Journal of Educational Psychology*, 108(4), 528–546. https://doi.org/10.1037/edu0000065.

Guttormsen Schar, S., & Zimmermann, P. G. (2007). Investigating means to reduce cognitive load from animations: Applying differentiated measures of knowledge representation. *Journal of Research on Technology in Education*, 40(1), 64–78. https://doi.org/10.1080/15391523.2007.10782497.

Hug, T. (2007). *Didactics of Microlearning: Concepts, Discourses, and Examples*. Germany: Waxmann Verlag.

Hug, T. (2010). Mobile learning as 'microlearning': Conceptual considerations towards enhancements of didactic thinking. *International Journal of Mobile and Blended Learning*, 2(4), 47–57. https://doi.org/10.4018/jmbl.2010100104.

Jahnke, I., Lee, Y.-M., Pham, M., He, H., & Austin, L. (2019). Unpacking the inherent design principles of mobile microlearning. *Technology, Knowledge and Learning*, 25(3), 585–619. https://doi.org/10.1007/s10758-019-09413-w.

Kapp, K. M., & Defelice, R. A. (2019). *Microlearning: Short and Sweet*. Association for Talent Development.

Mayer, R. E. (2009). *Multimedia Learning*. Cambridge, UK: Cambridge University Press.

Mayer, R. E. (2014). Principles Based on Social Cues in Multimedia Learning: Personalization, Voice, Image, and Embodiment Principles. In R. E. Mayer (Ed.), *The Cambridge Handbook of Multimedia Learning*, (pp. 345–370). Cambridge University Press.

Mayer, R. E. (2014b). Cognitive Theory of Multimedia Learning. In R. E. Mayer (Ed.), *The Cambridge Handbook of Multimedia Learning* (2nd ed., pp. 43–71). New York: Cambridge University Press.

Mayer, R. E. (2019). How Multimedia Can Improve Learning and Instruction. In J. Dunlosky & K. A. Rawson (Eds.), *The Cambridge Handbook of Cognition and Education* (pp. 460–479). Cambridge University Press. https://doi.org/10.1017/9781108235631. 019.

Mayer, R. E., & Chandler, P. (2001). When learning is just a click away: Does simple user interaction foster deeper understanding of multimedia messages? *Journal of Educational Psychology*, 93(2), 390–397. https://doi.org/10.1037/0022-0663.93.2.390.

Mayer, R. E., & DaPra, C. S. (2012). An embodiment effect in computer-based learning with animated pedagogical agents. *Journal of Experimental Psychology: Applied*, 18(3), 239–252. https://doi.org/10.1037/a0028616.

Mayer, R. E., Dow, G. T., & Mayer, S. (2003). Multimedia learning in an interactive self-explaining environment: What works in the design of agent-based microworlds? *Journal of Educational Psychology*, 95(4), 806–812. https://doi.org/10.1037/0022-0663.95.4.806.

Mayer, R. E., Fiorella, L., & Stull, A. (2020). Five ways to increase the effectiveness of instructional videos. *Educational Technology Research and Development*, 68(3), 837–852. https://doi.org/10.1007/s11423-020-09749-6.

Mayer, R. E., Mathias, A., & Wetzell, K. (2002). Fostering understanding of multimedia messages through pre-training: Evidence for a two-stage theory of mental model construction. *Journal of Experimental Psychology: Applied*, 8(3), 147–154. https://doi.org/10. 1037/1076-898X.8.3.147.

Mayer, R. E., & Moreno, R. (2003). Nine ways to reduce cognitive load in multimedia learning. *Educational Psychologist*, 38(1), 43–52. https://doi.org/10.1207/S15326985EP3801_6.

Mayer, R. E., Mautone, P., & Prothero, W. (2002). Pictorial aids for learning by doing in a multimedia geology simulation game. *Journal of Educational Psychology*, 94(1), 171–185. https://doi.org/10.1037/0022-0663.94.1.171.

Mayer, R. E., & Pilegard, C. (2014). Principles for Managing Essential Processing in Multimedia Learning: Segmenting, Pre-training, and Modality Principles. In R. Mayer (Ed.), *The Cambridge Handbook of Multimedia Learning* (2nd ed., pp. 316–344). Cambridge University Press. https://doi.org/10.1017/CBO9781139547369.016.

Mayer, R., Sobko, K., & Mautone, P. (2003). Social cues in multimedia learning: Role of speaker's voice. *Journal of Educational Psychology*, 95(2), 419–425. insights.ovid.com

MindToolsmindtools.com (n.d.). Cognitive load theory. www.mindtools.com/pages/article/ cognitive-load-theory.htm.

Moreno, R. (2007). Optimising learning from animations by minimising cognitive load: Cognitive and affective consequences of signalling and segmentation methods. *Applied Cognitive Psychology*, 21(6), 765–781. https://doi.org/10.1002/acp.1348.

Moreno, R., & Mayer, R. E. (2000). Engaging learners in active learning: The case for personalized multimedia messages. *Journal of Educational Psychology*, 92(4), 724–733. https://doi.org/10.1037/0022-0663.92.4.724.

Moreno, R., & Mayer, R. E. (2004). Personalized messages that promote science learning in virtual environments. *Journal of Educational Psychology*, 96(1), 165–173. https://doi.org/10.1037/0022-0663.96.1.165.

Nass, C., & Brave, S. (2007). *Wired for Speech: How Voice Activates and Advances the Human-Computer Relationship*. MIT Press.

Peper, R. J., & Mayer, R. E. (1978). Note taking as a generative activity. *Journal of Educational Psychology*, 70(4), 514–522. https://doi.org/10.1037/0022-0663.70.4.514.

Peper, R. J., & Mayer, R. E. (1986). Generative effects of note-taking during science lectures. *Journal of Educational Psychology*, 78(1), 34–38. https://doi.org/10.1037/0022-0663.78.1.34.

Pixabay.com (n.d.) Knitting from first person perspective. https://pixabay.com/photos/knit-sew-girl-female-make-craft-869221.

Pixabay.com (n.d) Knitting from third person perspective. https://pixabay.com/photos/knitting-knitting-needles-human-5447283.

Purushotma, R. (2007). When Remix Culture Meets Microlearning. In *Didactics of Microlearning* (p. 218).

Robbins, P., & Aydede, M. (2009). *The Cambridge Handbook of Situated Cognition*. Cambridge University Press.

Schmidt, A. P. (2007). *Microlearning and the knowledge maturing process: Towards conceptual foundations for work-integrated microlearning support*. Proceedings of the 3rd International Microlearning 2007 Conference, 99–105. www.researchgate.net/publication/229422972_Microlearning_and_the_Knowledge_Maturing_Process_Towards_Conceptual_Foundations_for_Work-Integrated_Microlearning_Support.

Shrager, L., & Mayer, R. E. (1989). Note-taking fosters generative learning strategies in novices. *Journal of Educational Psychology*, 81(2), 263–264. https://doi.org/10.1037/0022-0663.81.2.263.

Simon, H. A. (1974). How big is a chunk?: By combining data from several experiments, a basic human memory unit can be identified and measured. *Science*, 183(4124), 482–488. https://doi.org/10.1126/science.183.4124.482.

Sweller, J., Ayres P., & Kalyuga, S. (2011). Measuring cognitive load. In *Cognitive Load Theory* (pp. 71–85). New York, NY: Springer.

Talentcards.com. (n.d.). Talentcards. https://talentcards.com.

TED-Ed. (n.d.) How fast can a vaccine be made?https://ed.ted.com/lessons/how-fast-can-a-vaccine-be-made-dan-kwartler.

Terzopoulos, G., & Satratzemi, M. (2019). *Voice assistants and artificial intelligence in education*. Proceedings of the 9th Balkan Conference on Informatics, 1–6. https://doi.org/10.1145/3351556.3351588.

Winger, A. (2018). Supersized tips for implementing microlearning in macro ways. *Distance Learning*, 15(4), 51–55.

Zhang, J., & West, R. E. (2020). Designing microlearning instruction for professional development through a competency based approach. *TechTrends*, 64(2), 310–318. https://doi.org/10.1007/s11528-019-00449-4.

5

OPTIMIZING MICROLEARNING MATERIALS FOR MOBILE LEARNING

Lucas Kohnke

Introduction

In today's fast-paced digital world, technology can act as both a catalyst and an inhibitor of learning. The rapid developments in the technological landscape of the education and workplace sectors may transform teaching and learning methods from being dominated by long input sessions to instead, using bite-sized chunks known as *microlearning* experiences. This learning strategy allows learners to multitask anytime and anywhere (Coakley et al., 2017; Kukulska-Hulme & Traxler, 2005). Microlearning involves fairly small, focused learning units that consist of condensed learning events (Hug et al., 2005), which are typically around two to six minutes in duration. This functions as *snackable content*, which are concise nuggets that have been optimized for mobile learning (Jahnke et al., 2019). In this chapter, the term *mobile learning* is used to refer to any type of learning that relies upon, or is disseminated through, a mobile device. This definition is not connected to any preexisting pedagogical assumptions or underlying theories of learning, instead, it is associated with objects that are explicitly technological in nature. In addition, in this chapter, *learners* denote students in education or workplace employees and teachers who are working in an educational institute or as workplace trainers.

Today's generation of learners no longer carries heavy backpacks with textbooks to and from class, nor is its learning primarily reliant on long, face-to-face classes. Instead, learners carry mobile devices with them at almost all times. They interact, connect, and engage with classmates and teachers, and process and absorb information in vastly different ways (Kohnke, 2020; Torgerson & Lannone, 2019). As a result, microlearning has become an emergent practice not only in education, but also in corporate and workplace training (Clark et al., 2018). It has engaged and motivated employees (Callisen, 2016; Glahn, 2017) and helped them to fit learning into their demanding schedules by providing quick answers and solutions (Shank, 2018). The number of studies into competency training in the workplace and the impact of microlearning on learners continues to increase (Emerson & Berge, 2018; Nikou & Economides, 2018a, 2018b).

Having the ability to access relevant, engaging microcontent on their mobile devices can afford learners brief learning experiences while simultaneously allowing them to dig into particular areas of content in more depth. This method of learning caters specifically to the needs of the current generation of learners. It is, moreover, a more motivating type of learning experience than some traditional learning methods (Reinhardt & Elwood, 2019). Microlearning is not a new concept (Hug et al., 2005), though the increased number of mobile applications (or apps) has only scratched the surface of technology's full pedagogical potential (Goggins et al., 2013). Teachers in formal education environments and learning professionals in corporate settings will benefit from exploring the possibilities of microlearning to motivate and engage today's learners, thereby maximizing the number and quality of their learning experiences. This chapter provides suggestions for practical strategies, tools, and best practices in multimedia design. In doing so, it aims to help educators and learning professionals create and deliver microlearning mechanisms that are optimized for mobile learning.

Microlearning Philosophy

The adoption of microlearning techniques requires careful planning and the reimagining of conventional teaching approaches into alternative ones, specifically embracing and devising learning formats that consist of short, essential messages or bursts of information. The key tenet of microlearning is to create high-impact, highly engaging modules of learning that are accessible, and digestible, in a short timeframe (Kapp & Defelice, 2019). These bursts of learning are not short, self-contained events. Instead, microlearning deconstructs concepts or topics into meaningful chunks and focuses on single ideas to allow for a better learning pace that is tailored to, and by, the individual, thereby reducing the risk of cognitive overload (Demmans Epp & Phirangee, 2019). Microlearning introduces individualized learning paths by prioritizing the delivery of short, high-impact messages (Zoltan, 2017).

Several specific terms have been employed in the context of teaching and microlearning, and scholarship about these terms, to articulate the specific structures of such learning devices and strategies in more depth. The term *micro-level* represents the organization of an individual session, whereas the overall course structure is known as the *meso-level*, and the curriculum is described as the *macro-level* (Buchem & Hamelmann, 2010). In engaging with microlearning approaches, individuals can take control of their learning. This, in turn, facilitates the effective transmission and retention of information (Sun et al., 2015). Moreover, microlearning nurtures perpetual, life-long learning by bridging formal and informal learning experiences. The process of doing so involves the utilization of mobile technologies to create learning objects before integrating them into brief events. As with all pedagogical approaches, it is necessary to think carefully about whether particular learning objectives are suitable for, and transferable to, microlearning environments.

The concept of microlearning has become synonymous with bursts of high-impact learning that take place in media-rich environments, like those of video and e-learning, and in a diverse mix of modalities, such as through infographics and podcasts. These modalities provide learners with new forms of stimuli that increase levels of both engagement and learning retention. To introduce mobile microlearning and microteaching to learners successfully, it is crucial to consider which available apps are the most appropriate (e.g., the most visually impressive, the fastest running, requiring the least storage space) for mobile devices. Also, to create and deliver effective microlearning experiences, one thing is paramount: meaningful design. The next section presents four key strategies to optimize approaches to mobile microlearning.

Practical Strategies

The primary aim of microlearning is to teach a straightforward, engaging, and well-structured lesson, which allows learners to understand key concepts efficiently and effectively (Zhang & Ren, 2011). Mobile microlearning addresses learning topics with the goal of being understandable, easy to absorb, and having a correct answer available (Jahnke et al., 2019). Today, mobile devices (e.g., cellphones, tablets) are increasingly used in the workplace, which allows users to just as easily communicate with someone as find out how to complete a task. Mobile learning brings learning anytime and anywhere to learners without necessitating them to step away from their work environment. These microlearning objects "can be made available on demand to facilitate just-in-time learning" (Sun et al., 2015 p.123), such as offering at-a-glance information to teach or refresh prior learning (e.g., how to put on and remove a face mask). Mobile microlearning enables learners to learn on the go without information overload.

To achieve this when segmenting away from traditional workplace and classroom-based learning to bite-sized learning via mobile applications, it is important to: incorporate videos and other visual components; use minimal text; use responsive page designs; and ensure there are at least some consistent, recurrent elements. The key is to keep all the elements simple and to incorporate only what is essential. Remember: *less is more*. Microlessons require high-quality content to be effective in the same way as any other pedagogical material would (Zhang & Ren, 2011). Visual aids, interactivity, and simplicity can all contribute to effective learning practices. Likewise, setting small and specific learning objectives engages learners (Bratt, 2020). Consider taking the textbook or training manual and breaking it down into small, manageable chunks of short learning events that can be delivered via mobile devices. This could include a three-minute podcast or presentation using slides that provides an overview of the topic, followed by a two-minute flash-card event with learners' drills for factual information. Later, learners could have access to a video or infographic that helps them to remember what to do or shows them a process for completing a task. When segmenting content for mobile microlearning, focus on a single learning goal in manageable chunks for each goal.

When planning to use microlearning, educators and learning professionals should consider these questions:

- What is the learning aim for learners?
- How will microlearning help learners to achieve this aim?
- What form should the microlearning take?

The answers to these questions will help educators and learning professionals determine how to structure the mobile learning content. Added to this, the four key considerations below (learners' needs, medium, interactivity, and simplicity) can guide educators, learning professionals, and instructional designers and developers in creating successful mechanisms of microlearning for mobile use.

Learner Needs

Microlearning is about meeting learners' needs and delivering personalized, flexible learning in short, bite-sized learning chunks (Jahnke et al., 2019). When considering how to formulate a potential mobile microlearning event, it is first necessary to think about learners' needs and how to create possible mobile solutions that meet those needs. This should be the *red thread* upon which to focus: How is it possible to optimize the use of learners' time while effectively fulfilling their learning needs? This depends on the responses to three questions:

- What does the learner need to know or learn?
- Will the learner find this resource useful?
- How will it affect the learner's learning?

Forms of microlearning are often facilitated by mobile devices with relatively small screens. The first step in preparing a microlearning event is to decide its objective. Is the event going to form part of the preparation for the next class/training? Does it reinforce the input of learners in class discussions? Does it constitute standalone training? It is important to ensure that learners' needs have been carefully considered when designing the event, as well as how they might apply it. Doing so will ensure that both learning professionals and learners find significant value in the materials, and it will increase the likelihood of learners achieving the specific learning outcome. Finally, it is important for educators and learning professionals to consider how microlearning will affect their capacity as facilitators of knowledge and skills. For example, it is important to ask important questions, such as: Will it provide valuable instruction and enrich learning without taking up additional time or impeding pedagogical practice? And is it necessary to reinvent established pedagogical practices completely or can existing teaching materials and strategies be used?

Medium

There are many potentially useful forms of media for microlearning events. Video is often the preferred medium when designing microlearning events, as it can combine slides, audio, graphics, and video. However, many other media are available, such as podcasts, infographics, e-learning lessons or modules, blogs, social media, simulations, slideshows, and pdfs, which appeal to different types of learners. It is important to keep the educational message simple and engaging while still providing high-quality content, no matter which medium has been selected. When considering which medium would be most suitable for delivering the event, it is important to ask:

- What medium or format would be most relevant and specific to the topic?
- What should learners do before, during, and after the event?

Do not be afraid to include multiple learning elements (e.g., visuals, audio, quizzes, slideshows, pdfs, and links). However, it is recommended that only one medium be used for each microlearning event component. Events work best when they are short and focused and consequently, do not confuse learners. It is also recommended that every event explains the fundamental premise or concept clearly, summarizes all the key points, and includes details of resources through which learners may gain further information.

Interactivity

Interactivity and engagement are two vital components of any learning event to ensure that learners are participating actively. As microlearning events are brief, learners must be focused upon and interested in the event throughout. It is effective to embed a variety of features in the chosen medium to appeal to different learning style preferences. When developing an event, consider the type of features that will reduce levels of passivity and increase input from, and activity on behalf of, learners. For example, consider if the event should:

- Provide single choice questions? Alternatively, use multiple-choice questions?
- Use branching on learning decisions?

- Offer dropdown lists?
- Employ fill in the blank events?
- Use click and reveal exercises?

Given the multitude of different types of features available for mobile learning with which rich, efficient, and effective optimized events can be created, it is important to keep the focused learning outcome in mind at all times and to be clear about how the features help to achieve the outcome. It is, for example, a good idea to incorporate some review events as interactive features (e.g., digital flashcards) in microlearning mechanisms (Kapp & Defelice, 2019). For instance, learners could receive a checklist to complete to verify whether they have grasped the fundamental concept or premise, or they could be asked to write a short reflection on social media or websites such as *Padlet* or *lino* (Kohnke, 2019a).

Simplicity

Because the central tenet of microlearning is to deliver short and snappy lessons, simplicity is key (Jahnke et al., 2019). The message should be clear, targeted, and focused, presenting each concept or subject one step at a time to be manageable (Lindner, 2007). Information needs to be easy to digest and to hold the audience's attention, delivering immediate results. To achieve simplicity, consider the following questions:

- Who is the intended audience?
- What is the best way to present information without dumbing it down?

Simplicity does not mean that the microlearning event does not require learners to master complex knowledge of skills. Instead, as learners delve into additional microlearning events, the content could be designed to become increasingly more challenging, while the fundamental premise of the session remains simple. The events should be designed for a single purpose, have a sole learning objective, and be part of a larger course aim. Therefore, when deconstructing key concepts or larger topics, it might be necessary and, indeed, good practice, to develop a series of microlearning events. For example, mini e-learning modules with short burst of learning consisting of video tutorials, followed by infographics and social media, can be created and implemented.

It is important to keep in mind the four key considerations described above when designing and optimizing practical microlearning events for mobile learning. It is vital to remember that the process is not about *slicing and dicing* regular learning materials. Instead, it is about connecting with, and motivating, learners, ensuring that they are engaging in meaningful, active learning, while simultaneously tapping into available mobile resources to maximize the learning experience (Hwang & Chen, 2017). In addition, the intended practical strategies should be considered carefully, as well as ensuring that the primary purpose or objective has been determined and is understood. Microlearning is not a one-size-fits-all strategy, and it will not work for every kind of learning or all kinds of content. With the right strategy and planning, however, mobile microlearning events can positively enhance teaching practice. Additionally, microlearning caters particularly well to the learning capabilities and skills of the current generation of learners (Aitchanov et al., 2018; Dai et al., 2018). In the next section, the impact of specific tools and apps that can enrich, enhance, and optimize microlearning experiences for mobile use will be identified and explored.

Tools and Apps

In our fast-paced culture, mobile learning is both flexible and customizable. It creates immediate learning opportunities. Apps provide multisensory opportunities such as audio, text, visuals, and actions to complement and aid understanding of learning content. However, as there are millions of apps available, the challenge is deciding where to start. A good point of reference is to consider the responses to the following questions:

- How do I find high quality apps?
- Which apps are good aids for learning about this subject?
- Which learning apps do learners already use and like?

Deciding which app is the most suitable for delivering the key message is paramount for creating effective and engaging microlearning. The selected app must be able to deliver the key message in a simple, effective way, while simultaneously deepening the learning process. As a general rule, the tool or app should be easy to set up and to use inasmuch as task motivation is crucial for learning (Nikou & Economides, 2018a, 2018b). Apps can technically be divided into two groups: (1) those that offer automated practice and learning, and (2) those that enable users to create things themselves. The more artifacts learners can create (e.g., through word clouds or checklists), the more likely the app will prove engaging, and therefore, the more likely it is to increase levels of task motivation among learners.

In the next section, several tools, apps, and software that are easy to use and that require little technical knowledge are discussed. As there are so many tools and apps available for designing and optimizing microlearning events for mobile learning, this is not an exhaustive list but, rather, a general point of reference.

Podcasts

A podcast is an effective microlearning tool and a good starting platform from which to introduce microlearning using mobile devices. A podcast is, in essence, a micro-lecture on a given topic. Generally, podcasts rely on audio, are easy to create, and are effective in increasing levels of engagement with their audience (Drew, 2017). Podcasts can be created on any computer platform or mobile device using a host of commercial, free, or open-source programs such *Audacity* for Windows, *GarageBand* on MacOS, *Voice Memo* for iOS, or *Anchor* for Android. To optimize the production of podcasts, one can create a free account on *Soundcloud.com* (available on the web, iOS, Android or, alternatively, through *Simplecast* or *Captivate*). On *Soundcloud*, it is possible to host almost all podcasts, and learners can subscribe through the really simple syndication (RSS) function to receive automatic notifications whenever new podcasts become available.

Presentation Software

Presentation software, like Microsoft *PowerPoint*, Apple *Keynote*, and *Google Slides,* is available for most computers and can easily be used to create microlearning objects. For example, *Microsoft PowerPoint* comes with a built-in screen capture feature, which can capture videos from *YouTube* or *TED*, making it easy to attach the video's URL to the PPT(X) file. Moreover, *PowerPoint* can integrate animations, triggers, and feedback to present microlearning events as stories. Similarly, *Google Slides* can be used to create microlearning content. Collaboration is a major reason to use *Google Slides*, as both applications and presentations are saved in Google Drive. This allows learners, educators, and learning professionals to easily share and simultaneously edit and co-create learning content. For users of Apple products, *Keynote* is a good user-friendly alternative, and it comes with themes, animations, and effects. Additionally, with *PowerPoint, Google Slides*, and *Keynote*, it is easy to create checks, quizzes, surveys, and assessments, which can help to reinforce learners' knowledge. To produce more professional microlearning events, it is possible to add *iSpring*, an e-learning authoring tool that is available on Windows operating systems and that functions as a *PowerPoint* add-on. The software allows educators and developers to create and enhance their *PowerPoint* presentations by incorporating content such as videos, branched quizzes, simulations, and interactions. These presentations can also be packaged into mobile-friendly lessons and integrated into learning management systems.

Infographics

Infographics are visually appealing, and they can break complex data down into simple visual formats as quick reference materials. Infographics can be useful for reviewing larger courses or for providing a quick snapshot of new information (e.g., step-by-step instructions, timeline to illustrate how something has changed over time). To make infographics memorable, they should be made intuitively comprehensible. Thus, design considerations include carefully choosing visual elements, such as charts, graphs, and colors, and they should include minimal supporting text to convey key messages (Kohnke & Chan, 2019). Leaners will be able to gather information from images and texts that are easy to understand and comprehensible at a glance. *Canva* and *Piktochart* are two easy-to-use web tools for creating dynamic infographics. Infographics can be exported in JPEG or PNG picture format, making them easy to share.

Videos

Videos can be used in the context of microlearning either as a form of standalone learning or as part of a series of teasers, that is to say, quick introductions to key learning elements. According to Köster (2018), most learners find videos more interactive and compelling than podcasts, *PowerPoint* presentations, or infographics, as they stimulate deeper levels of recall and retention, thereby leading to more positive learning experiences. Videos are especially suitable for offering high-impact, just-in-time forms of learning, for example, to demonstrate how to carry out a detailed procedure (e.g., change a tire, put on safety gear, improve customer service skills). The key criteria in optimizing videos for learning are that they are engaging and immersive and that they offer the required support for learners at the moment of need. As with other microlearning events, it is necessary to match each video to a specific learning outcome. Videos make it easy for learners to pause and to watch the content multiple times to help them to grasp the topic. When designing videos, bear in mind that, as aforementioned, *less is more*. It is important to keep it focused and let the visual stimuli tell the story. To complete the microlearning event, additional resources can be included with which learners may access extra information, as well as quizzes, to reinforce learning. There are many video creation and editing tools available. IMotion HD for Apple IOS or Magisto Video Editor and Maker for Android are free and easy to use. Microsoft and Apple also offer video editing tools in their suite of software tools.

Flashcards

Interactive flashcards, which can be accessed on mobile devices, are easy to create, and use, and constitute an effective and relatively simple option for delivering microlearning for initial learning or review of key concepts and terms. Flashcards can allow learners to learn progressively, faster, and as active users (Nakata, 2019). They are easy to create using free online flashcard sites like *Flashcard.online, StudyBlue*, and *FlashDecks*. *Brainscape.com* is an excellent source for previously created flashcards across multiple disciplines and grade levels. Interactive flashcards can incorporate animations, sounds, and images. For example, a keyword, phrase, number, or image may be on one side of the flashcard, while, on the other side, there is explanatory text or animation. This mechanism helps learners to make visual connections with facts or the steps of a process, allowing them to quiz themselves on the topic in question, for example, if learners need to learn a large amount of factual information about new products or features.

Collaborative Spaces

Today's learners use various social media channels throughout the day. As such, social media can present opportunities for creating active learning communities through which instructors and facilitators may connect with learners, anytime, anywhere. It is possible to create closed *Facebook* groups in which learners can access and discuss course-related events and share a variety of media, including podcasts, videos, *PowerPoints*, and infographics. Similarly, microblogs like *Twitter* can be useful to summarize or reflect on events succinctly, due to character limitations on individual posts, called *tweets*. Another popular platform is *Instagram*, to which learners can upload word clouds to illustrate visual concepts. Social media allow learners to support each other and to feel more involved with educational communities (Trowbridge et al., 2017). Learners can also collaborate in real time to brainstorm ideas by using collaborative social sites like *Mindmeister, Bubble,* or *Cacoo*. Moreover, poll and survey tools such as *Kahoot!, Poll Everywhere, Mentimeter,* or *GoSoapBox* can increase levels of learner participation (Kohnke, 2019b; Moorhouse & Kohnke, 2020).

Before or after a microlearning event, educators and learning professionals can pose questions using a number of question formats, including open-ended questions, word clouds, true-or-false statements, and multiple-choice questions. Such pre- and post-practice exercises delivered via social collaborative apps can help to close the feedback loop and provide opportunities for learners to learn from and with their peers. As with all forms of social media, collaborative learning can provide learners with valuable opportunities to practice communicating knowledge (Göschelberger, 2016a, 2016b). Collaborative forms of microlearning deepen levels of learning and understanding as well as enabling learners to feel as though they are part of a community.

In summary, microlearning encourages the process of studying in short bursts, and it can be introduced through numerous platforms as illustrated above. When designing visually appealing and content-precise events, especially for mobile use, it is important to strive to keep learning events short and focused, encourage contributions to deepen learning, choose a delivery platform that is available anytime and anywhere, and create learning communities so that learners have opportunities to create, curate, deliver, and engage in learning events. The efficacy of microlearning events lies in the interactivity and simplicity of their design (Baumgartner, 2013).

Best Practices

Microlearning has the potential to revitalize professional development and education and to give learners what they need by using short, bite-sized chunks of learning content that can be delivered directly to learners' mobile devices. Learners can conveniently access and complete events during their daily commutes or during their breaks or free time. As microlearning takes place in small bites, learners can revisit any given content multiple times, and the retention rate is higher than that of learners who undertake traditional methods of learning (Kang, 2016; Shail, 2019).

While microlearning objects can stand alone as isolated learning events, they can also be part of a larger learning experience. If designed appropriately, microlearning can provide increased flexibility and lead to higher levels of engagement and productivity among learners (Nikou & Economides, 2018a, 2018b). Faced with an overwhelming volume of information in today's fast-paced, increasingly connected, and mobile society, educators and instructional designers must rise to the challenge of educating today's learners by integrating microlearning events into traditional and emerging online pedagogical practices. The following seven tips can assist with the design and optimization of microlearning events for mobile learning:

1. Make it focused – keep each event focused with one learning objective.
2. Make it simple – keep the text and layout simple.
3. Make it graphic – keep it visual to illustrate the topic.
4. Make it interactive – keep it interactive, increasing levels of engagement and memory recall.
5. Make it short – keep it around two to six minutes in length to maximize the concentration span and to increase levels of learner engagement.
6. Make it social – keep it social by incorporating social media, discussion forums, and polls.
7. Make it mobile adaptive – keep the design simple, clear, and adaptable.

Summary: Why Mobile Microlearning Works

The short, engaging, and interactive delivery of content that characterizes microlearning meets the information-retrieving style and needs of today's generation (Donahue, 2016; Winger, 2018). Instead of reading long sections of text in traditional textbooks or manuals to grasp a particular concept, learners can: (a) watch a short informative video, (b) access an interactive infographic that visually deconstructs complex ideas, (c) use interactive flashcards to make visual associations with facts or concepts, (d) work through branched simulations on slideshow presentations, (e) listen to authentic interviews or lesson summaries on podcasts, and (f) take collaborative quizzes or access additional learning resources, all within only two to six minutes. If microlearning events are optimized for mobile devices, learners can multitask, receiving short bursts of information while accessing information through digital platforms.

There are several benefits to adopting microlearning events on mobile devices, including the provision of just-in-time access to content or resources, the consolidation of key information, and the incorporation of many different modalities such as infographics, videos, podcasts, images, and word clouds (Souza & Amaral, 2014). By distilling key learning messages – conveying them in simple and clear ways through mobile devices using responsive designs and easy-to-remember visuals, microlearning enables learners to receive specific information through an interactive format, one that is highly motivational and rewarding.

The process of incorporating microlearning into traditional courses and professional development programs can initially seem daunting. However, by using the information in this chapter as a starting point and a guide, targeted microlessons that can take advantage of ubiquitous forms of technology can be created and delivered. By incorporating the tips and suggestions that have been outlined in this chapter, levels of learner engagement and active learning through the use of mobile microlearning events can be optimized. By optimizing microlearning materials for mobile learning, learners can be afforded the flexibility to fit learning into their busy schedules, anytime, anywhere. The incorporation of optimized microlearning materials for mobile learning is an exciting avenue to explore. It has great potential to lead to even more engaging and effective methods of learning in the future.

Discussion Questions

1. How can you align your learning outcomes with methods of microlearning? How will you determine if your content is suitable for microlearning?
2. What are the challenges you may face in optimizing microlearning materials for mobile learning in your particular context?
3. How can microlearning best be delivered for your specific learners? How could it suit your audience/learners?
4. In what ways can you optimize microlearning events for mobile learning to be used to create personalized events for learners?

References

Aitchanov, B., Zhaparov, M., & Ibragimov, M. (2018). *The research and development of the information system on mobile devices for micro-learning in educational institutes.* In 2018 14th international conference on electronics computer and computation (ICECCO) (pp. 1–4). IEEE.

Baumgartner, P. (2013). Educational Dimensions of Microlearning – Towards a Taxonomy for Microlearning. In P. Bruck & M. Sedlaczek (Eds.), *Designing Microlearning Experiences – Building Up Knowledge in Organisations and Companies,* Innsbruck University Press. https://pdfs.semanticscholar.org/836b/52598a2f1aca8a068c1a392a53e0b4ea55f5.pdf.

Bratt, S. (2020). *Essential strategies for developing mobile-based micro-learning.* Edmedia + Innovate learning proceeding. Waynesville, NC: Association for the Advancement of Computing in Education (AACE).

Buchem, I., & Hamelmann, H. (2010). Microlearning: A strategy for ongoing professional development. *eLearning Papers*, 21(7), 1–15.

Callisen, L. (2016). Why micro learning is the future of training in the workplace. https://elearningindustry.com/micro-learning-future-of-training-workplace.

Clark, H., Jassal, P. K., van Noy, M., & Paek, P. L. (2018). A New Work-and-Learn Framework. In D. Ifenthaler (Ed.), *Digital Workplace Learning* (pp. 23–41). Springer.

Coakley, D., Garvey, R., & O'Neill, Í. (2017). Micro-learning—Adopting Digital Pedagogies to Facilitate Technology-enhanced Teaching and Learning for CPD. In G. Teh & S. Choy (Eds.), *Empowering 21st Century Learners Through Holistic and Enterprising Learning* (pp. 237–242). Springer.

Dai, H., Tao, Y., & Shi, T. W. (2018). *Research on mobile learning and micro course in the big data environment*. In Proceedings of the 2nd international conference on e-education, e-business and e-technology (pp. 48–51). ACM.

Demmans Epp, C., & Phirangee, K. (2019). Exploring mobile tool integration: Design activities carefully or students may not learn. *Contemporary Educational Psychology*, 59. https://doi.org/10.1016/j.cedpsych.2019.101791.

Donahue, M. (2016). Microlearning and the incredible shrinking attention span. *Hotel Management*, 231(7), 27.

Drew, C. (2017). Edutaining audio: An exploration of education podcast design possibilities. *Educational Medial International*, 54(1), 48–62. https://doi.org/10.1080/09523987.2017.1324360.

Emerson, L., & Berge, Z. (2018). Microlearning: Knowledge management applications and competency-based training in the workplace. *Knowledge Management & E-Learning: An International Journal*, 10(2), 125–132.

Glahn, C. (2017). Micro learning in the workplace and how to avoid getting fooled by micro instructionists. https://lo-f.at/glahn/2017/06/micro-learning-in-the-workplace-and-how-to-avoid-getting-fooled-by-micro-instructionists.html.

Goggins, S. P., Jahnke, I., & Wulf, V. (2013). *Computer-Supported Collaborative Learning at the Workplace*. Springer.

Göschelberger, B. (2016a). A Platform for Social Microlearning. In K. Verbert, M. Sharples, & T. Klobučar (Eds.), *Adaptive and Adaptable Learning. EC-TEL 2016. Lecture Notes in Computer Science, 9891* (pp. 513–516). Springer.

Göschelberger, B. (2016b). Social Microlearning Motivates Learners to Pursue Higher-Level Cognitive Objectives. In G. Vincenti, A. Bucciero, M. Helfert, & M. Glowatz (Eds.), *E-learning, E-education, and Online Training. Lecture Notes of the Institute for Computer Sciences, Social Informatics and Telecommunications Engineering*, Vol. 180 (pp. 201–208). Cham: Springer.

Hug, T., Lindner, M., & Bruck, P. (2005). *Microlearning: Emerging Concepts, Practices and Technologies after E-learning*. Innsbruck University Press.

Hwang, G. J., & Chen, C.-H. (2017). Influences of an inquiry-based ubiquitous gaming design on students' learning achievements, motivation, behavioral patterns, and tendency towards critical thinking and problem solving. *British Journal of Educational Technology*, 48, 950–971. https://doi.org/10.1111/bjet.12464.

Jahnke, I., Lee, Y.-M., Pham, M., He, H., & Austin, L. (2019). Unpacking the inherent design principles of mobile microlearning. *Technology, Knowledge and Learning*, 24(2), 1–35.

Kang, S. H. (2016). Spaced repetition promotes efficient and effective learning: Policy implications for instruction. *PIBBS*, 3, 12–19. https://doi.org/10.1177/2372732215624708.

Kapp, K. M., & Defelice, R. A. (2019). *Microlearning: Short and Sweet.* Association for Talent Development.

Kohnke, L. (2019a). Use sticky-notes and make the content stick. *Teacher Trainer*, 33(1), 6–7.

Kohnke, L. (2019b). Tech review: GoSoapBox – Encourage participation and interaction in the language classroom. *RELC Journal*, https://doi.org/10.1177/0033688219872570.

Kohnke, L. (2020). Exploring learner perception, experience and motivation of using a mobile app in L2 vocabulary acquisition. *International Journal of Computer-Assisted Language Learning and Teaching*, 10(1), 15–26. https://doi.org/10.4018/IJCALLT.2020010102.

Kohnke, L., & Chan, B. (2019). Exploiting infographics. *Modern English Teacher*, 28(1), 67–68.

Köster, J. (2018). *Video in the Age of Digital Learning.* Springer.

Kukulska-Hulme, A., & Traxler, J. (2005). *Mobile Learning in Developing Countries.* Vancouver, Canada: Commonwealth of Learning. http://oro.open.ac.uk/49128/.

Lindner, M. (2007). *What is microlearning? (Introductory note).* In 3rd International Microlearning 2007 Conference. Innsbruck University Press.

Moorhouse, B., & Kohnke, L. (2020). Using Mentimeter to elicit student responses in the EAP/ESP classroom. *RELC Journal*, 51(1), 198–204. https://doi.org/10.1177/0033688219890350.

Nakata, T. (2019). Learning Words with Flash Cards and Word Cards. In S. Webb (Ed.), *The Routledge Handbook of Vocabulary Studies* (pp. 304–319). Routledge.

Nikou, S., & Economides, A. (2018a). Mobile-based assessment: A literature review of publications in major referred journals from 2009 to 2018. *Computers & Education*, 125, 101–119. https://doi.org/10.1016/j.compedu.2018.06.006.

Nikou, S., & Economides, A. (2018b). Mobile-based micro-learning and assessment: Impact on learning performance and motivation of high school students. *Journal of Computer Assisted Learning*, 34(3), 269–278. https://doi.org/10.1111/jcal.12240.

Reinhardt, K. S., & Elwood, S. (2019). Promising Practices in Online Training and Support: Microlearning and Personal Learning Environments to Promote a Growth Mindset in Learners. In J. Keengwe (Ed.), *Handbook of Research on Virtual Training and Mentoring of Online Instructors* (pp. 298–310). IGI Global.

Shail, M. S. (2019) Using micro-learning on mobile applications to increase knowledge retention and work performance: A review of literature. *Cureus*, 11(8): e5307. https://doi.org/10.7759/cureus.5307.

Shank, P. (2018). Microlearning, macrolearning. What does research tell us? https://elearningindustry.com/microlearning-macrolearning-research-tell-us.

Souza, M. I., & Amaral, S. F. (2014). Educational microcontent for mobile learning virtual environments. *Creative Education*, 5, 672–681.

Sun, G., Cui, T., Yong, J, Shen, J., & Chen, S. (2015). *Drawing micro learning into MOOC: using fragmented pieces of time to enable eBective entire course learning experiences.* In International Conference on Computer Supported Cooperative Work in Design (pp. 308–313). IEEE CPS.

Torgerson, C., & Lannone, S. (2019). *Designing Microlearning.* American Society for Training & Development.

Trowbridge, S., Waterbury, C., & Sudbury, L. (2017). Learning in bursts: Microlearning with social media. https://er.educause.edu/articles/2017/4/learning-in-burstsmicrolearning-with-social-media.

Winger, A. (2018). Supersized tips for implementing microlearning in macro ways. *Distance Learning*, 15(4), 51–55.

Zhang, X., & Ren, L. (2011). *Design for application of micro learning to informal training in enterprise*. In 2nd international conference on artificial intelligence, management science and electronic commerce (pp. 2024–2027). https://doi.org/10.1109/AIMSEC.2011.6011235.

Zoltan, R. (2017). *Exploitation of micro-learning for generating personalized learning paths*. DS 87–9. In Proceedings of the 21st international conference on engineering design (ICED 17), Vol 19: *Design Education*, pp. 129–138. Design Society.

6

ASSESSING THE LEARNING IN MICROLEARNING

Rita Fennelly-Atkinson and Renee Dyer

Introduction

How does one go about accessing the learning that participants acquire within microlearning opportunities? Like the assessment of effective learning in any setting, it all begins with the instructional design process and planning for learning in accordance with a selected instructional design model. While there are many instructional design models, most include components of analysis, design, development, implementation, evaluation, and revision (Roblyer, 2015). Minimal peer-reviewed research into microlearning is currently available to instructional designers. Thus, even less peer-reviewed research into the meaningful assessment of the learning occurring within microlearning opportunities is available to those designing instruction (Zhang & West, 2019). As such, a robust instructional design process becomes even more paramount when instructional designers create successful microlearning opportunities for participants.

This chapter will guide readers through a myriad of topics to consider when they begin planning each microlearning event and its corresponding assessment strategy. In addition, this chapter will guide readers on the design of effective microlearning assessments that are Inventive, Targeted, Specific, and Yielding (ITSY). Readers will learn more about the importance of robust instructional design at the foundation of microlearning to ensure assessments are aligned to the intended outcome. Readers will also learn more about aligning training preferences with various microlearning options before finally examining possible microlearning assessments through the tried-and-true Kirkpatrick Model for training evaluation.

Contextualizing Microlearning within the Instructional Design Process

When developing a strategy for effective learning in any setting, the instructional design process should be considered. While there are many instructional design models, most include components of analysis, design, development, implementation, evaluation, and revision (Roblyer, 2015). To assess microlearning successfully, this process becomes critical in creating effective microlearning instruction with tangible results. Currently, there is sparse peer-reviewed research into microlearning and even less of it addresses assessment in a meaningful way (Zhang & West, 2019). Hence, the tried-and-true processes of instructional design may be applied to ensure assessments are meaningful.

As a result, the assessment and evaluation of microlearning are essential to ensuring its successful application and effectiveness. The key to unlocking microlearning's potential lies in understanding the parameters and varying contexts unique to the microlearning experience. While there are differing definitions of microlearning, several of them (Buhu & Buhu, 2019; Hug & Friesen, 2009; Janjua, 2017; Kapp & Defelice, 2018; Lim, Ryu, Martindale, Kim, & Park, 2019; Orwoll et al., 2018; Winger, 2018) describe it as a learning experience that is:

- short
- focused
- relevant
- incorporates some technology
- is specific to the learning context or environment
- includes an assessment.

Let's take a more in-depth look at each of these characteristics and how they impact the development of assessments in microlearning.

Microlearning should be short. In microlearning, short refers to the length of the learning experience. Is it easily digestible by the learner? Microlearning events have been described to be as short as seconds and as long as up to 20 minutes (Buhu & Buhu, 2019; Gross et al., 2019; Hesse et al., 2019; Hug & Friesen, 2009; Janjua, 2017; Scaglione, 2019; Zhang & West, 2019). The length of the microlearning experience should include the time it takes for a learner to consume the learning materials (Hug & Friesen, 2009). This timeframe may also include an assessment and feedback portion, depending on the context of the learning event (Buhu & Buhu, 2019; Gross et al., 2019; Lim et al., 2019). In relation to assessments, the primary consideration is whether the assessment is occurring within or outside of the learning experience.

Microlearning should be focused. Due to the short nature of the microlearning experience, its effectiveness is primarily based on being focused on a specific instructional need. Hug and Friesen (2009) describe it as small units or narrow topics, while Khan (2019) refers to them as snippets. Gross et al. (2019) represent microlearning as "chunk[ing] the learning process into [small] episodes, skill elements, or 'knowledge nuggets'" (p. 3). Still others describe it as an independent unit focused on a single application, concept, skill, or task (Osaigbovo & Iwegim, 2018; Paul, 2016; Scaglione, 2019). Consensus indicates microlearning should be based on one learning objective or goal, but no more than three (Higgenbotham, 2019; Janjua, 2017; Kapp & Defelice, 2018; Lim et al., 2019; Paul, 2016; Winger, 2018).

Researchers further recommend microlearning avoid tackling concepts like theoretical knowledge or complex processes, and instead focus on skills, procedures, tasks, and reinforcement (Gross et al., 2019; Higgenbotham, 2019; Paul, 2016; Scaglione, 2019). Still, microlearning can be leveraged to support complex processes by focusing on the aspects that tend to be critical points of failure. Extending these ideas to assessments, the ideal assessment should also be short and targeted to the desired goal for the learning or larger organizational outcome.

Microlearning should be relevant. Relevance refers to the degree to which a microlearning session connects to the need of the learner. Buhu and Buhu (2019) describe relevance as being able to "offer just the right amount of information necessary to help a learner achieve a specific objective" (p. 374) in an immediately applicable manner. Learners experience yet another dimension of relevancy when the training design encourages them to search for information instantaneously online at their point of need. To further promote microlearning's relevancy, Paul (2016) asserts learners should be able to reference microlearning content on-demand whenever and wherever they may be working. Likewise, relevant assessment data should also be available on demand to provide the organization and learner with information on progress and future directions.

Microlearning should incorporate technology. Many current definitions of microlearning specify it should include a technological component for the delivery of instruction (Janjua, 2017; Winger, 2018; Zhang & West, 2019). Hesse et al. (2019) specify the use of any web-enabled device. Other researchers, however, specifically mention mobile phones and smartphones as the most readily available device for a learner interested in engaging in a microlearning event (Buhu & Buhu, 2019; Kapp & Defelice, 2018; Lim et al., 2019; Orwoll et al., 2018; Osaigbovo & Iwegim, 2018; Paul, 2016). The use of devices such as smartphones is based on the expectation that learners may need to access instruction on-demand or just-in-time; a tenet of microlearning (Kapp & Defelice, 2018; Orwoll et al., 2018; Paul, 2016). Depending on the goal of instruction, it is foreseeable that microlearning may include the use of devices such as smart wearable technologies, virtual reality, augmented reality, artificial intelligence, and other types of web-enabled equipment.

Because technology allows for a variety of formats, microlearning can be presented to learners in many ways. Microlearning instruction can be offered via text, audio, visual, audiovisual, mixed media, and interactive formats (see Table 6.1). Moreover,

TABLE 6.1 Examples of microlearning formats

Format	Examples
Text	Books, flashcards, handouts (Higgenbotham, 2019; Hug & Frieson, 2009)
Audio	Radio, podcasts, recordings (Higgenbotham, 2019; Hug & Frieson, 2009; Lim, et al., 2019; Winger, 2018)
Visual	Job aids, graphics, pictures, and infographics (Buhu & Buhu, 2019; Higgenbotham, 2019; Lim, et al., 2019; Winger, 2018)
Audiovisual	Video and animations (Buhu & Buhu, 2019; Gross et al., 2019; Higgenbotham, 2019; Lim, et al., 2019; Winger, 2018)
Mixed media	Computer-based learning, online learning, games, learning management systems, cloud-based authoring software, and presentations (Capuano & King, 2015; Hesse et al., 2019; Higgenbotham, 2019; Hug & Frieson, 2009; Winger, 2018)
Interactive	Games, quizzes, social media, puzzles, simulations, scenarios, and any interactively designed format listed above (Osaigbovo, 2018; Lim et al., 2019; Winger, 2018)

microlearning assessments can go beyond the traditional evaluation tools and utilize unique assessment data based on the type of technology being used and, consequently, the type of data being collected.

Microlearning should be specific to the learning context or environment. One of the beauties of microlearning is it can occur at any time in any environment. Whether it is a traditional classroom, corporate setting, or in the field, research supports microlearning can be used successfully. Paul (2016) states microlearning is ideal for decentralized learning. Kapp and Defelice (2018) consider microlearning ideal for meeting just-in-time performance needs, changing learner behaviors, refreshing previous instruction, or preparing for new or irregularly occurring events. Designers can also ensure the microlearning event meets the needs of learners by building on any pedagogical foundation best suited to the learning context (Hug & Friesen, 2009). Further, the learning context or environment may be considered formal or informal, optional or required, individual or organizational. All these factors will impact how the microlearning should be designed, delivered, and assessed.

Since the goals for microlearning are so varied and dependent on the purpose for the initial intervention, there are an infinite number of ways that organizations can assess the success of microlearning events. For example, if the goal of a microlearning intervention is to support a behavior change designed to improve performance, organizational learning leaders could choose to assess the learning through observation of the performed behavior, indirect performance metrics, or both.

Microlearning should be assessed. The variety of formats, technologies, and learning contexts means there are endless possibilities of how learning can be assessed. While this will be discussed in greater detail in the sections that follow, for now, it is sufficient to consider the potential overarching goals that will influence how microlearning can be assessed. If the goal is to track the successful completion of required training, a microlearning assessment might be as simple as a knowledge check with completion tracking. If the goal is to informally share knowledge or information to a nonspecific audience, an assessment might use the number of likes, followers, comments, or shares. If the goal is to reduce process inefficiencies or increase safety, an indirect assessment of organizational data may be used to assess the usefulness of the microlearning experience.

Assessing the Learning in Microlearning

Professional learning opportunities, be they macro or micro in size, exist to fulfill learning needs within an organization. That being said, how can organizational leaders gauge if the learning opportunities they provided actually worked? The simple answer is that the effectiveness of the learning solution can be determined by assessing the outcome of the training. Yet, this simple answer is not so simply accomplished. How can it be determined if employee professional development goals were met? In 1954, Donald Kirkpatrick developed the Kirkpatrick Training Evaluation Model as part of his dissertation. As part of the evaluation process, he called for training evaluators to examine four key elements when determining the effectiveness of trainings delivered to participants: (1) participant reaction to the training, (2) learning gained by the participants as a result of the training, (3) the change in participant behavior due to the training, and (4) the degree to which the results of the training reflect the original goals of the training (Kirkpatrick & Kirkpatrick, 2016). Its inherent simplicity has made it a highly adaptable model that can be used in any learning context (Kurt, 2018). Subsequently, it is not surprising that this model is useful and applicable to microlearning. If built on a solid instructional design foundation and evaluated using a time-tested method, like the Kirkpatrick model, microlearning developers can transcend the limitations of traditional professional learning opportunities to meet learners at their point of need, with instructional portions that accomplish organizational goals bite by bite.

When applying the Kirkpatrick model, it is crucial to remember that according to Kirkpatrick and Kirkpatrick (2016), in order for the assessment to be of value, the training must be well-designed from the start. This assertion takes on even greater importance for the design of more concentrated, microlearning events. For example, the table below summarizes the assessment purpose behind the four levels of The New World Kirkpatrick Training Evaluation Model. If the microlearning assessment was focused on behavior, which corresponds to Kirkpatrick's

Training Evaluation Level 3, then an appropriate microlearning assessment could be a performance observation as seen in Table 6.2 below.

It is important to remember that microlearning is often delivered and assessed within the context of more comprehensive training programs and is tied to long term organizational goals. As such, microlearning often serves to address needs that were uniquely suited for a focused microlearning event or an emergent need due to evolving circumstances. Assessing the learning attained from microlearning events, while similar in many ways to more traditional assessment structures discussed by Kirkpatrick and Kirkpatrick (2016), is different in that it includes assessment elements more unique to the developing microlearning field. Whereas traditional assessments may measure a greater breadth of learning, microlearning assessments will be highly targeted to precisely measure the microlearning goal.

These differences may be more easily remembered using the acronym ITSY. For this chapter, ITSY represents Inventive (thinking outside the box), Targeted

TABLE 6.2 Summary of *The New World Kirkpatrick Training Evaluation Model*

Level	Goal of Evaluation	Examples of Microlearning Assessments or Indicators
1. Reaction	• What were participants' reactions to the training? • Do participants regard the training favorably? • Did participants find the training engaging? • Did participants feel that the training was relevant to their work?	• Feedback surveys • Check-ins • Completion rates
2. Learning	• What were participants' reactions to the training? • Did participants obtain the intended skills, knowledge, and self-confidence from the training provided?	• Knowledge checks • Skill demonstrations • Surveys • Performance evaluations
3. Behavior	• To what degree did the participants apply what they learned in the training once they were back at work.	• Observations • Self-assessments • Performance indicators • Surveys
4. Results	• Did the training accomplish the outcomes desired when the training was created?	• Ratings • Productivity or production • Various organizational indicators of performance or success

Note. This table was adapted from Kirkpatrick and Kirkpatrick (2016).

(analogous and focused on the learning objective), Specific (distinct for each student and context), and Yielding (providing useful information to the learner and organization). Let's take a closer look at each element of ITSY.

Assessments should be Inventive. Due to the nature of microlearning, assessments tend to be more creative than those found in more traditional learning contexts. While short quizzes, surveys, and pre- and post-assessments might still be valuable tools to assess microlearning, the technology tools used to deliver microlearning affords trainers additional options. For example, social media is particularly well suited for delivering and assessing microlearning. In particular, social media has the advantage of being able to help people connect with peers and experts; these connections can then be leveraged into organic collaborations, learning moments, and networking (Fennelly-Atkinson et al., 2019). Adding to the value of social media as a tool for microlearning assessments, Osaigbovo and Iwegim (2018) highlight how engagement, satisfaction, and relevance can be assessed via the number of followers and likes microlearning content receives. Assessing learners' reactions provides many unique opportunities for microlearning. Paul (2016) also recommends using data, such as traffic or downloads, to evaluate the success of microlearning. This type of data can be extended to microlearning conducted on other platforms like learning management systems (LMS), software for delivering and tracking learning, apps, and website analytics, which can track information including the number of clicks, users, time spent, and other potentially useful information. LMSs generate learning analytics, data presented in specific ways that can provide a predetermined set of data by assignment, course, and institution. Although some of these platforms might be able to provide detailed and individualized user data, this type of microlearning assessment is particularly suited for assessing generalized information about all users engaging with the learning. A plethora of data, such as how many times a video has been viewed, for how long, on which type of device, and so much more can be gathered. These data can be used to assess which type of content is most engaging for learners or to provide real-time customer demographics that could inform future microlearning event decisions.

Assessment of learning can also be conducted via brief surveys and quizzes embedded within the content of the microlearning (Hesse et al., 2019; Higgenbotham, 2019; Kapp & Defelice, 2018; Zhang & West, 2019). Additionally, the evaluation of tasks can be a valuable form of assessing application skills (Zhang & West, 2019). However, self-assessments and self-reported compliance can also be used to evaluate the effectiveness of learning (Orwoll et al., 2018). For example, a survey could be used for learners to self-report their compliance with specific expectations. This type of assessment allows learners to evaluate themselves, while providing timely reminders for items they can double-check and correct if needed, which serves as an additional opportunity to reinforce learning.

According to Kirkpatrick and Kirkpatrick (2016), the assessment of behaviors is often overlooked even though it is critical to performance. In many ways, this is the area in which microlearning shines as it has many applications for helping professionals learn protocols and procedures. Capuano and King (2015) studied how games could be used for emergency training and ongoing assessment of skills. In this case, learners' actions within the game were continually assessed and used to determine whether the learner moved forward or engaged in skill reinforcement. This type of embedded assessment can be used for any adaptive microlearning experience that might be found in a game, adaptive learning apps, or personalized learning pathways designed within a learning management system. Social gamification can also be used to increase the desired behavioral performance through individual and team competitions (Orwoll et al., 2018). Orwoll et al. (2018) defined social gamification as the application of game mechanics, particularly competition, in a social media environment. In their study, individuals or teams would primarily document and report their progress and performance through formal or informal competitions facilitated on social media groups or platforms. The researchers used microlearning to decrease preventable infections through improved medical practices. Each nursing team earned points for each completed self-assessment and used a social media platform to track participants and determine winners and prizes. The informal competitions that resulted led to increased self-assessment, which reduced overall infection rates. Social gamification, such as the example described above, is an excellent example of how a targeted microlearning informal assessment can be creatively coupled with competition to yield a noticeable improvement in individual performance and, therefore, increase the quality of organizational services.

Likewise, observational data should not be overlooked. While it can be time-consuming, this type of assessment can be effective in evaluating mission-critical performance or behaviors. Kapp and Defelice (2018) recommend the use of comparisons of before-and-after performance evaluations or comparisons between learners who accessed the microlearning versus those who did not. Zhang and West (2019) also recommend using supervisor feedback on task performance and the use of awarding micro-credentials. Micro-credentials, in particular, offer a unique method of assessing behavior. Generally speaking, learners engage in a short, focused experience in which they will need to complete specific tasks or create specific artifacts to demonstrate their acquisition of a skill. Demonstration of microlearning competencies can often be tied to opportunities for advancement, compensation, or social prestige, which can help foster motivation to engage in the process while also assessing the effectiveness of the learning.

While the learning experience may be compact, there is no reason why microlearning assessments cannot be used to evaluate progress towards larger organizational outcomes. These types of outcomes can address organizational aspects such as costs, quality, efficiency, compliance, safety, and many more (Kirkpatrick & Kirkpatrick, 2016). It is here that the instructional design process is key in determining high-leverage targets ideal for microlearning interventions. For example, safety is a critical issue for many organizations. While most institutions provide staff with some type of formal training, safety is an ongoing concern that needs to be regularly addressed. For example, an organization might experience a surge in a certain type of accident and an analysis might reveal that they occurred in a particular area or during a specific type of activity. Microlearning might be used to provide a targeted refresher for staff most likely to be in these high-risk situations. One way that the success of this intervention could be assessed is by looking at whether the overall number or a specific type of accident decreased after the intervention was implemented.

Assessments should be Targeted. Chada et al. (2018) proposes that learning and development professionals in organizations focus on listening to, consulting with, and delivering small, social, and collaborative learning experiences that meet participants' swiftly changing needs. When professional learning developers become learning partners with their participants, they are better able to understand and address the performance areas that need further clarification or development. As such, developers and creators of microlearning events should provide learners with chunks of micro-content directly targeting learner knowledge in small, digestible portions that are task-oriented and focused on a particular skill or outcome (Simkins & Maier, 2009). If participants benefit from highly targeted microlearning instruction, it stands to reason that the assessments accompanying that learning should also be analogous, highly targeted micro-assessments. Multiple research studies have demonstrated the learning benefits associated with providing students, immediate feedback and step-by-step scaffolding of learning events (Hauk, Powers, & Segalla, 2015; Nikou & Economides, 2018). Further, microlearning events are often created as individual, scaffolded learning opportunities that, while standing alone, also build upon one another. For example, Brebera (2107) explored microlearning's potential uses in foreign language classrooms. The study concluded that individual microlearning events that scaffolded course material fostered increased learners' capacity for long-term language development by increasing their exposure to the increasingly sophisticated foreign language curriculum.

Assessments should be Specific. As the way people learn is changing, so too must the way we assess that learning. Microlearning events require learning and development professionals to create assessments that are congruent with each microlearning event, reflect the participants, and measure the learning objective (Nikou & Economides, 2018). One way in which microlearning assessments can match microlearning events is for learning and development professionals to plan assessments that are built around the shrinking attention spans of today's learners. Katherine Hayles (2012) reports that adult attention spans in the 1960s required approximately 20 seconds to recognize an image on a screen. Today, adults recognize images in 2–3 seconds and are ready to move on to the next image almost immediately.

Further, in 2018, The Nielsen Company reported the time spent with digital media for all generations within our current workforce. They found young adults (ages 18–34) spend 43 percent of their time ingesting media on digital platforms, adults (ages 35–49) reported spending approximately 45 percent of their time each day with media on digital platforms, and adults (ages 50–64) spend almost 55 percent of their time each day interacting with media on digital platforms (p. 8). From the percentages above, learning and development professionals clearly have stiff competition for their participants' time and attention. Learning and development professionals should then create microlearning content and assessments that specifically address the changing workforce, changing job requirements, new skills needed by veteran employees, and the limited time afforded to employees to learn new skills on the job (Javorcik & Polasek, 2019; Margol, 2017; Winger, 2018). For example, providing an infographic on how to complete a specific task as it is performed, allows an employee to access support, implement the skill, and ensure successful completion. In this case, the learning is assessed by whether or not the employee can successfully complete the task, which could be applicable to learning how to use a new copy machine or navigating the latest and more sophisticated security measures.

Assessments should be Yielding. Because microlearning is targeted and specific, assessments must be designed carefully to ensure that they are capable of yielding data that are informative and useful. Baker and O'Neill (1987) state that "[i]t is more important to think broadly first about information needed to make instructional decisions, and secondly, about the inferences one can draw from such information …" (pp. 343–344). This statement means that depending on the purpose of the microlearning, the assessment could consist of data that lie on the spectrum of whether learners viewed or liked the learning event and span the evaluation of whether the learning was applied and had the intended impact. Assessment can also vary from being very objective to highly subjective. Regardless of how formal or nuanced an assessment may be, the data yielded should be usable in some way that can inform future decisions. Consider the following when determining what type of assessment data to collect:

- Do we need data at the level of the individual, department, organization, or other classification?
- Do we need to measure the effectiveness of a specific microlearning event or a collection of learning experiences?
- Do we need to create an assessment to collect data, or are the data we need already being collected directly or indirectly?
- How will the data be used? Are the data reliable enough to use them in the manner we intend?

While a singular microlearning event may not satisfy all training needs, a microlearning strategy with well-designed assessments can offer robust learning interventions and data that can be used to increase overall organizational performance, while simultaneously scaffolding content for learners with the additional bonus of being able to iterate and pivot quickly.

Summary and Next Steps

The instructional design process is key to ensuring that microlearning and related assessments are effective. Understanding how to design effective microlearning assessments is inherently tied to the parameters of microlearning. Ideally, micro-learning events are short, focused, incorporate technology, include an assessment, and are specific to the learning context and environment. Assessments should also consider the variability of learners, their needs, and their experiences. Collectively, this will inform how to design an effective microlearning assessment that is ITSY. This means assessments are Inventive in how and what is evaluated, Targeted to a learning goal, context, environment, Specific to the needs of the learner, and Yield useful and informative data. While there is no road map specific to creating micro-learning, these practices and guidelines will ensure assessments are effective in mea-suring progress and informing later steps.

Discussion Questions

1. Reflect upon your last organizational training event. What data does your organization require at the individual, department, or organizational level to demonstrate proficiency and how could you restructure that training event to incorporated specific microlearning experiences to gather this data?
2. If you were to more closely consider one of Kirkpatrick's four levels of training evaluation throughout the planning and development stages of your next microlearning event, which level would facilitate participant learning more authentic and applicable to the achievement of organizational objectives?
3. Thinking of the acronym ITSY for planning of microlearning assessment. List one way you can incorporate *inventiveness* into the assessment of future microlearning events. List one way you can ensure your microlearning assessments are *targeted*. List one way you increase the *specificity* of your microlearning assessments. Finally, describe the changes you can make to microlearning assessments that can increase result *yields*.

References

Baker, E. L., & O'NeillJr., H. F. (1987). Assessing Instructional Outcomes. In R. M. Gagné (Ed.), *Instructional Technology: Foundations* (pp. 343–378). Hilldale, NJ: Lawrence Erlbaum Associates.

Brebera, P. (2017). *Microlearning in foreign language courses: A threat or a promise?* Proceedings of the European Conference on E-Learning, 85–93. https://search.proquest.com/doc view/1968935592/fulltextPDF/F5CC706C6464451AP Q/1?accountid=36196.

Buhu, A., & Buhu, L. (2019). *The applications of microlearning in higher education in textiles.* Proceedings of the 15th International Scientific Conference "ELearning and Software for Education,"3, 373–376. https://doi.org/10.12753/2066-026X-19-189.

Capuano, N., & King, R. (2015). Knowledge-based assessment in serious games: An experience on emergency training. *Journal of E-Learning and Knowledge Society*, 11(3), 117–132. https://doi.org/10.20368/1971-8829/1058.

Chada, S., Kumar, S. A., Achar, S. A., Hasteer, R., Singh, J., Maheshwari, S. K., & Rajiv, R. (2018). From macro to micro. Human Capital, 22(2), 24–27. http://search.ebscohost.com. ezproxy.shsu.edu/login.aspx?direct=true&db=bth&AN=130634646&site=eds-live& scope=site.

Fennelly-Atkinson, R., Dyer, R., & Laprairie, K. (2019). *It's a small world after all: Decreasing the distance one tweet, snap, & post at a time.* In M. R. Simonson & D. J. Seepersaud (Eds.), 42nd Annual AECT Proceedings (pp. 57–68). Association for Educational Communications & Technology. https://members.aect.org/pdf/Proceedings/proceedings19/2019/19_09.pdf.

Gross, B., Rusin, L., Kiesewetter, J., Zottmann, J. M., Fischer, M. R., Prückner, S., & Zech, A. (2019). Microlearning for patient safety: Crew resource management training in 15-minutes. *PLoS ONE*, 14(3), 1–21. https://doi.org/10.1371/journal.pone.0213178.

Hesse, A., Ospina, P., Wieland, M., Yepes, F. A. L., Nguyen, B., & Heuwieser, W. (2019). Short communication: Microlearning courses are effective at increasing the feelings of confidence and accuracy in the work of dairy personnel. *Journal of Dairy Science*, 102(10), 9505–9511. https://doi.org/10.3168/jds.2018-15927.

Higgenbotham, E. (2019, March). Bringing manufacturing L&D into the 21st Century. *TD: Talent Development*, 73(3), 58–63. www.td.org/magazines/td-magazine/bringing-manufacturing-l-d-into-the-21st-century.

Hauk, S., Powers, R. A., & Segalla, A. (2015). A comparison of web-based and paper-and-pencil homework on student performance in college algebra. *Primus*, 25(1), 61–79. https://doi.org/10.1080/10511970.2014.906006.

Hayles, N. K. (2007). Hyper and deep attention: The generational divide in cognitive modes. *Profession*, 187–199. Retrieved December 23, 2020, from www.jstor.org/stable/25595866.

Hug, T., & Friesen, N. (2009). Outline of a microlearning agenda. *ELearning Papers*, 16, 1–13. www.researchgate.net/publication/255582537_Outline_of_a_Microlearning_Agenda.

Janjua, N. (2017). Piloting surgical near-peer microlearning sessions: Lessons learnt from students and teachers. *Education in Medicine Journal*, 9(2), 65–68. https://doi.org/10.21315/eimj2017.9.2.8.

Javorcik, T., & Polasek, R. (2019). *Practical application of microlearning in education of future teachers.* Proceedings of the European Conference on E-Learning, 254–259. https://doi-org.ezproxy.shsu.edu/10.34190/EEL.19.031.

Kapp, K., & Defelice, R. (2018, July). Elephant-sized impact. *TD: Talent Development*, 72(7), 26–30. www.td.org/magazines/td-magazine/elephant-sized-impact.

Khan, B. (2019). Microlearning: Quick and meaningful snippets for training solutions. *International Journal of Research in Educational Sciences*, 2(2), 275–284. https://doi.org/10.29009/ijres.2.2.7.

Kirkpatrick, J. D., & Kirkpatrick, W. K. (2016). *Kirkpatrick's four levels of training evaluation.* Alexandria, VA: ATD Press.

Kurt, S. (2018). Kirkpatrick Model: Four levels of learning evaluation. https://educationaltechnology.net/kirkpatrick-model-four-levels-learning-evaluation/.

Lim, C., Ryu, J., Martindale, T., Kim, N., & Park, S. (2019). Learning, design, and technology in South Korea: A report on the AECT-Korean Society for Educational

Technology (KSET) panel discussion. *TechTrends*, 63(5), 503–505. https://doi.org/10.1007/s11528-019-00418-x.

Margol, E. G. (2017). *Microlearning to boost the employee experience*. Alexandria, VA: Association for Talent Development. http://search.ebscohost.com.ezproxy.shsu.edu/login.aspx?direct=true&db=nlebk&AN=1447365&site=eds-live&scope=site.

Nielsen Company. (2018). Nielsen total audience report [webpage]. www.nielsen.com/us/en/insights/article/2018/time-flies-us-adults-now-spend-nearly-half-a-day-interacting-with-media/.

Nikou, S. A., & Economides, A. A. (2018). Mobile-based micro-learning and assessment: Impact on learning performance and motivation of high school students. *Journal of Computer Assisted Learning*, 34(3), 269–278. doi: 10.1111/jcal.12240.

Orwoll, B., Diane, S., Henry, D., Tsang, L., Chu, K., Meer, C., *et al.* (2018). Gamification and microlearning for engagement with quality improvement (GAMEQI): A bundled digital intervention for the prevention of central line–associated bloodstream infection. *American Journal of Medical Quality*, 33(1), 21–29. https://doi.org/10.1177/1062860617706542.

Osaigbovo, I. I., & Iwegim, C. F. (2018). Instagram: A niche for microlearning of undergraduate medical microbiology. *African Journal of Health Professions Education*, 10(2), 75. https://doi.org/10.7196/ajhpe.2018.v10i2.1057.

Paul, A. M. (2016, May). Microlearning 101. *HR Magazine*, 61(4), 362–342. www.shrm.org/hr-today/news/hr-magazine/0516/Pages/0516-microlearning.aspx.

Roblyer, M. D. (2015). *Introduction to Systematic Instructional Design for Traditional, Online, and Blended Learning Environments*. Upper Saddle River, NJ: Pearson Education.

Scaglione, C. (2019, September). 9 reasons why you should use microlearning in your training program. *EHS Today*, 12(7), 17–20. www.ehstoday.com/safety-leadership/article/21920368/9-reasons-you-should-use-microlearning-in-your-training-program.

Simkins, S., & Maier, M. (Eds.). (2009). *Just-in-time Teaching Across the Disciplines and Across the Academy (New Pedagogies and Practices for Teaching in Higher Education)*. Stylus Publishing, LLC.

Winger, A. (2018). Supersized tips for implementing microlearning in macro ways. *Distance Learning*, 15(4), 51–56. http://search.ebscohost.com.ezproxy.shsu.edu/login.aspx?direct=true&db=eft&AN=136816983&site=eds-live&scope=site.

Zhang, J., & West, R. E. (2019). Designing Microlearning Instruction for Professional Development Through a Competency Based Approach. *TechTrends*. https://doi.org/10.1007/s11528-019-00449-4.

PART III

Microlearning in Academic, Corporate, and Personalized Learning Contexts

7

MICROLEARNING AND MICRO-CREDENTIALS IN HIGHER EDUCATION

Megan Kohler, Chris Gamrat, Victoria Raish, and Elizabeth Gross

Introduction

Since the mid 1800s, academia has been pursuing more effective ways of quantifying the value of an educational experience for students (Heffernan, 1973). The traditional credit hour was initially established by Andrew Carnegie as a means to more effectively pay faculty rather than measure student learning (Laitinen, 2012). However, as time has progressed, education has become more expensive and numerous questions have been raised about the efficacy of the credit hour. Harris (2002) states:

> Even if major higher education stakeholders and leaders realized that the problem lies in awarding degrees on banked credits, they would be reluctant to attempt changing the academic currency and banking system. Not only does the credit support provide the basis for determining qualifications for degrees, it is also the basis for fiscal management, e.g. student payments, state appropriations, and Federal financial aid. Through it administrators determine faculty workloads.
>
> *(p. 8)*

Knowing that higher education as a whole relies on the credit hour as the primary form of educational currency, it provides educators with a major challenge as they explore new avenues for delivering, capturing, and measuring student learning.

As we begin to look at microlearning and the promise it holds for making learning more approachable for students, it is important to note that the concept of microlearning isn't new. It has more commonly been referred to as *chunking*.

Research on chunking shows that more expert learners perceive situations differently than novice learners. (Chase & Simon, 1973) Novice learners do not have the mental models to make sense of content in a similar manner to more expert learners. Scaffolding students in small segments and prompting them to make meaningful connections improved the output of student work (Butcher & Sumner, 2011). Microlearning fits into this type of learning because the learning experience is broken down into a smaller unit with dedicated objectives, activities, and goals.

Several factors have contributed to the revival of the microlearning approach in higher education. A key consideration is the increasing interest in learning sciences, instructional design practices, and other teaching and learning processes by which we can make learning more effective for students. The influence of the zone of proximal development (Vygotsky, 1978), the idea that a learner can achieve more with support rather than on their own or with great effort, has been translated into a higher education context in many college course designs. The structure in microlearning allows for students to begin in a topic that is close to their current knowledge and abilities and, with designed educational supports, increase their abilities. In this design, the small scope of microlearning acts as the support in that it requires less effort on their part and is within the range of the student's zone of proximal development, and the stacking of microlearning acts as a mechanism for progressive progress in an area of study. This progress allows for a learner to no longer need the initial supports as they are increasingly more capable.

Microlearning elements in a course also support the visibility of a course's trajectory, making visible the purpose of each element of a course to students. By breaking down large courses into discrete and complete learning objects, students can progress through coursework with a greater understanding of the intended outcome for the course. These pieces can be designed to have greater clarity and focus, while at the same time further providing the ability for each element to be designed with a greater degree of quality. In doing so, instructors can more easily support student progression and reduce a feeling of overwhelm in the learning journey.

The advances in technology are also a key factor, impacting both the delivery and the tracking of student learning. Advances in technology provide the ability to offer microlearning elements in various formats including videos, podcasts, lightboard recordings, animations, gamified activities, and more. As the technology advances, the barriers for creating and distributing microlearning elements is reduced. With the increased ability to build systems that can manage and store vast amounts of data, new technology also provides the ability to offer microlearning elements in a way that can be tracked for each individual who participates or completes an activity. Over the past few years, we have witnessed the development of micro-credentialing platforms, eportfolios, short courses, workshops, and many other systems for managing the delivery and storage of data pertaining to microlearning. These systems offer students the ability to collect and display completed work as a product of participating in a microlearning experience. What was lacking in this environment was a place to store and display evidence of these microlearning experiences. *IMS Global* has established an initiative known as the *Comprehensive Learner Record* as a means by which microlearning and micro-credentials can be transferred, stored, and retained. While there are many other factors to consider for the growth of microlearning, one thing remains clear, the practice of chunking was previously considered a good design practice but has now gained traction as a stand-alone learning experience, not just as part of the traditional credit course.

While microlearning may not be a new concept, this chapter will offer perspectives on why the time is right for microlearning as a powerful approach in academia and how innovative approaches to microlearning have the ability to transform our students' learning experiences.

For the purposes of this chapter, we offer the following definition to highlight the affordances of microlearning in higher education: microlearning is the combination of techniques and technology to support student learning through the chunking of learning on a scale smaller than course objectives, scaffolding these experiences, and capturing the learning to articulate students' accomplishments. It is helpful to consider microlearning in terms of its differences from traditional learning in higher education. For example, it might entail changes in learning design: instead of the common pattern of a long chapter or a long semester with a test at the end, microlearning might design focused activities with practice and assessment for each learning objective. The potential of microlearning goes beyond design to changes in capture and scope, such as implementing badges for key learning objectives and accomplishments within a course, across multiple courses, or expanded to co-curricular learning, such as workshops, to capture and recognize accomplishment at a more granular level.

This chapter will provide an overview of the current state of microlearning in higher education. We begin by discussing the contexts in which microlearning offers potential solutions to qualifying student learning in academic settings. Next, we will identify limitations of current implementations and how they fall short of providing students with a framework that effectively communicates the value of a degree. Through this discussion we examine the question of what types of learning and currency should become universally accepted by higher education institutions. After reading this chapter, we hope to instill in the reader a sense of urgency that higher education needs to engage with the microlearning ecosystem, both for student learning and for the health of the institution as a whole.

The Currency of Microlearning in Higher Education

The world we live in is full of bite-sized pieces of information and nuggets of knowledge. Learning can happen at any time and any place. While credit courses and traditional measures of learning are not going anywhere for the time being, microlearning has emerged as a logical addition to the learning ecosystem. Students might be learning from a service experience or listening to the latest podcast and applying it. Microlearning creates a space for educators to structure these information encounters that students have.

Education Today: Understanding the Context

A scholarly search using the keywords "challenges *and* higher education" reveals numerous articles and predictions, some positive and some negative, about the future of higher education. Guthrie's work (2019) stands out among the others for its systems perspective and acknowledgement of the context of challenges. These challenges include unsustainable cost models of traditional instruction; a changing student population; new educational technology; balancing curricular choices and offerings; unbundling and rebundling of education; credentialing; talent selection; and an extreme focus on the whole student experience. From these challenges comes opportunity.

There is an incredible amount of diversity in the types of institutions that exist in the higher education landscape. This richness is an asset and means that many people can find the higher education institution that works for them. With the increasing costs of education, students will become more judicious when choosing an institution, opting for one that will offer them the best opportunity to support their learning goals (Seltzer, 2017). Regardless of the type of institution, most are feeling increased pressure upon and scrutiny of the product they deliver. A report published from the *American Council of Education, Huron Consulting*, and the *Georgia Institute of Technology* found that leaders of four-year institutions are not confident in their institution's ability to lead into the future. In particular, these leaders are very concerned about the ability to compete with national university expansion like *Western Governors University*, a competency-based online university, or microdegrees from places like *MIT*, for example, which allows students to earn credentials through MOOC-style courses and apply them to degrees. (Stokes, Baker, Demillo, Soares, & Yager, 2019).

These administrative challenges are further complicated by increasing pressure from society to draw clearer connections between the value of a degree, increased job opportunities, and the relevance for both students and their potential employers (Jaschik, 2019a). Existing research still shows the value of earning a bachelor's degree over only a high school diploma (Jaschik, 2019b). What is not known from existing information is the role of microlearning and micro-credentials in the educational ecosystem. What is known is that the needs for lifelong learning, skilling, and res-killing are recognized as necessary by CEOs (Gallagher, 2019). Currently, microlearning and micro-credentials are on the fringe, looking at higher education. DiSalvio (2018) notes the parallels between microlearning and online learning, which also started on the fringe, but is now accepted as a key piece of an institution's strategy for excelling in the 21st century and beyond.

Limitations of Traditional Credits

Historically, students have received transcripts upon graduation from an institution. The transcripts typically consisted of abbreviated course titles and codes followed by a series of letters or numbers to denote one's level of mastery with the subject matter they were evaluated on. Yet, these transcripts in no way communicate the skills or knowledge acquired by a student. Foerster (1937) elaborates on this notion by saying:

> Once a credit was earned, it was as safe as anything in the world. It would be deposited and indelibly recorded in the registrar's saving bank, while the substance of the course could be, if one wished, happily forgotten.
>
> *(p. 97)*

The difficulty with transcripts is they are merely a summation of grades achieved via course assessments. However, we know that there are known issues with these course assessments including test construction, test anxiety, measuring learning, and if students can perform on an applied learning task with transfer. Given this insight, it is natural to question whether the student is actually acquiring the knowledge and skills relevant to their degree. This gives way to even broader questions about how to effectively measure the actual quality of learning available from one institution or another when a student evaluates which option will best support their future career goals.

Transcripts are the primary method by which institutions are able to track and record student learning during their time in academia. The majority of registrars' offices do not yet have the capacity or the technology to manage this information in a different format than the traditional credit course. As microlearning continues to gain traction as a valuable methodology, this limitation will need to be resolved.

A Potential Solution

In response to the increasing pressures described above, higher education institutions may benefit by scrutinizing the viability of microlearning. Microlearning has the potential to enable students to see direct connections between the skills and knowledge that comprise a degree and their employability in the professional field. This enables a unique opportunity for both students and employers to more clearly understand the value of a degree.

To reiterate our definition, microlearning is the combination of techniques and technology to support student learning through the chunking of learning on a scale smaller than course objectives, scaffolding these experiences, and capturing the learning to articulate students' accomplishments.

Based on the above definition, microlearning:

- **Provides focused learning experiences**. Microlearning creates focused learning opportunities for students by breaking down learning into smaller and more manageable pieces. This offers students learning opportunities which may seem like a less daunting task instead of a towering accomplishment to be achieved over a span of months or years. Moreover, the implementation of smaller milestones in learning also affords the student opportunities for feedback and constructive criticism, which allows the student to adjust if needed.

- **Removes extraneous content**. An added benefit of microlearning is the ability for an instructor to remove content that may detract from the overall learning goal. In a less-is-more approach, microlearning offers more concise and focused experiences tied to learning outcomes. An excess of information may lead to cognitive overload and complicate the learning process unnecessarily. Additional microlearning modules can also be created to elaborate on or bolster points.

- **Increases quality through more intentional design**. Gamrat, Bixler, and Raish (2016) describe many possible considerations for the design of digital badges, a form of microlearning. In their chapter, they explain that microlearning can be approached as competency-based, allowing students to demonstrate an expected level of mastery. Whereas, other methods of achievement are also possible in the design but would depend on the use of this microlearning into the scope of the follow-on credential awarded for completion. Instructors and administrators would need to consider the needs of their students, program, and institution to provide a well-designed microlearning experience.

- **Can be incorporated into the educational experience in a variety of ways**. Microlearning naturally lends itself to a variety of formats and can easily be incorporated into the educational experience in a variety of ways. Microlearning elements can be delivered via text, video, audio clips/podcasts, and more. An instructor may create a lightboard video to provide instruction on how to solve a challenging equation and ask the student to demonstrate their understanding by explaining their work in a physics problem, or a dance instructor can demonstrate proper positioning of the body when performing a dance combination and the student can demonstrate their developing skill in providing feedback to their peers using the instructor as a model. Microlearning elements offer greater flexibility than traditional courses and can be easily integrated or removed as part of an experience.

- **Creates a learning experience that is comparable to that of a course**. By designing microlearning elements as a thoughtful collection of connected concepts, educators can create a learning experience that is comparable to that of a course. Through thoughtful curation of the concepts which construct microlearning elements, one can craft a more robust and focused learning experience, rather than a playlist of elements. (While someone may be able to create an arguably well-constructed playlist, it is not as carefully thought out as the album). This approach can reduce excessive and unnecessary information while providing a comprehensive and complete course offering.

What Type of Learning Should Higher Ed Recognize?

As previously established, institutions are not yet equipped to transition to microlearning to replace the traditional academic transcript. This raises the questions of what types of learning and measures best reflect a student's acquisition of knowledge, and how should this learning be captured and communicated? If the traditional transcript measures student learning in the format of a credit hour as the primary educational currency, how can a disruption like microlearning improve the methods by which academia awards "degrees"?

Since the concept of a college credit was introduced in the 1800s, it measured the educational experience in terms of the number of hours a student dedicated to their studies. (Harris, 2002). The credit hour arose as a method by which to measure learning, but in reality, it measures only time in seat, not the actual knowledge acquired. Harris (2002) further argues that the method of a credit hour, a course elective system, and educational accreditation have given rise to a system which is detrimental to a student's overall education. With this in mind, it is easy to see why higher education as a whole is exploring alternate options for measuring student learning. Faculty have been actively pursuing options such as eportfolios and micro-credentials (digital badges) as alternate options for enabling students to demonstrate their success through competency-based learning.

The case for traditional credit hours presents further challenges when considering prior learning assessments. Higher education struggles with these forms of recognition with the argument that it is difficult to offer credit for experiences because it is hard to know exactly what was learned. However, with microlearning, students can more easily provide detailed explanations of what they learned and how they demonstrated this growth.

Microlearning as a Disruption

As microlearning and specifically micro-credentialing continue to gain traction in higher education, they can provide new opportunities for more effectively communicating acquired skills and knowledge between academia and industry. By more clearly articulating the competencies a learner acquires, micro-credentialing allows industry to see how the skills and knowledge apply to the field. This achieves a long-standing goal of higher education to close the skills gap which occurs when students transition from college to the professional field. Industry has been able to see the value of microlearning as a just-in-time learning solution and has begun initiating partnerships with academia to develop more targeted competencies related to the field. The most prominent partnership today is between *IBM and Northeastern University*. Employees who earn IBM badges for skills and competencies on the job can apply them towards a Northeastern University degree. *IMS Global* is another organization which is investing in microlearning, specifically micro-credentialing, with an initiative called the *Comprehensive Learner Record*.

Affordances

Microlearning offers a number of affordances for both students and educators. Students can be more effectively engaged in the learning experience while educators can be more effective in the teaching and design strategies implemented as part of the learning. Examples of these benefits will be discussed in the sections below:

- **More approachable for novice learners**. Microlearning is particularly suited to reaching novice learners, or those beginning their learning journey for whom the chunking of objectives and achievements offers a clear and rewarding path. With more concise chunks of information accompanied by opportunities for practice and feedback, it allows learners to better understand their progress in an otherwise abstract learning process. This in turn allows the learner to feel more enthusiastic, motivated, and to have a greater sense of achievement while completing learning modules.
- **Modularity**. The affordances of using microlearning in a modular fashion, and the flexibility of this approach, is one of the strongest benefits. From an educational perspective, course materials can be reused, re-combined, and updated more efficiently. This benefit transcends a single course experience and can be applied to an entire program and across relevant curricula within an institution. One can think about microlearning as comprising building blocks, which can be leveraged or referenced through a course. They can be used to shore up insufficient prerequisite knowledge, reinforce new concepts, and to scaffold learning designs to support later objectives.
- **Transferability**. The modular nature of microlearning elements offers greater opportunities for transferability. The capacity for reuse and redeployment is a quality unique to microlearning. As previously mentioned, microlearning "building blocks" can be redeployed throughout a course or throughout a program curriculum in higher education, such as a higher-level advanced course that offers review content. In this sense, microlearning elements act as a type of open educational resource. While microlearning elements may only be reused within a program, college, or university, their ability to be reused for multiple purposes affords benefits to students, faculty, and administrators. This transferability serves these stakeholders much more effectively by offering greater consistency in the information presented.

- Another aspect of transferability is the clarity of the design. Since microlearning diminishes the capacity for "filler" or extraneous information, it provides learning that is more concise and easily applied to a variety of contexts. This varies greatly when compared with a textbook, a hallmark of information dissemination for higher education. A textbook, for example, provides a very specific and directed pathway of learning where students learn about a concept as it applied in the provided scenario, but there is little to no capacity to transfer the concept to other contexts. Microlearning elements are more easily portable to be redeployed or connected to varied other scenarios.

- Similarly, institutions should not overlook the potential benefits of microlearning to be deployed beyond the traditional "credit" academic environment as well. The possibilities of microlearning elements allow higher education institutions the ability to engage with a broader public in terms of offering non-credit or professional learning opportunities that can draw from the same material as academic programs, but packaged and leveraged for different audiences. This capacity for reuse or repackaging can be critical to allowing higher education institutions to compete in the growing arena of micro-credentials in addition to traditional degree programs.

- **Flexibility**. Returning to the student perspective, microlearning affords considerable flexibility to students to accomplish learning objectives in a more self-directed and clear manner. Given the competency-based nature of microlearning, students can engage in activities as needed in order to ensure a complete understanding of the information. If struggling with a concept, students can pursue supplementary resources until sufficient competency is acquired. Likewise, students who excel and wish to move forward have the ability to do so. Students can also explore both course-related and independent concepts to support their personal passions and interests, while also (potentially) gaining credit for their work.

The Currency of Microlearning: Conclusion

In higher education, microlearning can provide higher quality learning experiences over traditional courses due to the concise nature of the objects created. Because smaller snippets of resources are being produced, it provides the ability for a more focused design strategy to be established and implemented. Microlearning makes every single learning moment meaningful by prompting intention and precision in design. Both students, faculty, and other creators of microlearning elements need to carefully consider the intended use and educational outcomes of each object. It is the careful design and institutional strategies behind microlearning that enable its affordances for students and institutions alike.

Designing Microlearning for Higher Ed Contexts

When engaging in the design process for microlearning and associated methods of recording the skills acquired, we can look to four main categories of classifications: curricular, cross-curricular, co-curricular, and open curricular. This framework provides guidance to faculty, designers, students, administrators, partnering corporations, and others as they begin to establish microlearning experiences. While this method was primarily developed for micro-credentials, it can be applied to all microlearning which occurs both internal and external to education contexts. In the following sections we will discuss these classifications, provide examples or sample use cases, and discuss how information is captured, the intent and design of the elements, and finally the key points of consideration for each type.

The Design and Intent is Key

What makes microlearning effective is the intentionality of the design and strategy. An example will help to illustrate. First, let's consider what is not microlearning in an academic context. Contrast a textbook chapter or a long classroom lecture on a topic for a course, such as an introduction to horticulture. A textbook might discuss plant classification and its history, the conventions of genus and species, then the main plant families and classification categories and subcategories, all of which could run 25 to 30 pages. This same topic might unfold as an explanatory lecture that runs one to two class periods. A traditional accompanying assessment might be a quiz or test at the end of the chapter or end of the week. Neither of these are atypical approaches to undergraduate learning: to deliver a lot of information, all at once, to students who are viewed as empty vessels who are expected to contain and retain it all. How could we transform this into microlearning?

First, by bringing intentionality to one specific learning objective at a time, such as to explain the history and use of the binomial system of plant classification based on genus and species. Next, by presenting this content, such as via lecture, video or reading. Then, by allowing students to actively engage with this "chunk" and practice it, such as by identifying the parts of plant names and their correct and incorrect use, and finally, by assessing them on this portion of knowledge and capturing this assessment.

The technology used to present the information and capture the learning record does not matter greatly, but digital learning tools are particularly suited to it. They have affordances for designing and organizing course content in smaller sections, tools for easy production of multimedia, allowing students to easily navigate and self-pace through information, as well as tools to easily deliver assessment and capture it. In this context, microlearning can deliver a complete learning experience, with the aim being a demonstrable change in knowledge.

The learning event is crafted carefully with intention to be smaller and more tightly focused. One might envision a traditional chapter being replaced by a series of microlearning objects, well-curated and organized, with sufficient connection to each other, with structured repetition and context to support learner retention.

Curricular-Based Microlearning

Curricular-based microlearning elements are woven directly into the curricula. They can be implemented in two primary ways, the course content and the assessment strategy. The best way to understand these integrations is by looking at examples.

Example 1. Curricular-based microlearning examples can be provided in a variety of formats including text, video, audio, and other forms. Within a course a faculty member may choose to create a video tutorial to demonstrate the proper positioning of the body when completing a dance step or combination of steps. Students can review the video created by the instructor then record their own as they perform the dance steps. Students can then view their own recordings with the option to practice a bit more and rerecord a video or submit the original in order to receive feedback from a fellow student or the instructor. This enables the students to engage in critical thinking and self-evaluation among field-specific skills.

How it's being captured. In video format, completed student work can be captured through various technologies such as *Voicethread, Kaltura, YouTube, Vimeo*, or any other platform that supports video. Ideally the technology used has an integration option for the CMS/LMS used by the institution.

Intent and design. Through content-based microlearning, students are given very specific guidance through video instruction. In doing so, the students are able to review the video as many times as needed in order to fully understand the correct body positioning and placement. This also provides an aspect of personalized learning. In a face-to-face class of 15–30 students, not all learners may be able to clearly see the instructor perform the dance combination. The microlearning video enables the instructor to describe proper body positioning with close-up views on aspects that need specific attention.

Recommendations. Microlearning can support curricular-based instruction while providing on-demand guidance and feedback for students.

Example 2. An example of an assessment-focused microlearning element is a course activity designed to allow students to work through learning and applying concepts as they complete the course assignments. Students are asked to complete a course assignment in which there may be various steps of completion. For example, a student may be tasked with completing an interview of a leader in a fortune 500 company. In order to prepare for the interview, students may have to review a series of tutorials on interview techniques, such as types of questions to ask, structuring the timing and flow of an interview, ethics regarding recording interviewees, or professionalism tasks such as sending a thank you note following the interview. Students are able to engage in a competency-based approach for the completion of course work. The design of this strategy pairs especially well with micro-credentials or digital badges.

How it's being captured. Penn State developed a system to support faculty, staff, and student-driven micro-credentialing initiatives through Penn State's micro-credentialing system and the *Canvas* LMS. Students submit the assignments to *Canvas*, then the badges are awarded through PSU's micro-credentialing system, similar to the way *Credly* awards digital badges. No direct evidence is displayed with the work as all students must submit their homework to *Canvas*. Once the teachers grade the work, the badges become available for students to add to their professional profiles.

Intent and design. Each microlearning element is created to provide students with a concise, yet comprehensive understanding of a specific skill within the course. The microlearning elements in this example are directly associated with micro-credentials (digital badges) as an optional activity for the students. Once a student has completed the required course work, the micro-credential becomes available for download within the university's digital badging platform. Students are able to build a profile which lists all of the skills they are competent in. A link to this page can then be shared with potential employers as the student interviews for a professional position in the industry.

Recommendations. The assessments in this example were designed to be very "hands on" with a goal of extending the learning beyond the classroom into real-world contexts. With the use of microlearning elements embedded within a course, students have the ability to directly explore and apply the information learned in the course. The tutorials and text-based resources provided support to learners to help them prepare to engage with professionals in the field and to engage in meaningful conversations.

Cross-Curricular Microlearning

Microlearning offers a unique opportunity to reuse existing resources across the curricula of various programs within an institution. These reusable microlearning objects allow greater use of the materials, ensure consistency in the presentation of common concepts, and maximize the returns on financial investments incurred during the creation of these resources.

Example. Information and digital literacy are becoming an area of increased focus for institutions. A series of microlearning modules to support students in learning about this important topic has the ability to transcend various programs and support overall student learning and research efforts. When designing cross-curricular microlearning objects, it is important to be discipline agnostic to have the greatest applicability and relevance to the highest number of students.

Context. Cross-curricular microlearning modules offer institutions a unique option for maximizing the funds and resources invested into creating learning materials for students. The concise design of each learning module enables a number of programs to share relevant pieces across the curricula. In doing so, a program or multiple programs across the institution can benefit from well-designed, high-quality elements, which can easily be added as core curricula or supplementary resources.

How it's being captured. Cross-curricular work is often not captured from course to course. This results in a repetition of work such as multiple courses that require students to become familiar with library resources in multiple writing classes. Through the development of microlearning modules and captured recognition as micro-credentials, students and instructors would then be able to more easily document and track competencies achieved across and between courses and what may still need to be completed. This would be of particular benefit for any learning that is not linear in nature as students may be asked to complete the same cross-curricular work at different points in their academic careers.

Intent and design. The intent and design of cross-curricular microlearning needs to be carefully considered from both a content perspective as well as the context. Content should be free of specific references to a singular course while still providing significant value. With the example of the information literacy badges illustrated above, students are able to gain value from acquiring the badges regardless of the information discussed in the course.

Recommendations. Instructors and administrators may benefit from considering the development of resources that can exist beyond any single course as both an investment in quality and consistency of resources developed to support a program, college, or a whole university. Cross-curricular microlearning can also help to bolster student remediation, where necessary. Since these microlearning modules exist outside any one course, they can then be used to refresh student understanding in any number of areas.

Co-Curricular Microlearning

Professional perspective. While having a strong education background makes for a solid job candidate, achievements and activities completed outside the classroom can make a significant difference. Students can stand out from the crowd by getting involved in co-curricular and open-curricular activities.

For the purposes of this text, we refer to a learner's related learning experiences that are germane to their professional growth but exist outside of their prescribed curriculum. This can include but is not limited to informal learning experiences such as clubs, workshops, guest lectures, field experiences, and job shadowing. Each of these types of activities provides students with an opportunity to further develop their expertise with experiences that are related to a major or field of study.

Example. As an example, Penn State University's College of Information Sciences and Technology hosts a *Penetration Testing Competition* for undergraduate students studying in cybersecurity and related majors. While related to the College's curriculum, this event is entirely voluntary, but through a series of preparation meetings and the event itself, students develop additional skills that will enhance what they are already learning in their course work.

Context. The context of co-curricular microlearning is similar to that of academic clubs, research labs, and other organizations in higher education. That is, they exist in parallel to current courses and curriculum and offer additional mechanisms for students to explore the content in greater breadth, depth, and often in ways that are more hands-on than is typical for a course. This track, or organization of parallel study, also supports students in a broader area of study than in most courses. That is, students in the groups can range from freshmen through graduate students.

How it's being captured. This learning is not usually recognized with the exception of leadership positions, major projects, and publications. This documentation also ranges considerably in the permanence of record for achievement. On one side, a record of leadership roles for clubs may only exist on a website. Whereas on the other end of the spectrum, a student participating in a research lab would have the opportunity to be part of a published article, which is then archived and made available for all future researchers.

Intent and design. The intent of this example is to give students exposure to real-world problems in the area of cybersecurity and provide motivation for students through a competitive atmosphere. Each of these competitions offers a unique learning experience and requires students to participate in preparation events leading up to each competition. During these preparation activities, students are meeting regularly as a club to learn more about cybersecurity techniques that can be added to their knowledge.

Recommendations. While the meetings for students preparing for and participating in cybersecurity competitions are small in duration, they may be daunting to the novice learner. By ensuring that barriers to entry are sufficiently low for freshmen, clubs like this can encourage participation from new students to continue to develop outside learning and sharing across students of all seniority. With some careful strategy and planning, university faculty and programs can leverage co-curricular microlearning experiences for students, in a manner more nimbly than adapting a traditional curriculum, into strong program enhancements that can benefit students, the reputation of the program itself, and also possibly even alumni and professionals.

Open-Curricular Microlearning

The authors of this text refer to "open-curricular" resources as formalized curriculum that is available to anyone and exists outside of a traditional academic course or program. This might include resources such as LinkedIn learning videos (or other available tutorials), *Massive Open Online Courses* (MOOCs), articles, textbooks, seminars, and conferences.

Example. Online and in-person informal instruction is another way for students to continue their development. Colleges, universities, and other institutions may offer additional educational experiences for students beyond the scope of regular coursework requirements of a degree. As an example, a student could participate in education programming to help prepare for a job or internship interview. This type of session would be publicly advertised to students and available for all or on a first-come, first-served basis. Because of the openness of these resources, students are able to pick and choose which of these types of learning experiences might best fit their needs and schedules.

Context. The context of open-curricular microlearning is independent learning or self-directed learning. That is, students are actively making decisions about what other resources to leverage for their education. This style of independent learning affords significant learner personalization (Kearney, Schuck, Burden, & Aubusson, 2012), to determine what and when they pursue additional learning opportunities. However, this context also requires students to have a greater knowledge of what they want to learn (Butcher & Sumner, 2011).

How it's being captured. Open-curricular activities are recognized in a variety of ways including certificates, badges, or nothing at all. In all of these cases, the capture or recognition is dependent on students' ability to represent their achievements to others.

Intent and design. The design of these open-curricular opportunities is often self-paced, with an asynchronous structure to support personalized learning. This design structure affords a high degree of learner decision-making in terms of what to learn and when. While open-curricular opportunities provide maximum flexibility, one byproduct for some students is being able to carve time into their busy schedules to complete the activities. An analogy could be made between open-curricular opportunities and exercise, where some people may be strongly self-directed in their workouts, while others may require the structure and shared meaning-making that comes with taking a synchronous course.

Takeaway. Students can benefit from various types of open-curricular learning but there are examples that work for some and not for others. The authors recommend that learners explore various types to get a sense of what works for them.

While both co-curricular and open-curricular efforts are, in many cases, options for students, they can also set students up for long-term good practices in lifelong learning. Students who invest time into extra-curricular areas of study will reap the benefit of making themselves stand out when they get to their first interviews. Moreover, engaging in co-curricular and open-curricular opportunities can help students explore new areas for growth and expand on their existing skillsets.

Considerations for the Future

The affordances of microlearning have the capacity to significantly transform the versions of higher education learning experiences that have evolved from traditional structures and artifacts such as seat time, classroom schedules, the linear nature of textbooks and lectures, and the credit hour. With digital technologies so thoroughly transforming the limitations of learning by time and space through the rise of online learning and ease of multimedia authoring technologies, it makes sense that the systems for delivering, tracking, and storing learning also evolve.

What may be challenging for educators is not the design of learning – faculty educators are skilled at creating learning opportunities and all that they entail, including content delivery, practice, and assessment. Arguably, the challenges to educators based on the need for multimedia and technology skills are diminishing, for multimedia authoring tools and deployment are becoming so much easier, more commonly used, and increasingly supported institutionally. What may be challenging is the framework of mind and intent to design smaller, more focused, and more flexibly, which requires a different outlook and different goals. As this chapter has discussed, the affordances of designing microlearning are powerful when coupled with the institutional strategy to promote and deploy it to maximum effect, whether within curricular and co-curricular academic arenas or in the space of non-credit and continuing education. It is our hope this chapter motivates educators to consider the value of microlearning coupled with micro-credentials as worthy of the design challenge as well as their advocacy in the institution.

Opportunities for Universities

Historically, partnerships between higher education and corporations have been viewed with skepticism and an affront to the core of higher education. Recently, however, the conversation has shifted, and now higher education and corporations work together from streamlining administrative tasks, to collaborating on research, to managing student data privacy, to co-developing curriculum. There are inherent challenges within these partnerships, but corporations are feeling similar pressures of reskilling workers for changing jobs as higher education is with preparing career-ready students. The line between who is responsible for providing educational opportunities is blurring and now there are many cross higher education-industry learning partnerships. It is relatively common now for universities to invite industry leaders to sit on their boards.

This changing environment is challenging the identities of both corporations and higher education institutions. Corporations have to see themselves as providers of learning opportunities, and higher education institutions need to see themselves not as the exclusive holders of information, access, and learning. The influence of microlearning in corporations has trickled down to higher education and some institutions are being responsive in how they are packaging learning opportunities for their learners.

One notable example is how *Northeastern University* partnered with *IBM* to award course credit to students who successfully completed *IBM* modules and earned micro-credentials. There are three majors for which students can apply badges towards course credit. IBM badges are grouped under five categories: knowledge, skills, proficiency, certifications, and general.

While institutions of higher education hold deep expertise in pedagogy, learning sciences, and research, they play a critical role in shaping the educational landscape. Stakeholders need to critically evaluate how they are designing responsive instruction that prepares students to thrive in a rapidly changing marketplace of skills, competencies, and job requirements while staying true to their institutional missions and visions.

Summary

While the apprenticeship of observation, continuing to teach how we are taught (Lortie, 1975) is a strong inclination for many in higher education; faculty, staff, and administration are becoming increasingly interested in the application of microlearning in multiple contexts. Adopting an innovation is not a simple and linear process. However, higher education is not an island, but rather, a partner with elementary and secondary school systems, and with industry as well. The needs of students and lifelong learners will continue to exert a greater influence on the ways higher education adjusts and adapts approaches to teaching. Human capital is a critical piece of the overall plan for business leaders and higher education institutions and carry their reputations as quality learning places. Accordingly, including microlearning as an instructional strategy is imperative for institutions who want to be responsive to today's learning ecosystems.

Discussion Questions

1. Is microlearning a disruption to higher education?
2. Is the skills gap argument legitimate? What biases might influence people's perceptions on this gap?
3. What trends can you predict in the future of adoption and perception of microlearning?
4. What are all of the factors you need to consider when adding microlearning as an overall learning strategy? As an institutional strategy?

References

Butcher, K. R. & Sumner, T. (2011). Self-directed learning and the sensemaking paradox. *Human-Computer Interaction*, 26(1–2), 123–159. doi:10.1080/07370024.2011.556552.
Chase, W. G. & Simon, H. A. (1973). Perception in chess. *Cognitive Psychology*, 4(1), 55–81.

DiSalvio, P. (2020). Microcredentials: On the outside looking in. https://evolllution.com/programming/credentials/microcredentials-on-the-outside-looking-in.

Foerster, N. (1937). *The American State University its Relation to Democracy.* Chapel Hill, North Carolina: The University Of North Carolina Press.

Gallagher, S. (2019). A new era of microcredentials and experiential learning. www.universityworldnews.com/post.php?story=20190213103113978.

Gamrat, C., Bixler, B., & Raish, V. (2016). Instructional Design Considerations for Digital Badges. In *Digital Badges in Education: Trends, Issues, and Cases,* (pp. 71–81). Taylor and Francis. https://doi.org/10.4324/9781315718569.

Guthrie, K. M. (2019). Challenges to Higher Education's Most Essential Purposes. Ithaka S+R, *Issue Brief.* https://doi.org/10.18665/sr.311221.

Harris, J. (2002). Brief history of American academic credit system: A recipe for incoherence in student learning. *Information Analysis.* https://files.eric.ed.gov/fulltext/ED470030.pdf.

Heffernan, J. M. (1973). The credibility of the credit hour: The history, use, and shortcomings of the credit system. *The Journal of Higher Education,* 44(1), 61–72. www.jstor.org/stable/1980626.

Jaschik, S. (2019a). 2019 survey of admissions leaders: The pressure grows. www.insidehighered.com/news/survey/2019-survey-admissions-leaders-pressure-grows.

Jaschik, S. (2019b). Is college worth it? Yes. www.insidehighered.com/news/2019/06/10/new-data-show-economic-value-earning-bachelors-degree-remains-high.

Kearney, M., Schuck, S., Burden, K., & Aubusson, P. (2012). Viewing mobile learning from a pedagogical perspective. *Research in Learning Technology,* 20(14406), 1–17. doi:10.3402/rlt.v20i0/14406.

Laitinen, A. (2012). Cracking the credit hour. New America Foundation and Education Sector. https://eric.ed.gov/?id=eD540304.

Lortie, D. C. & Clement, D. (1975). *Schoolteacher: A Sociological Study (21).* Chicago: University of Chicago Press.

Seltzer, R. (2017). Turning down top choices. www.insidehighered.com/news/2017/03/23/study-shows-how-price-sensitive-students-are-selecting-colleges.

Stokes, P., Baker, N., Demillo, R., Soares, L., & Yager, L. (2019). The transformation-ready higher education institution. www.acenet.edu/Documents/The-Transformation-Ready-Higher-Education-Institution-Huron-ACE-Ebook.pdf.

Vygotsky, L. S. (1978). *Mind in Society: The Development of Higher Psychological Processes.* Cambridge: Harvard University Press.

8

MICROLEARNING IN K-12 SETTINGS

Laura Sheneman

Introduction

Teaching and learning are in the forefront of many Kindergarten-12th grade (K-12) educators' minds. Trends come and go, but research-based best practices in curriculum and instruction have remained strong over the years. John Hattie and Robert Marzano are two names many education leaders are familiar with due to their ideas about teaching strategies that have the most impact. Killian (2019) summarizes Hattie and Manzano's common teaching strategies as: having a clear focus, providing overt instruction, engaging students, providing feedback, building in opportunities for repeated exposure, applying new knowledge, facilitating cooperative learning, and building students' self-efficacy.

Microlearning, which began to appear in education circles in the 1990s, offers the benefits of most, if not all, of these powerful teaching strategies. By its very nature, microlearning must have a clear focus since the pedagogy consists of short bursts of learning delivered through any platform. Microlearning has the ability to engage students, provide immediate feedback, can be used repetitively, provides learners the opportunity to apply their learning, and can demonstrate to students their self-efficacy. Depending on how the microlearning event is developed, there may even be an opportunity for students to work collaboratively.

In a traditional classroom, educators tend to prescribe structured learning sequences to their students. They want their instruction to be engaging and result in a specific educational outcome. One attractive feature of microlearning is the flexibility it offers learners by enabling them to choose the segments and sequence of learning during their own time or classroom time. Strategic educators see the value of flexibility in sequencing and selecting and can think back to what they learned from Piaget's idea of unstructured play in a structured environment. To achieve these ends, the classroom teacher can create a web portal of some sort (structured environment) to house microlearning content for their students to serve as part of the scheduled learning process or as a just-in-time resource (unstructured play). These microlearning segments can create informal learning opportunities that can be stand-alone or bundled into sequential learning modules designed by the teacher to achieve specific learning outcomes.

According to Major and Calandrino (2018),

> [s]tudents need a design that gives them easy access to the information, smaller contexts that keep them engaged, allows for remediation as needed, quick assessments that build on the whole, and a course engagement that allows for the students to apply the knowledge they have gained or draw conclusions.
>
> *(p. 28)*

Kapp and Defelice (2018, p. 26–30) sum up the main features of microlearning that also hold true in the K-12 setting:

- focused on one to two learning objectives
- brief and typically between two and seven minutes in duration (though this varies up to 15 minutes)
- action-oriented in the sense that there is a specific achievable purpose or goal.

Microlearning in the Lesson Cycle

A lot has changed in the past decade as curriculum content began to move away from print-based textbooks as the sole source of content. Mobile technology entered the classroom picture and created an environment where classrooms have the ability to offer interactive and self-paced learning opportunities (Tan, 2016, p. 6). While there is still a time and place for *macrolearning*, heavy content delivered face-to-face through direct instruction, microlearning is making inroads in education, due in large part to the emergence of e-learning. Microlearning can be delivered in a variety of formats including, "video, self-paced e-learning, visuals (e.g., memes, infographics, images, or visual presentations), podcasts or audio, and messaging requiring short durations of attention from learners, as well as interactive forums" (Major & Calandrino, 2018, p. 29). It provides an avenue for students to access what they need to know, when they need to know it.

Borrowing from adult education and workplace training, educators have the opportunity to implement microlearning in many effective ways. Educators can create learning segments that offer a preview of upcoming content, like an explainer video. Educators can pique students' interests with small pieces of information to foreshadow the lessons to come. In a flipped classroom environment, they can use microlearning to lay a foundation that future lessons will build on. It is even possible to use microlearning as a pre-assessment. Teachers can provide students with a microlearning segment that includes a quiz to identify learning gaps prior to starting a new lesson or module.

In a blended classroom, microlearning can be used during instruction as a time to practice the content that was delivered face-to-face. This allows the learners time to reflect on the instruction and work further on areas where they may need additional support. This type of microlearning during instruction can include quizzes, games, or even simulations.

Microlearning can also be used to reinforce content post-instruction to review material that was just taught. Through a post-instruction microlearning event, students can review bite-sized nuggets of information to self-assess their grasp of the materials. Educators can also create simple recall microlearning lessons that are reintroduced throughout the year to help keep material fresh in the students' minds. Using microlearning in this way, one can begin to envision a spiraling microlearning curriculum that repeats throughout the year and gets more complex as time passes.

Educators can also prepare microlearning events to address specific tasks or for performance support for students who are struggling with a process or skill associated with a current lesson of study. For example, imagine sending students to a web site where they can watch tutorials on decimals to enable them to progress through a math unit on adding and subtracting decimals.

Now that we can visualize how microlearning can be embedded throughout the entire lesson cycle, and even outside of the classroom, the rest of this chapter will focus on examples of microlearning in the K-12 setting.

Online Tutorials

One well-known example of a site that provides online tutorials for education is *Khan Academy*, a web-based resource that provides microlearning tutorials at elementary, middle, and high school levels. According to its "About" page, Khan Academy offers, "practice exercises, instructional videos, and a personalized learning dashboard that empower students to study at their own pace in and outside of the classroom" (Khan Academy, 2020, para.1). Through the website, students are free to browse topics and select tutorials as needed. They may seek out information as problems become apparent, or they can participate in work assigned by the teacher, or both.

Khan Academy uses instructors to introduce an educational objective through a screen capture video program. An educational objective may include short instructional microlectures, review articles, practice sections, quizzes, and unit tests. To motivate learners, gamification strategies are applied to allow students to demonstrate mastery and earn points, and by answering practice questions and taking quizzes before progressing to more advanced levels.

Students can work through Khan Academy on-demand when they are self-seeking assistance. This form of self-directed learning facilitates self-paced practice on topics of interest to students. Educators can create accounts and upload their student data to facilitate the use of Khan Academy content during instructional time. Educators can also focus on one to two learning objectives by using brief tutorials for guided practice and homework. Teachers can also integrate micro-learning tutorials into their lessons to provide differentiation or remediation as needed.

Microlectures in the Flipped Classroom

Another possibility for microlearning is the idea of using microlectures in the flipped classroom. Sweet (2014) states it "is important to ensure that microlectures are used to create a learning environment where students take some responsibility for their own learning" (p. 52). Sweet argues that microlectures do not provide videos as a way to replace instructors, but instead allow for differentiation and increased engagement during class time.

Using microlectures in a flipped classroom setting provides students time to prepare ahead of face-to-face class time, thus freeing the instructor to use class time to work on boosting problem-solving and skills development. Instructors have access to a variety of video creation tools from paid products like *Adobe Premiere Pro* to free online tools such as *Screencast-O-Matic* and animated video creator *Powtoon*.

Since students will be working independently for significant periods of time, it is important to engage them in the flipped learning environment. Potentially, students' use of smartphones, tablets, or computers can facilitate engagement through microlectures that provide audio and visual stimulation. To further enhance student engagement, instructors can embed quizzes to videos using open-source tools like *Vizia* and *Edpuzzle* to make them interactive. These quizzes can be used for review or as pre- or post-test assessments of the lesson objectives.

Another strategy for using microlectures in the flipped classroom is to address common misconceptions that act as barriers to students' understanding of key concepts. A web portal aligned to a course can provide students access to micro-lectures that can be watched and re-watched anytime as needed. Accordingly, through microlectures, differentiation can take place at the remediation or even advanced levels. Access to microlectures through a course portal can engage students' curiosity about new topics or allow advanced students to move ahead of the class to continue learning on their own.

Lastly, in support of the flipped classroom, school librarians, who are often certified educators, can also use microlectures in response to requests for assistance from teachers or students. For example, librarians might create a series of videos to highlight various scenarios that repeatedly occur in the library, such as how to use the *Online Public Access Catalog* to find a specific book by title or author or how to find the location of a specific book using the library's numbering system. Microlectures could also be developed to facilitate library orientations or to share common library services and procedures to new students on campus.

Mobile Language Learning

Students who are learning a foreign language need repeated opportunities to hear and speak a foreign language. Unless they are situated in an environment where this naturally occurs, then alternative ways of creating this environment should be sought such as the use of mobile language learning applications. Often these mobile applications offer an engaging and gamified opportunity for students to immerse themselves in a foreign language. Through short bursts of learning with repetition and practice, mobile language learning applications can increase learning for students wanting to master a new language (Demmans Epp & Phirangee, 2019, p. 1).

Some mobile language learning applications guide students through a series of sequenced vocabulary building opportunities, like the free app or web-based version of *Duolingo*. This app allows users to take an initial placement test or test out of easier lessons and advance to more challenging lessons. The self-paced lessons are organized into modules with multiple short lessons in each module.

These small bursts of information, that repeat and cycle back as learners move through the modules provides a classic example of microlearning's strongest attributes for promoting language learning. Mobile language learning apps primarily help the users to learn, study, and practice a foreign vocabulary at their own pace. These apps can help build a base vocabulary that can be further developed in the classroom setting where the teacher can also work on fluency.

Digital Textbooks and Open Educational Resources

Technology has had a huge impact on the textbook industry. Over the past several years the traditional textbook has undergone major changes from static physical books, to inactive digital copies, to fully interactive, multimedia-rich print and digital texts. Another recent advancement in the evolution of the textbook is the emergence of *Open Educational Resource (OER)* textbooks, media, and other digital assets, which are cost-free to the consumer and openly licensed for use in and outside the classroom.

One example of an OER textbook initiative is *OpenStax*, which provides OER resources for high school, college, and university students. This OER project is funded through Rice University and philanthropic partners like the Bill & Melinda Gates Foundation. One of *OpenStax's* partners is *Blending Education, LLC* that boasts over 3,000 microlearning lessons that are self-grading and can be easily uploaded for use in most Learning Management Systems (LMS). "Each microlearning product can be used and re-used freely year after year on unlimited students, resulting in an ultimate cost-savings" (Blending Education, 2018, para. 7).

With the availability of microlearning and OER textbooks, educators can easily provide differentiation for their diverse students. Microlearning can boost the skills and basic understandings of at-risk students in need of remediation to fill in learning gaps. It can also provide support for general education students, and advanced students can quickly make their way through more rigorous and advanced content. Microlearning and OER textbooks also open the door for personalized learning where the learners can choose their own courses and work their way through mastery.

These OER microlearning products with grade *passback* capability can provide instant feedback to students and potentially ease teachers' workloads when integrated into a campus or school district's learning management system. Students' grades can be linked to the district's grading program or downloaded to a spreadsheet that can be transferred into the grading system at a later point in time.

Professional Development

Another important aspect of education revolves around the professional development of educators who serve the K-12 students. Ask teachers about their availability of time for professional development and they will profess that there are not enough hours in the day to get everything done, much less, to find time to learn something new. In addition to teaching, teachers have additional duties and responsibilities being added to their plates all the time. Their work often extends beyond the school day into evenings and weekends. To address this issue, some districts have found creative ways to add professional development time back into teachers' schedules through professional development days added to district calendars or adjusting teaching schedules to allow for professional development during the regular work hours.

Czyz (2017) provides several examples of microlearning being used for teacher professional development, including *lunch and learn* programs. Since school lunch periods are relatively short, lunch and learn events can be used to provide short and quick learning segments to faculty. While teachers eat, they can watch or participate in short learning activities that are provided individually or in small groups, through online or in person gatherings. Short video trainings are another suggestion from Czyz (2017). For example, when a campus or district adopts a new platform like *Google for Education*, a series of short how-to videos could be created to cover the fundamental elements of the platform with tips for teachers on how to perform the skills they will need to master.

A third idea shared by Czyz (2017) is Rob Sahli's *1-5-15 Bulletin*, which he creates weekly on the digital newsletter *S'more*. Sahli identifies one professional development topic and then curates three microlearning segments that will individually take 1, 5, or 15 minutes to review. Through the *1-5-15 Bulletin*, Sahli is meeting the need for his teachers to select their own professional development track based on the time they have available during the week to engage in professional learning. While teachers recognize the need to improve their teaching skills, they often have a hard time fitting it into their schedules. Additionally, due to lack of time and resources, some teachers may be restricted from traveling to off-site events for professional development. Microlearning may be able to help in these situations and others.

Micro-Credentials

To incentivize professional development efforts, micro-credentials or digital badges can be adopted by schools and districts to enable educators to demonstrate competency in specific knowledge and skills. The need for targeted microlearning can be assessed by the administration or central office personnel who identify key skills or competencies educators may require a greater understanding of, or for individuals who want to master a new skill. To allow for maximum flexibility the micro-credential program should be accessible, just-in-time, and on-demand, 24 hours a day, seven days a week. To earn a credential or badge, educators would need to complete a microlearning unit and submit evidence of their work to a validator who will review it and award credit.

With access to micro-credentials, educators can take the lead in their own learning. School districts can recognize these efforts and award educators for their efforts. This type of on-demand professional development is ideal for busy educators because it provides personalized, mini-bursts of learning on concentrated skills that can be completed anytime, anywhere. If set up appropriately, this form of professional training can provide a foundation for the development of key competencies, skills, and understandings across a campus or district.

Design and Delivery Options

There are a variety of tools available to the educators who want to implement microlearning in their classrooms. To get started, they will first need to determine the outcomes needed for students to be able to meet the learning objectives.

Video needs can be met through a variety of tools. Screen capture can be accomplished through free versions of *Screencast-o-matic* or *Screencastify*. Live-action videos are easily made using a tablet, cellphone, or web-camera. If animation videos are appropriate, the teachers and students can use web-based apps like *Biteable* or *Powtoon*. Completed videos can be housed on platforms like *YouTube, Vimeo, Merlot,* or *Wakelet*.

Graphic applications are plentiful and often come at no cost. Pictures can be created using *Canva* or stock photos can be used from sites like *Unsplash* or *Pixabay*. Meme makers include *Google Draw* or *Adobe Spark*. If educators want to add a little humor to their videos, they can make their still images talk using tools like

Talkr, Chatterbox, or *Chatterpix*. And finally, GIF makers include *Giphy, imgflip,* and *Brush Ninja*.

Text-based microlearning can be provided in multiple ways. Educators can create short articles for the student to read on paper on any platform available to them, be it a *Google Classroom, Edmodo*, or even a social media post that requires the student to read and respond.

Summary

As noted in the chapter, microlearning is an instrumental tool for both educators and students alike. Microlearning can be delivered in a variety of formats including short videos, e-learning lessons, infographics, images, and podcasts. Through a spiraling microlearning curriculum that repeats and gets more complex as time passes, microlearning objects can be used throughout the lesson cycle to pre-assess students' knowledge of a concept during instruction to introduce new concepts and lay a foundation for future lessons, and to reinforce concepts post-instruction.

Yet, microlearning places a heavy emphasis on technology applications and devices. When considering the use of microlearning in teaching and learning, there are some things to consider in advance. For example, do teachers have access to microlearning content through their textbook publishers or OER resources, or will they need to create it themselves? Accordingly, will teachers have the ability to integrate microlearning content into their lessons? More importantly, will students have the capability to access these resources at school and at home?

There are a variety of tools available to teachers who want to implement microlearning in their classrooms. Some possible introductory steps could include things like installing interactive screensavers on school computers that prompt students to solve puzzles or review definitions of key course-related terminology. Teachers could also conduct anonymous polls on a topic of the day using free apps like *Poll Everywhere* or offer quick challenge quizzes through apps like *Quizziz* or *Kahoot* where students can use their cellphones or mobile devices to respond. Students can even receive a SAT or content area word of the day via tools like *Remind*. As they gain experience and confidence, teachers can begin to develop more advanced mircolearning objects through a variety of video creation, screen casting, and web-design tools. In addition to developing their own microlearning objects, the ultimate aim would be to enable students to develop their own mircolearning products and learning aids.

To aid in professional development and incentivize self-directed learning, microlearning and micro-credentials could be used by organizations to promote self-directed, personalized, professional learning to all educators. Potential technology leaders on the school campus like the school librarian or instructional technologist may be able to offer educators guidance as they explore and create their own microlearning units.

In summary, microlearning creates many opportunities for educators to engage with their students in new and innovative ways. The microlearning events they create can consist of small learning segments and short-term focused activities that can stand-alone or support the daily classroom curriculum.

Discussion Questions

1. What is a major learning hurdle your staff needs to master this year? How can you break it up into a series of microlearning professional development events?
2. What digital tools are accessible on your campus for educators to use in creating microlearning segments for their students?
3. What digital tools are available to your students so they can access the microlearning units? Are the tools readily available or can they be checked out from the library on an as-needed basis?

Resource List of Microlearning Tools for the K-12 Classroom

- Adobe Premiere Pro – www.adobe.com/products/premiere
- Adobe Spark – https://spark.adobe.com
- Biteable – https://biteable.com
- Brush Ninja – https://brush.ninja
- Canva – www.canva.com
- Chatterbox – www.getchattering.com
- Chatterpix – https://apps.apple.com/us/app/chatterpix-kids-by-duck-duck/id734046126
- Duolingo – www.duolingo.com
- Edmodo – https://new.edmodo.com
- edpuzzle – https://edpuzzle.com
- Giphy – https://giphy.com
- Google Classroom – https://classroom.google.com
- Google Draw – https://docs.google.com/drawings
- Poll Everywhere – www.polleverywhere.com
- imgflip – https://imgflip.com
- Kahoot – https://kahoot.com
- Khan Academy – www.khanacademy.org
- Merlot – www.merlot.org/merlot
- openstax – https://openstax.org
- Pixabay – https://pixabay.com
- Powtoon – www.powtoon.com
- Quizziz – https://quizizz.com
- Remind – www.remind.com
- S'more – www.smore.com

- Screencastify – www.screencastify.com
- Screen-casto-matic – https://screencast-o-matic.com
- Screencast-O-Matic https://screencast-o-matic.com/screen-recorder
- Talkr – https://talkrapp.com
- Unsplash – https://unsplash.com
- Vimeo – https://vimeo.com
- Vizia – https://vizia.com
- Wakelet – https://wakelet.com
- Youtube – www.youtube.com

References

Blending Education. (2018, June 27). OpenStax Textbooks Teams with Blending Education, LLC to introduce content-driven microlearning. www.prnewswire.com/news-releases/openstax-textbooks-teams-with-blending-education-llc-to-introduce-content-driven-microlearning-300577987.html.

Czyz, R. (2017). Four o'clock faculty: A rogue guide to revolutionizing professional development. Place of publication not identified: Dave Burgess Consulting.

Demmans Epp, C. & Phirangee, K. (2019). Exploring mobile tool integration: Design activities carefully or students may not learn. *Contemporary Educational Psychology*, 59. https://doi-org.ezproxy.shsu.edu/10.1016/j.cedpsych.2019.101791.

Kapp, K., & Defelice, R. (2018). ELEPHANT-SIZED impact. *TD: Talent Development*, 72 (7), 26. http://search.ebscohost.com.ezproxy.shsu.edu/login.aspx?direct=true&db=f6h&AN=130402054&site=eds-live&scope=site.

Khan Academy. (2020). www.khanacademy.org/about.

Killian, S. (2019, November 22). 8 strategies Robert Marzano & John Hattie agree on. www.evidencebasedteaching.org.au/robert-marzano-vs-john-hattie.

Major, A., & Calandrino, T. (2018). Beyond chunking: Microlearning secrets for effective online design. *Distance Learning*, 2(27). http://search.ebscohost.com.ezproxy.shsu.edu/login.aspx?direct=true&db=edsgov&AN=edsgcl.560418414&site=eds-live&scope=site.

Spangler, D. (2019). Micro approach, major impact: With microcredentials, educators can tailor their learning to their specific needs. *Learning Professional*, 4(60). http://search.ebscohost.com.ezproxy.shsu.edu/login.aspx?direct=true&db=edsbl&AN=RN621279610&site=eds-live&scope=site.

Sweet, D. D.-S. (Ed.) (2014). Microlectures in a flipped classroom: Application, creation and resources. *Mid-Western Educational Researcher*, 26(1), 52–59. http://search.ebscohost.com.ezproxy.shsu.edu/login.aspx?direct=true&db=eue&AN=98710275&site=eds-live&scope=site.

Tan, T. (2016). Unfolding the next chapter in digital content proposition: Reimagining, retrofitting, revamping, restrategizing, oh my! *Publishers Weekly*, (18), S4. http://search.ebscohost.com.ezproxy.shsu.edu/login.aspx?direct=true&db=edsglr&AN=edsgcl.452884075&site=eds-live&scope=site.

Winger, Amy. (2018). Supersized tips for implementing microlearning in macro ways. *Distance Learning*, 15(4), 51–55. http://search.ebscohost.com.ezproxy.shsu.edu/login.aspx?direct=true&db=eft&AN=136816983&site=eds-live&scope=site.

9

MICROLEARNING IN CORPORATE SETTINGS

Pamela S. Hogle

Introduction

Across industries, workers are pressed for time. Their jobs are changing rapidly; new technologies and tools demand constant upskilling. Automation, mergers, and layoffs, whether industry-wide or organization-specific, are changes that often lead to a smaller number of workers who take on increased workloads or new tasks.

Training is essential at all stages of professional life. However, conventional training, whether instructor-led or comprehensive e-learning courses, takes time that workers do not feel they can spare. According to an infographic published by Bersin by Deloitte (n.d.), employees spend only 1 percent of a typical workweek on training and development activities. Microlearning offers a solution for time-crunched employees. Managers and executives are increasingly turning to microlearning in response to workers' need for efficient, focused training, and learning and development (L&D) teams are expected to provide microlearning solutions.

Benefits of microlearning include its ability to engage learners and improve learning and retention; flexible options for format and delivery; ease of personalizing professional development and delivering adaptive training; and speed of development, deployment, and updates. Some see it as a bridge between formal and informal learning that can be integrated easily into the workday (Buchem & Hamelmann, 2010).

Moving learning into the flow of work is a paradigm shift that, according to talent management expert Josh Bersin (2018), reflects a need for immediate information, a need that microlearning excels at meeting. The emergence of microlearning, alongside platforms like *Spotify* and *Netflix* that make it easy for consumers to instantly find appealing content, make this new paradigm of on-demand, in-the-workflow learning possible.

Corporate training diverges from *Netflix, Spotify,* and similar platforms in its ultimate objective though. Rather than trying to get learners to consume as much content as possible, corporate training professionals seek efficiency. As Bersin (2018) wrote, "We don't want people to be 'addicted' to the learning platform; we want them to *learn something, apply it,* and then **go back to work**" (Explaining The Shift: Learning In The Flow Of Work, para. 8). Microlearning can help L&D professionals achieve this in corporate settings.

This chapter will describe the appeal of microlearning in corporate settings and the problems and pain points it addresses. It will present best practices for designing and using microlearning with corporate learners. Finally, the chapter will share examples of microlearning in a variety of fields and use-case applications.

Why Use Microlearning?

Employee training is a fact of life for many corporations and organizations. New employee onboarding requires teaching new hires the ropes: rules and regulations, company culture, the specifics of their jobs. Employees seeking to advance need new and improved skills. Changing technology requires training. Federal or state laws, industry regulations, or company rules might mandate training on safety best practices, emergency response, safe use and handling of equipment or materials, harassment prevention, and more. Customer-facing employees or managers might need training on soft skills ranging from leadership to effective communication to recognition and mitigation of implicit bias.

Challenges in Corporate Learning

Conventional approaches to training include in-person courses or workshops, single or multi-session classes taught by an instructor, and e-learning. A blended learning solution might combine instructor-led sessions, in person or online, with asynchronous e-learning. Conventional e-learning tends to follow a predictable format of text, video, and interactive activities, divided into chapters or sections. Each section, and the course as a whole, may be followed by a quiz.

While these approaches to instruction are familiar and time-tested, and they are effective for many types of training, they have significant drawbacks. For example, designing and developing courses is costly in time, resources, and budget; materials are not easy to update; any sessions with a live instructor must be scheduled, often far in advance; sessions and courses tend to be long, sometimes several hours or even days, and during training time, workers are not productive. (Zhang & Ren, 2011).

Perhaps most significantly, the courses demand a large investment of worker time, time that is difficult for many employees to schedule while also remaining productive and executing the essential tasks of their jobs. Therefore, most learners complete comprehensive training courses only once — and they are "done." However, learners, especially adult learners, do not master content after a single exposure.

Global organizations and those that hire large numbers of seasonal workers might need to train large numbers of workers at once or in widely dispersed locations. These obstacles also make conventional training problematic.

A Solution for the Modern Learner

Microlearning, which appeared on the L&D radar screen in the early 2000s, offers solutions to many of these challenges. Its popularity dovetails with changes in consumer behavior that are spilling over into workplaces as well.

As consumers, parents, citizens, and simply innately curious individuals, modern digital learners seek quick answers online. Questions arise in day-to-day life, such as where the nearest supermarket is, who starred in a film, or how to repair your leaky faucet. The typical response is to whip out a mobile device, tablet, or smartphone, and *Google* the answer. Whether the answer is packaged as a *Google Snippet*, a *YouTube* video, a *Wikipedia* article, or some other format, it is **not** a 30-minute course or a two-day in-person workshop.

At work, as in non-work situations, learners want quick information, answers to their questions, or solutions to a problem. They want to find that answer and get on with their work. Microlearning brings quick learning **into the workflow** to support their performance and minimize disruption of their work. According to Major & Calandrino (2018), modern employees, who comprise the majority of corporate learners, are "overwhelmed, distracted, and impatient," (para. 1) and they are accustomed to accessing information on-demand and through networks of colleagues or peers. They added, microlearning aims to "deliver material in short, manageable, readily attainable bursts" (para 4).

Microlearning offers additional significant contrasts with conventional training:

- Unlike a required multi-part course that covers a complex topic, each unit of microlearning is narrowly focused and relevant or immediately useful (Tipton, 2017a).
- Learners do not have to schedule the training and take time away from work.
- Short, focused, and searchable, microlearning does not force learners to cover material that they already know or don't need to learn.
- Much microlearning is packaged and delivered in ways that promote retention. Rather than a single exposure to a vast amount of information, learners often get repeated exposure and on-demand access to microlearning content.

The appeal of microlearning stems from its flexible and modern approach that simply works for adult learners in our digital information age.

Not Simply "Chunked" Content

A common misperception about microlearning is that it is simply long-form e-learning "chunked" into bite-size lessons. However, the utility of microlearning, especially to busy professionals, comes from its completeness.

Chunked content refers to "one long program/course/video broken into bite-sized pieces, primarily to help with cognitive load. Each content piece is connected to the other and therefore, acted on in a linear fashion" (Tipton, 2017a, para. 6). In contrast, each unit of microlearning must stand alone and form a complete learning unit.

Neither is microlearning "dumbed-down" e-learning. "When appropriately applied, microlearning can allow for deeper encoding, reflection and practice retrieval – all necessary for the successful exchange of knowledge and learning application" (Tipton, 2017a, para. 12). Corporate microlearning is right-sized content designed to completely meet a learning need in the moment.

Where Microlearning Excels

Microlearning is not the answer to every corporate training question, of course. It excels in these four common corporate training scenarios:

1. Preparation for Longer Training Courses

Learners taking a comprehensive course or workshop will be dedicating significant time and effort to mastering the material. Preparatory microlearning can ensure that all learners are exposed to foundational concepts and have the same basic information prior to the first day of formal learning. Preparatory microlearning, whether pretests, assessments of prior knowledge and experience, or introduction of key terms and concepts "provides an opportunity to set up a series of planned learning initiatives to prepare for a larger learning event" (Kapp & Defelice, 2018, Preparation-based microlearning, para. 1).

2. Review and Reinforcement of Prior Learning

Added to conventional training, a microlearning solution extends learning and aids retention. Using microlearning to review and reinforce learning is an ideal complement to formal training. It "distills the key concepts" and breaks them into "bite-size pieces," which can then be delivered to learners on a regular schedule and/or made available on demand (Kapp & Defelice, 2018, Post-instruction microlearning, para. 1).

In workplaces ranging from factories to banks to vast cubicle-filled offices, deploying microlearning as a follow-up to conventional training is a way to improve the ROI (return on investment) that management has made in creating the original training. Microlearning of this type ranges from subscription delivery of activities that ask employees to recall and apply training content to job aids that offer a quick reference.

3. Teaching Dense, Fact-Based Content

Spaced repetition and *spaced practice* are terms used to refer to repeated exposure to training content, over time. This is a proven approach to building mastery and long-term retention (Kelley & Whatson, 2013; Tabibian et al., 2019). In fact, practicing recalling some information can cause other, less-frequently used information to become "inaccessible" (Storm, 2011).

Repeatedly studying the same information in a single sitting, "has its limits" Malamed (2012, para. 2) states, pointing to "practice with retrieval" (para. 3) over time as a more efficient alternative. Thus, using microlearning, "[e]mployees can expand their knowledge incrementally for effective knowledge retention" (Emerson & Berge, 2018, para. 5) by reviewing content repeatedly at spaced intervals.

This is partly due to the format of microlearning. Designed as short, focused units of instruction, and, generally, available on demand, microlearning is easy for learners to use over and over. Employees can quickly locate the correct microlearning unit, in a well-designed platform with robust search, and remind themselves of details they are having trouble recalling. They can also use these microlearning units to learn the material, reviewing and drilling themselves on facts or concepts repeatedly until they remember the information.

4. Supporting Workers in Applying Training

"[M]icrolearning is a strategy that complements more comprehensive classroom and web-based training by reinforcing concepts between tasks in the office or working as job aids on the production floor," Emerson and Berge (2018, para. 4) wrote, citing the advantages of moving learning into the workplace. Unlike instructor-led training or longer e-learning courses, employees do not have to schedule microlearning or block out a chunk of their workday to dedicate to training. They can use post-training support or job aids that are available on demand, integrating learning with the performance of their jobs.

This performance-based microlearning is often termed *performance support* or *workflow learning*. It might consist of a poster or quick-reference card or a series of short videos and texts that a worker can quickly access, using a learning management system (LMS), to look up seldom-used or highly detailed information. It could take the format of an app, accessed using a regular computer or a mobile device, that allows workers to quickly search for and locate short articles, diagrams, or other narrowly focused content. The short format and instant access provide answers and solutions without pulling the employee away from a work task. This type of learning supports performance while enabling learners to easily transfer learning from a formal instructional setting to on-the-job application — the ultimate goal of corporate training.

Microlearning Best Practices in Corporate Settings

As with any successful e-learning, designing and developing effective microlearning starts with knowing your audience. A key driver of corporate microlearning's popularity is its flexibility and fit with how people learn and use digital content when they are *not* at work. Keeping the behavior of digital consumers and citizens in mind helps when considering *best practices* for the design of corporate microlearning. Some guiding principles are described in the following subsections.

Maintain Good ID Practices

ID (instructional design) is the creation of instructional materials that will transfer knowledge, teach skills, or change behavior. In a corporate e-learning context, it requires identifying specific business needs, goals, or problems, and defining what meeting the goal or successfully resolving the problem would look like. In creating a solution that leads toward that success, an instructional designer must consider the learners' environment, their existing knowledge and experience, and the technology and tools available to them. Creating successful microlearning requires the same considerations as creating other effective e-learning. And, the steps in analyzing needs, goals, and environment must be repeated for each microlearning unit, which must be usable and useful on its own, even if it will also be used as part of a more comprehensive course of study comprising multiple microlearning units.

Make It Easy to Find Useful Content

Microlearning should be quick to find and to consume. A microlearning app or platform must have outstanding search capabilities, and content should be thoroughly indexed so that learners can find and access the information they need in seconds (Tipton, 2017a). Creating or packaging e-learning materials in ways that make learners work hard just to find what they need contributes to what Malamed (2011) calls "extrinsic" cognitive overload and reduces the effectiveness of the instructional materials because "it uses up cognitive resources that learners could direct at the learning task" (para. 8). Extrinsic cognitive load "is a result of poor learning design that can have a negative effect on learning" (Malamed, 2011, para. 8).

Focus Each Lesson Narrowly

A unit of corporate microlearning is laser-focused, often answering a single narrowly drawn question. It should have one to three learning objectives mapped to a specific KPI or *key performance indicator*, a business-critical performance criterion (Kapp & Defelice, 2019) and cover "[o]ne idea, one concept. No exceptions," according to Tipton (2017b, Is Microlearning the Solution? para. 1). When creating microlearning mini courses, each lesson should have three to five screens of content with no more than about 50 words per screen, according to Jimenez (2006). Key ideas must be immediately visible. Jimenez also suggests ending each lesson with a recap.

Know Your Audience

"Deliver the right training to the right learners at the right depth," Belhassen and Hogle (2019, Tenets of the agile microlearning philosophy, p. 10) advise. This requires knowing both what your learners need to be able to do at the completion of their training and how much knowledge they already have. Do not waste people's time with content they already know or have no need to learn; instead, make it easy for them to choose which content to use and which to ignore. Knowing your audience also means creating microlearning that works for learners' work environment and habits.

According to instructional design director Carla Torgerson, when *Bull City Learning*, a company that creates e-learning courses, microlearning, and other digital learning assets, worked with a client to turn a two-day sales skills workshop into e-learning, the design team initially considered a series of 30-minute e-learning courses. As the team analyzed the learners' needs, though, they realized that busy sales personnel needed training that they could fit into the short breaks between calls and meetings. The learners did not want to spend time on extraneous content, so each module had to be highly focused. These learners had different levels of experience, so they also needed the ability to do lessons in any order, skip lessons, and review content on demand. The *Bull City Learning* team realized that flexible microlearning was a perfect fit for both the learners and the content. They created a combination of short videos, two- to eight-minute e-learning courses, and PDFs with additional information that learners could use anytime, in any order (C. Torgerson, personal communication, January 9, 2020).

Understand How Your Learners Access and Use Content

Think about how digital learners use and master content. Jimenez (2006) uses the analogy of *pyramids with points*. The points are key ideas in the content that the learner can use immediately. "It is only when 'application points' are easily identified and accessible that learners can learn in 3 minutes and achieve results quickly. In essence, this is the highest form of learning quality and value" (Jimenez, 2006, p. 31). If your learners are *deskless* workers, on a warehouse or retail floor, or constantly traveling between customer sites for example, be sure to create mobile-first learning that works well on smartphone and tablet screens. This demands small, simple images and short text blocks. If you know that your learners will all be using tablets, design for that platform, consider podcasts for learners who drive a lot, delivery workers or traveling sales personnel, for example.

Remain Grounded in Science

Though concise, microlearning content is still **instructional** content; the instructional design and cognitive science principles that govern planning and designing longer-form learning content still apply. These principles include using instructional scaffolding to guide learners from basic to complex content or when introducing new concepts, and applying spaced repetition, rather than one-time exposure, to teach content and build long-term retention (Belhassen & Hogle, 2019). Quiz questions can reinforce learning and offer recall practice; deeper questions designed to spark reflection, presented as self-assessments, offer opportunities for learners to reflect on what they've covered. Both of these strategies deepen retention, as does "the use of interleaving, or mixing up information in unexpected ways" (Emerson & Berge, 2018, p. 127).

Give Learners Some Autonomy

Microlearning should be "device agnostic" (Tipton, 2017a). It should be usable on a desktop or laptop computer as well as any tablet or smartphone. This flexibility makes it easier for busy employees to integrate training into their workday. In addition, learners should be able to use microlearning units in any order and move forward and backward, skip content, review content, and start and stop learning as they choose (Belhassen, 2019; Jimenez, 2006). Flexible access to content allows learners to use it as training, to reinforce learning, or as performance support or job aids — all ways to facilitate retention and on-the-job application of content.

Remember That Learning Goes Both Ways

Microlearning can originate from the learning and development (L&D) team with content created at the request of managers or executives, or it can germinate from the employees themselves. Emerson and Berge (2018) note that "[s]martphone video technology gives just about any employee the ability to capture in-depth institutional knowledge and share that information formally or informally throughout the organization" (p. 127). This is yet another way to offer learners autonomy and give them a stake in their learning. Buchem and Hamelmann (2010, p. 7) go further, stating that "microlearning materials should be actively co-produced, assembled, and modified by learners" and designed as "learner-driven or user-generated" activities.

Forget the Flash

When creating microlearning, follow sound design principles, including visual design. Design for the environment. For example, if learners will be using mobile devices, keep a small screen in mind, and do not feel compelled to use graphics, video, or interactivity in every lesson. Interactivity is best used for lessons that require hands-on practice and for skills that are essential to on-the-job performance and are complex or difficult to master (Jimenez, 2006, pp. 101–102). Similarly, media assets like graphics or video "should be purposeful and used only where they will add instructional value," (Belhassen, 2019, p. 24) such as showing where a button or menu item can be found or demonstrating a process. They should show a level of detail appropriate to the learner's level of knowledge (Belhassen, 2019; Kapp & Defelice, 2019).

Keep Microlearning Easy to Develop and Easy to Update

"Time is of the essence for creation" (Tipton, 2017b, Is Microlearning the Solution? para. 1), so microlearning should be designed in such a way that development is quick and content is easy to update. This requires knowledge of budget, project scope and timeline, and the client's expectations. Microlearning developers are advised to analyze the learners' environment, tasks, goals, and prior knowledge, and to test extensively throughout design and development (Kapp & Defelice, 2019). Once deployed, microlearning content should be equally quick and easy to access and consume —*view and go* — not buried in an LMS or an Intranet shared drive. It should also be, "fit for mobile, desktop, tablets, and/or digital files" (Tipton, 2017b, Is Microlearning the Solution? para. 1).

Focus on Organizational Needs

Above all, effective microlearning "focuses on meeting the organization's performance needs" and "identifies the quality outcomes suitable to e-learners" (Jimenez, 2006, p. 50). Many microlearning platforms that target corporate training include sophisticated data collection and analysis capabilities. When designing microlearning, ask focused questions about the goals of the training, the problems it will solve, the desired post-training behavior and performance, and identify metrics that can measure changes. Then, use the narrow focus and flexibility of microlearning to home in on those behaviors and metrics. This is a 180-degree shift from designing comprehensive training that covers everything any employee might need to know and a way to fully exploit the differences and key advantages of microlearning.

Microlearning in Action

The flexibility of microlearning, the way it slips into workers' routines without disrupting their workflow, and the ease of creating micro-sized training in any media format make it a versatile solution for common training needs. Employee-learners are increasingly likely to encounter microlearning in typical corporate learning *use cases*. This section provides a few examples.

Onboarding

New employees have a lot to learn. In addition to the tasks and concepts and processes related to their new roles, they have to learn about the corporate culture and its rules and regulations. They may need to enroll in benefits and learn their way around the office and figure out who does what. It is possible to integrate microlearning into onboarding training in these ways:

- A microlearning app can summarize key policies and procedures that are explained in detail in the employee handbook, offering a quick way to search for relevant sections. It can also introduce the office culture and share examples and anecdotes about how things are done.
- Microlearning in the form of an app, chatbot, or text-messages can guide new hires through important first steps like filling out paperwork, meeting with the HR officer, enrolling in their retirement plan, etc. It can send them reminders, show them where to go, and nudge them to meet deadlines.
- Large companies can create mobile-friendly interactive maps of the corporate premises, helping newbies find their way around or figure out where people sit.
- Introductory training aimed at all new hires can convey core values and practices that company leaders see as an integral part of the organization's mission and brand. Offering content in digital flash cards, a game, or questions encourages employees to drill and quiz themselves, helping them learn and retain key information.

Microlearning developed for onboarding may be flexible enough to use with experienced personnel who need to upgrade skills as well. Rather than call a mixed population of new and experienced technicians away from work for training, a heating and air-conditioning company worked with *Vignettes Learning*, a company that designs and delivers e-learning platforms, to develop a microlearning strategy that combined videos explaining new features and installation procedures, quick-reference documentation, a link to contact tech support, and coaching for problem resolution. They found that 80 percent of the technicians got the information they needed from the microlearning; only 20 percent requested coaching. The blended approach saved money and reduced disruptions to work (R. Jimenez, personal communication, January 8, 2020).

Upskilling and Behavior Change

In a tight job market, more employers are seeking to *upskill* existing employees rather than, or in addition to, hiring additional workers. This focus on training to add or extend employees' skills provides an opportunity for microlearning to shine. Microlearning on its own, or as an adjunct to a more comprehensive course of instruction, can play a useful role when employees are adding or updating skills, learning to use new software, and reviewing fact- or information-dense material that helps them perform role-related tasks. Microlearning can help in these ways:

- Used as preparation for a training course, a microlearning flashcard, game, or quiz app can help employees master vocabulary and concepts that prepare them for deeper learning.
- When skills are new, employees might not remember every detail from their training. They can refer to the same microlearning materials that introduced these concepts, using them as job aids and performance supports. The microlearning materials make it easy to look up and review content, as often as they need to, until they master it.
- Short microlearning videos can show employees how to do something, and they can replay the video over and over, as they practice the new skill, until they are comfortable doing it on their own. It does not matter what the skill is, whether the employee needs to use a new or updated software program, install a product at a customer site, or help a customer with a complex bank transaction, reviewing a step-by-step video can boost their confidence and remind them of key details.
- Spaced review of material covered in training aids long-term retention and increases mastery of the content over single-exposure learning.

Organizations of all sizes are seeing successful results with this approach.

A business skills training company that had a comprehensive library of video training worked with *Artisan E-Learning*, an e-learning development company, to add microlearning, creating short, interactive skill-building activities to help their learners put the concepts into practice. The pilot included 30 microlessons that had an 86 percent completion rate, higher than any other e-learning format they had used. In addition, 60 percent of learners' custom learning paths included at least one microlesson, and in the first 90 days, more than 8,000 completions were recorded (D. Elkins, personal communication, January 10, 2020).

When the *Cleveland Clinic* added *OttoLearn Agile Microlearning*^{TM} to their *Communicate with H.E.A.R.T.* health-care-provider training as a post-training knowledge retention strategy, knowledge gaps shrank dramatically. During a three-month period, the percentage of incorrect responses dropped from 34.3 percent to under 1 percent as learners progressed to a mastery level of four (out of five), or what *OttoLearn* calls "Proficient – Learners will exhibit accurate and rapid recall with few errors" (D. Belhassen, personal communication, January 8, 2020).

Compliance, Safety, and Sales – Boosting Performance

On its own or as a follow-up to conventional e-learning or face-to-face training, microlearning is useful as compliance or safety training, to teach sales teams about product features, to help customer service personnel practice interactions and scenarios they might encounter with customers, and much more. As a result, corporations that have long used an annual training approach to compliance training or safety training are turning to continuous microlearning instead. This holds true whether the training is harassment-prevention training for managers, teaching employees how to respond to an emergency situation, or safety training for forklift operators. Benefits of this approach include:

- Employees get constant, low-dosage exposure to important information and are more likely to remember and use it than when they get a huge amount of information delivered all at once.
- Materials are easy to update, since each unit is small and self-contained. This means employees can access the most current processes and content, rather than having to wait perhaps several months, until the next annual update.
- By encountering microlearning via a short lesson every morning or three times a week, all year long, rather than a single session once a year, employees review the material constantly.
- Microlearning platforms with data collection and analysis can show that employees have eliminated knowledge gaps and learned essential compliance content.

The continuous or *subscription* approach to microlearning uses the principle of spaced repetition or *the retrieval spacing effect*, which leads to better retention than *massed* study, learning a large amount of information in a single long session (Kelley & Whatson, 2013).

In addition, by *regularly pinging* learners, training administrators, and managers keep key information *top of mind* for learners, ensuring that the most important information is not forgotten (Thalheimer, 2014).

Thus, microlearning has the potential to be a more effective way to ensure that employees learn and remember key safety, compliance, or customer-focused skills and content than conventional e-learning alone. It can also be more efficient and cost-effective, making it possible to offer in-person or traditional e-learning less often, saving money and reducing the amount of time employees are away from their jobs (Thalheimer, 2014).

For example, a large health-care company found all of this to be true when it rolled out new *APEX* software, according to Ray Jimenez, chief learning architect at *Vignettes Learning*. Even though they provided training, the company realized that doctors and nurses were not able to keep up with changes and updates. It was costly and impractical to call the professional staff together for frequent training, though. They turned to *Vignettes Learning* to develop a microlearning program to introduce quick updates and provide necessary training within the workflow. The medical director told *Vignettes Learning* that staff used the micro-learning updates 8,000 times in a single month — "8,000 opportunities that could have led to disastrous outcomes without the proper knowledge" (R. Jimenez, personal communication, January 8, 2020).

In another example, when retailer *Bloomingdale's* needed training for thousands of employees of all ages and backgrounds, the company partnered with *Axonify* to introduce microlearning as the foundation of their frontline training, The solution supported more than 10,000 employees in retail stores across 12 U.S. states and saved millions of dollars, including $2.2 million in reduced safety costs in 2015 alone (McIntosh, 2015).

Bloomingdale's leveraged the *Axonify* learning solution to deliver gamified safety training to retail associates, integrated into their everyday workflow. In sessions that lasted just three to five minutes, associates completed training that focused on a balance of business priorities and personal development needs. Rather than leave the store floor to complete training in a back office, associates completed sessions during downtimes in their departments using tablets or point-of-sale devices (McIntosh, 2015).

Over 90 percent of *Bloomingdale's* associates voluntarily completed regular train-ing, and 86 percent reported an increase in job confidence (J.D. Dillon, personal correspondence, January 15, 2020). An added benefit was machine learning in *Axo-nify* that connected data captured from microlearning sessions to key performance indicators, allowing *Bloomingdale's* to clearly see how training impacted their business results, including reductions of 36 percent in general liability and 24 percent in worker's comp claims (J.D. Dillon, personal correspondence, January 15, 2020).

Summary and Next Steps

Microlearning is increasingly recognized as an effective solution for time-crunched employees who need to learn new concepts or information, reinforce training, or seek quick answers to questions that come up during their workflow. On its own or as part of a blended solution that combines instructor-led training, in person or online, with microlearning as preparation, additional resources, or part of a post-training retention strategy, the flexibility of microlearning is appealing to learners, executives, and L&D teams.

Microlearning offers numerous benefits in a corporate learning environment, including the fact that most microlearning platforms offer on-demand, mobile access. The short, narrowly focused learning units are easy to update. Their brevity also makes it easy for learners to quickly find the content that is relevant to them. Corporate microlearning is often offered as a continuous training approach as corporate training professionals realize that annual training is ineffective for long-term retention and that one-time exposure to information-dense instructional content is insufficient for most learners.

However, learning technologies evolve quickly, often following the lead of entertainment or marketing tools and technologies. Next steps for microlearning, as with much corporate learning, are likely to include increased use of immersive and scenario-based learning. Two developing technologies that offer great potential for use as microlearning and in-the-workflow learning, and support tools are augmented reality tools and voice computing:

- Augmented reality or AR overlays digital information on top of real-world tools and environments. AR already powers job aids like 3D diagrams that assist airplane mechanics as they work on complex wiring. It is also present in tools that use QR codes or other triggers to display content on demand, a functionality used in interactive maps, for example, to provide context-specific information as part of an onboarding *tour* of an office.
- Voice-based computing tools are constantly improving and can automate or assist with tasks like scheduling meetings. In a corporate microlearning context, voice-activated tools can provide hands-free assistance, enabling shift supervisors to track task progress and inventory on a warehouse floor or allowing employees to *look up* information in a reference manual without having to stop their work or even have the manual at hand.

Employees are eager to learn at work (LinkedIn Learning, 2019), and microlearning offers engaging options that meet their needs. As remote working gains acceptance, the gig economy continues to grow, and exciting new technologies emerge, the future for microlearning appears to have tremendous potential.

Discussion Questions

1. A corporate client has provided annual harassment-prevention training to all managers for the past several years. Their L&D (learning and development) team is eager to try a continuous microlearning approach to this and other training. How would you approach this project and what type(s) of learning materials would you suggest they develop?
2. How does corporate microlearning differ from conventional e-learning courses in its design and use? Identify and describe two specific training scenarios where microlearning would be a good choice and one where an instructor-led training or comprehensive e-learning course might be more suitable.
3. What characteristics of microlearning make it a good fit for adult learners in a professional setting? How does the paradigm of the *digital consumer* influence the popularity and effectiveness of microlearning for corporate e-learning?
4. How would you suggest using microlearning as part of a learning retention strategy for professionals in a highly regulated industry, like banking or health care?

References

Belhassen, D. (2019). Creating effective content. www.ottolearn.com/microlearning-resources/creating-effective-training-content.

Belhassen, D. & Hogle, P. (2019). The case for agile microlearning. www.ottolearn.com/microlearning-resources/why-agile-microlearning.

Bersin by Deloitte. (n.d.). Leading in learning. www2.deloitte.com/content/dam/Deloitte/global/Documents/HumanCapital/gx-cons-hc-learning-solutions-placemat.pdf.

Bersin, J. (2018, June 3). A new paradigm for corporate training: Learning in the flow of work. https://joshbersin.com/2018/06/a-new-paradigm-for-corporate-training-learning-in-the-flow-of-work.

Buchem, I. & Hamelmann H. (2010, Sept. 1–15). Microlearning: A strategy for ongoing professional development. *eLearning Papers*, 21.

Emerson, L. & Berge, Z. (2018, June). Microlearning: Knowledge management applications and competency-based training in the workplace. *Knowledge Management & E-Learning*, 10(2). www.researchgate.net/publication/326317952_Microlearning_Knowledge_management_applications_and_competency-based_training_in_the_workplace.

Jimenez, R. (2006). 3-Minute eLearning. Vignettes for Training, Inc. https://www.vignetteslearning.com/download/3-Minute-e-Learning-booksample.pdf.

Kapp, K. & Defelice, R. (2018, July). Elephant-sized impact. *TD Magazine*, Association for Talent Development. www.td.org/magazines/td-magazine/elephant-sized-impact?fbclid=IwAR1wEzW-p_iDWOG9gXSjii1gmImS8AUojpVHEZCQyLQ-XwRGKnTCI_hIB6Q.

Kapp, K. & Defelice, R. (2019). *Microlearning: Short and Sweet*. Alexandria, VA: ATD Press.

Kelley, P. & Whatson, T. (2013, Sept. 25). Making long-term memories in minutes: A spaced learning pattern from memory research in education. *Frontiers in Human Neuroscience*. www.frontiersin.org/articles/10.3389/fnhum.2013.00589/full.

LinkedIn Learning (2019). Workplace learning report. https://learning.linkedin.com/blog/learning-thought-leadership/2019-workplace-learning-report.

Major, A. & Calandrino, T. (2018, Winter). Beyond chunking: Micro-learning secrets for effective online design. *FDLA Journal*, 3. https://nsuworks.nova.edu/cgi/viewcontent.cgi?article=1013&context=fdla-journal.

Malamed, C. (2011). What is cognitive load?http://theelearningcoach.com/learning/what-is-cognitive-load.

Malamed, C. (2012). The power of retrieval practice for learning: An instructional strategy for long-term retention. http://theelearningcoach.com/learning/retrieval-cues-and-learning.

McIntosh, C. (2015, November 2). Bloomingdale's saves millions through revolutionary approach to employee training. *Learning Solutions*. https://learningsolutionsmag.com/articles/1844/bloomingdales-saves-millions-through-revolutionary-approach-to-employee-training.

Storm, B. (2011). The benefit of forgetting in thinking and remembering. *Current Directions in Psychological Science*, 20(5), 291–295. https://people.ucsc.edu/~bcstorm/s_2011b.pdf.

Tabibian, B., Upadhyay, U. De, A., Zarezade, A., Schölkopf, B., & Gomez-Rodriguez, M. (2019, March). Enhancing human learning via spaced repetition optimization. *Proceedings of the National Academy of Sciences*, 116(10), 3988–3993.

Thalheimer, W. (2014). Stuck in an e-learning box? Try subscription learning. *ATD Insights*. www.td.org/insights/stuck-in-an-e-learning-box-try-subscription-learning.

Tipton, S. (2017a). Microlearning: The misunderstood buzzword. https://learningrebels. com/2017/07/17/microlearning-the-misunderstood-buzzword.

Tipton, S. (2017b, May-June). Maximizing microlearning. *Training*. https://trainingmag. com/trgmag-article/maximizing-microlearning.

Zhang, X. & Ren, L. (2011). Design for application of micro learning to informal training in enterprise. IEEE. https://ieeexplore.ieee.org/document/6011235.

10

MICROLEARNING FOR PERSONAL AND PROFESSIONAL DEVELOPMENT

Tracy King

Introduction

The rapid pace of change and technological disruption in the labor market have necessitated continuous learning for professionals to remain competitive in their fields. Trend watchers call it an economic imperative (Campanella, 2018). Yet the press for time between work and life responsibilities does not allow the luxury of long-form learning to fill every gap. Bersin by Deloitte estimates knowledge workers can carve out about five minutes each workday for learning, which makes micro-learning the perfect size bite for pressing learning needs (Bersin, 2019). Those needs may be prescribed training offered by one's employer, but they may also be minutes in demand for one's own personal and professional development.

There is often a generous overlap between the operational goals of corporate training and a professional's personal investment in succeeding in their role by pursuing outside professional development (PD) opportunities. However, PD is far broader and more strategic than the knowledge and skills required to perform a job function. Microlearning offers an array of learning moments to deepen personal interests enriching our lives. It also may be harnessed as a powerful means for achieving our professional goals. Microlearning dots our learning pathway between and within formal professional development to shape our transferable skillset, positioning us to succeed in our current role as well as win-ning the next. These opportunities may range from learning a feature in excel to create an impressive report in one's current job, polishing podcast editing skills to launch a side gig, realizing through self-assessment that consultative skills will be vital to achieving the next job role, or following the curated content conversation of experts in the industry to stay on top of where the future of the profession is going so one can pivot with it.

The Association for Talent Development's recent report, *Upskilling and Reskilling: Turning Disruption and Change into New Capabilities*, points out 44 percent of organizations are not providing upskill or reskill opportunities (ATD Research, 2018). Couple this with the World Economic Forum's *Future of Jobs Report* prediction that employees will require 101 additional days of learning by 2022 to address the upskill and reskill demands in the rapidly evolving workforce (Ratcheva & Leopold, 2018). This requires professionals to take initiative to prepare *themselves* for the emerging global labor market.

As a result of these pressures, the consumerization of learning has shaped how education is presented and accessed within the professional development industry. Consumer learners are hailed with urgent messages about what to learn now and next, which sources to trust, and how to join others on the skill quest. This means joining others' ranges from liking and subscribing, to enrolling on email lists, to purchasing a membership. Together this collective of consumer learners taking responsibility for their professional development present their own requirements as a market. Oliver Craddock, CEO of Mind Tools, calls out five demands of the self-directed, self-improvement learner: (1) training when I need it; (2) quality resources I can trust; (3) lots of different formats, please; (4) give me broad options to pick from; and (5) I want total control over my training and learning (Craddock, 2018). These demands are now a well-documented consumer behavior: *I want what I want when I want it in a convenient format.*

Pursuing one's personal and professional interests takes many forms in the globally networked digital-mediated infosphere. Short-form content has become a gateway to larger learning commitments, as well as a means for incremental learning at the point of need. The intrinsically motivated learner must simply turn on their device and tap a query to access an entire ecosystem of succinct problem-solving resources they can leverage for personal or professional development. These micro assets may stand alone as information for some, but when applied toward one's personal or professional goals, they become fuel for learning and development.

Let us explore the landscape of three common contexts for accessing microlearning for personal and professional development, and then reflect upon how this impacts how to design impactful micro assets to serve this constituency.

Three Common Contexts

Some who participate in microlearning for personal and professional development may not even be aware they are because it is as effortless as asking a question and finding a solution. What the consumer learner does with that solution determines whether it serves as information or learning. If learners reflect upon the content, integrate it into their knowledge structure and apply it, the learning cycle has been engaged. Not all questions require a formal training response and not all curious questioners begin their quest seeking to pay for the answer. We turn to

Google, our handheld answer machine, to survey the options (Bersin, 2014). A search on how to invest money for retirement will return a variety of resources such as YouTube videos, magazine money quizzes, microtutorials from investment firms, a finance expert's podcast, to professional associations offering a variety of content and credentials in financial planning. How does one choose? It more than not, depends upon the axis of *free to fee* and the gradient of reputable expertise of the source ranging from the informal offerings of the Info Industry to the formal continuing education programs facilitated by Professional Associations. Three common contexts for accessing microlearning for personal and professional development have emerged and continue to evolve in the competitive realm of Business-To-Consumer (B2C) learning. They are: (1) Info Industry, (2) Expert Industry, and (3) Professional Associations.

Info Industry

More than half of the global population is online, equating to approximately four billion users engaging in the commerce of goods and content (Evans, 2018). YouTube alone claims two billion logged in users globally each month (YouTube, 2019), and according to Pew Research, captures approximately 73 percent of U.S. adults, more than Facebook (Perrin & Anderson, 2019). Alongside music and unboxing videos, education and how-to's are among the most frequently accessed content categories on YouTube. This represents a lot of content providers and consumer learners connecting to solve problems – everything from lifting weights and unclogging drains to Articulate 360 triggers and conflict resolution.

Granted, microlearning is not restricted to video. Combining WordPress, Tumblr, and other large platforms, there are an estimated 600 million blogs globally (Petrov, 2020) and over 1,000,000 podcasts (Winn, 2020). While education does not dominate the podcast medium, if you were someone looking to start a new business, you would likely access blog and podcast content. Online articles are also ever present and challenge their print counterparts for reads.

Information is clearly ubiquitous. When professionals desire a quick take on a question, there are numerous free resources available upon a click. But who is producing this content? The answer to that question is, anyone can. Social media has given rise to generations of individuals who are both creators and consumers of content, and channel, or category-based, learning online is frequently the first stop in answering a learning question (Bersin, 2018).

Many participate in the Info Industry, but chief among them are individuals with niche content expertise and corporations engaged in content marketing. While anecdotally there are individuals who simply desire to create community around a content, there is money to be made in content sharing. Transitioning from casual sharer to paid content creator is as simple as an affiliate link. Sponsorships, ads and Patreon, an online service allowing content creators to offer membership subscriptions to exclusive content and community, allow individuals to create a content business. Economics then becomes a factor in what content is prepared and how it is shaped to meet audience demands in the B2C consumer learner industry.

Corporations also figure prominently in social media and blogging micro content. According to the Content Marketing Institute, B2C marketers leveraging content seek to primarily create brand awareness (84 percent), educate audiences (75 percent), and build creditability (65 percent) (Rose, 2019). Delivering value through micro-content helps them build the critical currency of trust necessary to convert a prospect to a customer. For example, after learning so much about social media marketing from Sprout Social and earning some quick wins, how hard would you actually look for another service provider in your comparison shopping? It starts out being useful how-to content, but when the provider helps you realize how their solutions could level up your returns, you are probably farther into the customer journey than you realize.

Regardless the source and one's attitudes toward self-serve content on a spectrum from pure opinion to substantiated fact, the Info Industry serves a daily potluck of easy-to-access micro content that may contribute to self-serve learning outcomes in personal and professional development. As instructors and learning designers, knowing your learners will (and likely already are) accessing this content, how will your designs account for the influence of the Info Industry in formal and informal learning?

As you answer this question for your microlearning content targeting professional development learner consumers, consider the learner motives accessing informal micro-content as well as provider motives of Info Industry contributors in competition with your offerings.

Learner motives: Access free short-form resources to answer a question, solve a problem, and assess what knowledge and skill they may wish to pursue next.

Provider motives: Drive engagement, grow a following, generate brand recognition, and ultimately deliver a call to action ranging from like and subscribe to buy our product.

Expert Industry

According to a Civic Enterprises report, a bipartisan ideas company specializing in innovative initiatives at the cutting edge of domestic, economic, and international policy, there are now approximately 1.5 million experts sharing their expertise for a living in an estimated billion-dollar industry (Civic Enterprises, 2018). This represents as many as the combined total active Uber and Lyft drivers, they report. While this insight is groundbreaking, it only accounts for experts who are networked through an expertise broker, matching experts to companies with a problem they want to solve such as Gerson Lehrman Group (GLG). GLG experts include consultants, scientists, executives, and specialized professionals such as physicians and lawyers serving on a freelance basis.

In addition to these experts, there is an untallied number of authors, speakers, coaches, consultants, and online trainers independently marketing their programs and services. One of the primary means of marketing their expertise is through valuable online content. Consider Brendon Burchard's extensive video library on productivity and high performance. Consider Deepak Chopra's free meditation guides or Brooke Castillo's podcast on life coaching. Countless other experts utilize social media channels, blogs, and learning management systems to deliver freemium content, sharing their expertise as a means to attract their ideal clientele and for those prospects to get to know them, and most importantly, the problem they solve and the results they deliver. Their content may be presented side-by-side in a Google search along with their Info Industry counterparts. What is different is their level of expertise and hard-won experience backing the content they offer. Blog tips on easing hip pain may lead you to an offer to work with a trainer who specializes in hip mobility. Videos on mastering your personal budget may lead to an offer from a personal finance coach. Infographics and Facebook live interactions on scaling your small business may lead to an offer from a seven-figure entrepreneur. All entail quality micro-content paving the way to an opportunity to continue learning directly from the expert to achieve a personal or professional result.

Micro how-to and personal improvement content appeals to the consumer learner who does not just want to hear from the person who trains on the learning result they desire, but someone who has actually solved the problems and achieved the results they desire. They want direct access to the expert, and more than ever, this level of expertise is available not only to corporations seeking expert consultation through expert networks like GLG but to individuals for their personal and professional development. The gateway for many consumer learners who connect with an expert is through microlearning.

Experts serve their constituencies and attract new clients by teaching the initial steps toward a goal prospects want to achieve through short-form learning. There are no traps, just an invitation to buy a ticket for the full-length trip to that ultimate result. Because they have lived the journey and taken so many others to the destination in demand, they serve as a powerful force for learning in the personal and professional development market. As instructors and learning designers, how might you partner with experts to elevate the expertise allure and direct-from-expert quality of your training offerings?

As you consider your answer, think about the learner motives accessing expertise-backed micro-content as well as provider motives of Expert Industry contributors in partnership with your offerings.

Learner motives: Access a solution via learning from someone who has direct experience solving the problem or achieving a particular result.

Provider motives: Grow a client-based business by providing their expertise via micro-content to qualify them as a respectable service provider the consumer learner prospect will now know, like, and trust.

Professional Association Industry

There's a common refrain in the professional development industry: *there's an association for everything*. While AARP, NRA, and AMA, that are among the most recognized, professional associations serve nearly every industry from entrepreneurs (EO), to criminal defense lawyers (NACDL), to Minnesota soybean growers (MSGA); professional associations are membership organizations that exist to provide education, advocacy, networking, industry standards, and practice resources to advance the professionals and industries they represent. It's challenging to tally the number of professional associations in the U.S. as the federal government tracks charitable and philanthropic nonprofits as a group, but according to ASAE's Power of Associations Study, at last reporting the IRS recognized 1.2 million 501(c3) and (c6) organizations. In addition, according to the same source, there are approximately 64,000 trade associations. Since trade associations serve corporations as their members vs. individuals seeking personal or professional development, we'll focus upon professional associations and from this point forward in the chapter refer to them as "associations" or "membership organizations."

The American Society of Association Executives (ASAE) serves as the membership organization for the association profession, representing executive directors and their staff. According to ASAE, "each year, associations provide millions of American workers across every industry and state with critical post-college skills training required for professional success and career advancement" (Power of Associations Research). This programming entails conferences, training programs, centralized curricula, and certifications. Often these learning programs are accredited as continuing education (CE). Regulated industries such as medicine, law, and finance must meet rigorous accreditation standards specific to their industry to offer credit-bearing learning for their constituents to maintain their certification and licensure necessary to practice.

In 2016, ASAE Foundation established a multi-phase, future-focused research initiative entitled ASAE ForesightWorks to provide a longitudinal environmental scan that would reveal the change drivers for the association profession. The first 41 drivers were released March 2018, among them microlearning (ASAE Foundation, 2018). The work lays out a case for investing in microlearning programming as part of a comprehensive professional development learning portfolio.

While there has been interest among associations in developing microlearning, a few conditions have made this simple ask a challenging task. First, producing professional microlearning assets driving learning outcomes within an established curriculum thoughtfully connected to the current learning portfolio can be resource intensive. How will they recoup the expense when the Info Industry and Expert Industry have trained consumer learners that microlearning access is often free? Second, membership organizations by nature reserve their best content behind a pay wall for members only. Even if they adopted a business model to monetize microlearning, how can they earn widespread engagement with it if only members within their proprietary platforms can see it? And finally, perhaps one of the greatest challenges is the tension with accrediting bodies and industry regulators who have historically viewed microlearning as an informal learning engagement versus a training opportunity tied to measurable outcomes that may offer formal credit. Couple that with the member preference to spend precious learning minutes on programming that will earn formal CE credit toward industry requirements they are incentivized to meet. But the tides on these challenges are turning.

Exemplars are emerging among associations mastering microlearning challenges within their market. The Association of Fundraising Professionals (AFP) has circumvented the deep-pocket expense and the pay wall issues by crafting a library of microlearning videos produced and submitted by members. A selection of the library is free for the public to discover while the balance remains behind the member paywall requiring a log-in to access. Similarly, while the American Academy of Neurology's NeuroBytes is produced for members, a selection of full-length examples is discoverable on their YouTube channel poised to reach a broader audience.

Continuing professional education for Certified Public Accountants (CPAs) is accredited and tracked by the credit hour. CPAs must collect a minimum number of credits to maintain a license to practice depending upon their requirements within their state. For example, in Minnesota, CPAs earn 120 CPEs over a three-year period in approved formats within prescribed technical and non-technical fields of study. Because of the rise in prominence of microlearning for in-time learning and performance support, state-based CPA associations have advocated on behalf of their members to revise accreditation standards to include microlearning as an option; the first to succeed was Ohio (Athitakis, 2018). When the Ohio Society of Certified Public Accountants (OSCPA) began advocating for short-format learning in 2014, the Accountancy Board of Ohio only accepted learning delivered in at least one-hour or more increments. Now OSCPA offers a Quick Byte series of ten-minute accredited learning modules, and thirteen additional state CPA societies are following suit (Athitakis, 2018) Other examples of microlearning making its way into regulated industries include the American Board of Anesthesiology MOCA Minute® and the American Nephrology Nurses Association CExpress programs.

Microlearning offered by associations is positioned to serve several strategic roles within the learning portfolio beyond curated content and quick credits. As more associations experiment with micro assets as point-of-need toolkits, priming and reinforcement within formal learning pathways, micro-credentialing, and peer learning exchanges, microlearning is at the ready to be galvanized for just-in-time expert vetted learning.

Learners and Professional Association microlearning providers approach professional development within this market context with different motives than the Info or Expert Industries. How do these motives impact how you may participate or partner within this context?

Learner motives: Access vetted microlearning options with the lens of professional development within their industry of interest.

Provider motives: Advance the professional workforce they represent through a variety of opportunities within their learning portfolio, which increasingly includes microlearning.

Designing Microlearning for Professional Development

The proliferation of online content for personal and professional development has shifted the spotlight on microlearning design because outside of the formal classroom and office hours, it is commonly how the public acquires new knowledge, and sometimes, skills. But given these microlearning opportunities are not assigned by an instructor or corporate training division, designs must account for the requirements of self-initiated learning. One lens is to view target learners as a customer segment; in order to win engagement in microlearning content, you must understand your market.

Let's examine five *asks* beneath the microlearning trend and how they inform the opportunities and constraints for PD content providers as you consider positioning microlearning within this market.

The Ask Beneath the Trend

As colleagues in this book have shared, microlearning is not a new concept, but it has adapted through new technologies to become an important gateway of learning. Its endurance as a format tells us microlearning is not a flash-in-the-pan fad. In fact, there are several key asks beneath it.

First, modern empowered learners require *access*. Microlearning is available in the palm of one's hand, or whichever device is most convenient at the moment a question arises. Well-produced microlearning is an enjoyable experience on any device. Whether the leaner is in the breakroom, boardroom, train, museum, home or beach, learners expect to be able to get at a small-format solution with their device of choice.

Question for designers: What components of curricula or priority content can be made freely accessible across devices? What experience design considerations must be part of your screen optimization production process?

Second, modern empowered learners require microlearning at the *point of need*. They seek on-demand immediacy. It is just enough, just in time. The power of microlearning is accessing single objective training and immediately applying it within the context of practice. It is the right-sized support for the task at hand. The learner rapidly transitions from consuming content to trying it on and refining their practice.

Question for designers: What keywords are your learner prospects using to describe their problems or ideal solution so you can title and tag your work to be present at the point of need?

Third, modern empowered learners are seeking *just enough* to take the next step. For example, when creating a branched interaction in Rise for the first time, a designer may opt for a few YouTube demos before enrolling in a full-length seminar simply because of the constraints they are operating within. They need just enough right now to accomplish a task given their project deadline. Their self-initiated process of finding prospective solutions paired with trying and refining their applied approaches to the design problem right in front of them, advance their skill far faster than sixty minutes of lecture listening. Not to mention, not all learning questions require lengthy formal training.

Question for designers: When creating microlearning assets, what parameters can ensure the end product is just enough and no more to meet the learning objective?

Fourth, modern empowered learners expect microlearning will solve a problem. Naturally, all learning solves problems by either closing a knowledge gap or improving a skill so participants can be or do something new or better. Micro assets that do not solve a problem are information, not learning. Clearly, an intrinsically motivated learner can access a piece of information and initiate their own learning cycle around it, transitioning it from purely information to a part of their learning journey. But if providers intend learning is the ultimate goal of the personal and professional content they are producing, they must create it with solving a specific problem in mind.

Question for designers: How can we ensure our microlearning assets clearly articulate the problem learners seek to solve, connecting the dots between learner questions to solutions?

Fifth, modern empowered learners expect to access micro-content for *discovery learning*. When someone wants to learn how to pin curl their hair, they may spend hours exploring different takes on achieving the look to find the just-right approach for the desired aesthetic for their hair texture. When someone wants to grow their online business, they may invest weeks in the wealth of content available on social media marketing, sales funnels, optimizing conversions, and all the technology one must master to execute skillfully. Before committing to buying a course, working with an expert, or joining an association, the modern empowered learner expects to conduct their own investigation of a topic of interest through readily available microlearning. Discovery learning assists in refining the problem they may want solved through a formal learning opportunity.

Question for designers: How can you position your microlearning library to become the rabbit hole for discovery learning? How can you position your micro-content to then invite learners to invest in the next step with you through a formal learning engagement?

PD Provider Constraints and Opportunities

Microlearning functions beautifully for readiness, elaboration, practice, reinforcement, and performance support in formal learning. However, the consumer behaviors of learners accessing microlearning for personal and professional development crisscross the informal and formal learning boundaries. For micro-content providers in the Info, Expert, and Professional Association Industries, this introduces unique constraints and opportunities.

Constraint: Microlearning in the personal and professional development market is not required training, so it may be consumed out of sequence and out of context resulting in inefficiency and misconception.

Opportunity: The PD provider may choose to visually depict how this micro piece fits into a larger curriculum and offer their learning service as a solution to filling in that larger picture efficiently to achieve the larger result.

Constraint: Because microlearning in the personal and professional development market in large part functions as a giant self-serve buffet, self-selected microlearning may ultimately address a symptom and not the core problem.

Opportunity: Incorporate self-assessment into your microlearning cache to illuminate blind sides and open an opportunity to recommend solutions based upon the assessment results.

Constraint: Short-format learning is inherently limited because it is required to be succinct.

Opportunity: Assist learners in realizing that microlearning is a step, not the journey, toward a larger learning outcome they are seeking.

Constraint: Microlearning in the personal and professional development market often addresses hot topics or trending issues – it is not evergreen and requires frequent review and updates to remain relevant.

Opportunity: The great news is microlearning is easy to update. Create a review workflow that flags short shelf-life content and master a repeatable production format to push out fresh and timely micro modules.

Constraint: Just chunking existing long-form learning content does not result in a pleasing or popular microlearning experience; getting started creating a successful microlearning initiative can be labor and resource intensive.

Opportunity: Begin curating what you already have created and assess what gaps need to be filled by new microlearning opportunities. Share intentional and timely curated groupings of content around solving a common learning question with your target learners. Creating stockpile resource libraries may sound wise, but remember most learners start with Google and not your library to answer a question. When creating a library of micro-content, help learners quickly find what they are looking for through robust browse/search capabilities and intuitive organization to win their respect and return visit.

Constraint: In the personal and professional development market, it is challenging to measure the effectiveness of microlearning.

Opportunity: Metrics should be based upon your strategy and expected outcomes. For informal microlearning, that may mean likes, subscribes, comments, downloads, plays, and call-to-action response rates. For formal microlearning, that may mean utilizing an API like Tin Can, adding course evaluation questions directed at the utilization and effectiveness of the micro components, or selectively studying performance outcomes in the context of practice with an employer partner. While learning is the ultimate objective, there may be other metrics that signal microlearning content is considered valuable and is indeed used by consumer learners.

Constraint: Many accrediting bodies still do not allow credit for the microlearning format.

Opportunity: Leverage microlearning as an informal discovery vehicle that offers recommendations for deeper accredited learning; or, incorporate microlearning within an e-learning course or learning pathway which is accredited for total contact hours.

Summary and Next Steps

Effective microlearning begins with strategy, which informs the design crafted to deliver the promised results. The self-motivated consumer learner has created a market where PD providers must position their learning resources as a solution to a specific problem to win their engagement. While there are many contributors in this space, a majority of personal and professional development providers fall into three common contexts: Info Industry, Expert Industry, and Professional Association Industry. Each positions microlearning as a gateway to a call to action ranging from a like to a purchase of a product, service or membership. The consumerization of learning in personal and professional development in turn likely impacts learner expectations for academic and corporate training micro-content.

Because microlearning within this context may be in fact more influenced by content marketing than education standards, there is exciting experimentation in content delivery but a wide variation in the quality of content. Visual impact, tech aesthetics and click bait titles are tools for engagement, but not necessarily learning engagement. We rely on the discernment of consumer learners to select quality content, thus the appeal of expert produced and vetted micro programming. Design standards and best practices for the continuing education space widely accessible to informal microlearning producers would improve the overall quality and potentially consumer discernment. These standards should include recommendations for diversity, inclusion, and equity of access, producing and distributing microlearning.

The easy accessibility of technology and platforms to produce microlearning has made way for a creative explosion of digital how-to and educational content, the best of which can inspire learning design for both formal and informal engagements. Producers of content are also consumers; content consumers can easily select a social media platform and become producers. Microlearning is the right size, at the right time learning for intrinsically motivated individuals seeking to improve themselves or simply explore an area of interest. There is great potential yet to be explored for academic institutions, corporate training divisions, and associations to collaborate on vetted, industry specific microlearning initiatives assisting professionals as they navigate the complexities of a successful and satisfying career.

Discussion Questions

1. How does designing for a consumer-learner shift your microlearning instructional design choices and success measurement?
2. What opportunities for partnerships can you imagine bridging corporate or academic training to personal and professional development providers?
3. The quality of microlearning online for personal and professional development varies widely with no objective standards. What are the challenges and advantages of free-range content sharing for B2C learning?
4. What additional constraints and/or opportunities do you notice for microlearning PD providers in the current learning market?
5. What measures can be put into place to ensure equity of access to online microlearning?

References

American Society of Association Executives (ASAE). Power of Associations Research. (n.d.). www.thepowerofa.org/power-of-a-research.

ASAE Research Foundation. (2018). ASAE ForesightWorks: Content, learning and knowledge action set. https://foundation.asaecenter.org/foundation-home/research/research-methodologies/env-scanning-research-program/asae-foresightworks-action-sets.

ATD Research. (June2018). Upskilling and reskilling: Turning disruption and change into new capabilities. www.td.org/research-reports/upskilling-and-reskilling.

Athitakis, M. (January–February2018). Microlearning: Responding to new learning styles. *Associations Now.* www.asaecenter.org/resources/articles/an_magazine/2018/january-february/microlearning-responding-to-new-learning-styles.

Bersin, J. (2014). Meet the modern learner: Engaging the overwhelmed, distracted, and impatient employee. Bersin by Deloitte.

Bersin, J. (July 8, 2018). A new paradigm for corporate training: Learning in the flow of work. *Josh Bersin Insights on Corporate Talent, Learning and HR Technology.* https://joshbersin.com/2018/06/a-new-paradigm-for-corporate-training-learning-in-the-flow-of-work/.

Bersin, J, Zao-Sanders, M. (February 19, 2019). Make learning part of everyday work. *Harvard Business Review.* https://hbr.org/2019/02/making-learning-a-part-of-everyday-work.

Campanella, E. (July 6, 2018). To succeed in the changing job market, we must embrace lifelong learning. *World Economic Forum.* www.weforum.org/agenda/2018/07/the-cognitive-limits-of-lifelong-learning.

Civic Enterprises. (May 24, 2018). For up to 1.5 million experts in the little-known expert economy, sharing wisdom is the next great gig: First comprehensive study of billion-dollar expert industry examines implications and disruptive potential of fastest-growing professional learning sector. *Business Wire.* www.businesswire.com/news/home/20180524005337/en/1.5-Million-Experts-Little-Known-Expert-Economy-Sharing.

Craddock, O. (March–April2018). Managing the demands of today's consumer learner. *Training Industry Magazine.* https://trainingindustry.com/magazine/mar-apr-2018/managing-the-demands-of-todays-consumer-learner.

Evans, M. (December 17, 2018). 5 stats you need to know about the digital consumer in 2019. *Forbes.* www.forbes.com/sites/michelleevans1/2018/12/17/5-stats-you-need-to-know-about-the-digital-consumer-in-2019/#2e8b1bdd636b.

Perrin, A., & Anderson, M. (April 10, 2019). Share of U.S. adults using social media, including Facebook, is mostly unchanged since 2018. *Pew Research.* www.pewresearch.org/fact-tank/2019/04/10/share-of-u-s-adults-using-social-media-including-facebook-is-mostly-unchanged-since-2018/.

Petrov, C. (July 25, 2020). How many blogs are there and do they make money in 2020. *Techjury.* https://techjury.net/blog/how-many-blogs-are-there/#gref.

Ratcheva, V. S., & Leopold, T. (September 17, 2018). 5 things to know about the future of jobs. *World Economic Forum.* www.weforum.org/agenda/2018/09/future-of-jobs-2018-things-to-know.

Rose, R. (December 11, 2019). 2020 B2C content marketing: An excellent adventure. *Content Marketing Institute.* https://contentmarketinginstitute.com/2019/12/b2c-content-marketing-research-2020/.

Winn, Ross. (April 21, 2020). 2020 podcast stats & facts (New research from Apr 2020). *Podcast Insights.* www.podcastinsights.com/podcast-statistics.

YouTube. (n.d.). YouTube for Press. www.youtube.com/about/press.

PART IV
Microlearning Today and Tomorrow

11

CREATING MICROLEARNING OBJECTS WITHIN SELF-DIRECTED MULTIMODAL LEARNING CONTEXTS

Jako Olivier

Introduction

Learning is becoming increasingly multimodal in terms of individual preferences, interactions, modes of instruction, and delivery at the course and institutional level. Accordingly, technology and educational needs require different modes of interaction and learning. Within this dynamic context there is a need for student-centered, self-directed learning (SDL) (Bosch, Mentz, & Goede, 2019; Mentz, Bailey, Verster, & Breed, 2018) where students become active creators of knowledge. Often this sharing of knowledge through reusable learning objects happens as systematic micro-sharing (Aitchanov, Satabaldiyev, & Latuta, 2013). Thus, the reusability of knowledge though microlearning objects will be a focus of this chapter.

In this chapter, learning is regarded as being multimodal as the learning itself is a process of meaning-making (cf. Kress & Pachler, 2007, p. 145) within a context of different modes of communication, learning, and delivery. Therefore, *multimodal learning* can be defined as an approach to education where individual modal preferences, communication through different modalities, as well as learning, teaching, and delivery by means of different modes are considered. It is proposed that microlearning objects are not only delimited by duration, outcomes, or content, but also in terms of semiotic and semantic value. In other words, microlearning objects should be considered in terms of the meaning they convey. These objects in themselves become communicative acts.

The idea of learning in smaller units is not new, and Hanshaw and Hanson (2019) trace it back to the work of Dewey, who presented a philosophical framework in terms of learning through the use of smaller chunks. Moreover, Kapp and Defelice (2019) observe that using smaller meaningful chunks for learning has been done for centuries. Additionally, publications on microlearning from the past 15 years continued to illustrate the importance of this approach, especially in terms of changes in technology and the needs of students and life-long learners. Yet, within a context where anyone can be an author, the ease of creation and openness requires a critical approach to content, whether it is microcontent or not, the reliability of information needs to be interrogated consistently.

This chapter provides a short illustrative case study to explain the main themes discussed and further, aims to provide practical steps to guide the construction of learning opportunities that facilitate effective student self-directed multimodal learning through microlearning object creation for teaching and learning. To this end, the chapter will include a conceptual literature review of pertinent scholarship on communal constructivism, contribution-oriented pedagogy, self-directed multimodal learning, and microlearning.

Theoretical Framework

Self-directed multimodal learning will be analyzed through the learning theory lens of communal constructivism, which also links closely with contribution-oriented pedagogy within a constructivist pedagogy, for which the concept of "generative learning activities" (Collis & Moonen, 2009, p. 328) is central. Despite the use of the teacher-centered word "pedagogy," student-centered learning is regarded as the aim of multimodal learning, and consequently, of self-directed learning, which in contemporary learning environments takes place in a multimodal manner. For the purposes of this chapter, *pedagogy* relates to the process and the practice of teaching. Buchem and Hamelmann (2010) also emphasize this student-centeredness in terms of microlearning activities where such activities should be planned as either learner-driven or even being user-generated. According to Holmes et al. (2001), communal constructivism also emphasizes the role of the student, as it "is about empowering the learner[s] to allow them to reclaim a role in their own education" (p. 6).

Communal Constructivism

An ideal is for students to not only create content but also do that within the context of a community and for the benefit of a community. Communal constructivism builds specifically on the constructivist and social constructivist learning theories, where students are central to the construction of knowledge. Ershler and Stabile (2015, p. 6) observe that "[c]onstructivism requires the learner to engage in interpretation, organization, and inference creation about knowledge, with the cognitive structures they have previously constructed." Additionally, Collis and Moonen (2009) state that in terms of constructivism, the need exists for learners to actively construct meaning in order to learn, and that it also implies active learning, setting goals, and self-directed and authentic learning.

This approach to learning also resonates with the aims of self-directed learning, and as Mentz et al. (2018, pp. 171–172) observe that "[t]hrough social construction of knowledge, meaning should thus emerge for active participants." However, in terms of communal constructivism, the focus shifts to not just creating, but also sharing. Therefore, in this context, students take charge for their own learning, but also ultimately for the community's learning.

The concept of communal constructivism is ascribed to Holmes et al. (2001, p. 1), referring to "an approach to learning in which students not only construct their own knowledge (constructivism) as a result of interacting with their environment (social constructivism), but are also actively engaged in the process of constructing knowledge *for* their learning community" [emphasis in the original]. Consequently, with a communal constructivist approach, every person who is part of such a community, learns from others in the community, and also contributes towards the learning resources of the community (Rothkrantz, 2016) Furthermore, Jones (2017) emphasizes that with communal constructivism, the focus is not on the individual learning from the environment, but rather on constructing knowledge for the sake of the community.

The link between constructivism and microlearning was clearly established by Mosel (2005). Buchem and Hamelmann (2010, p. 7) also note the importance of learners as producers of microcontent, observing that "[m]icrolearning materials should be actively co-produced, assembled and modified by learners." Thus, in terms of the scholarship around microlearning, communal constructivism can involve not only individuals using microcontent, but also individuals and communities creating them for communal use. A logical extension of the communal constructivist approach is a pedagogy that is contribution oriented. In this regard, the work by Mosel (2005) ties in with the basic tenets of communal constructivism as the focus is not just on creating knowledge but also the contributions made by the learners.

Contribution-Oriented Pedagogy

The learning process can actively involve contributions or inputs from learners in order to avoid a teacher-centered approach. In contribution-oriented pedagogy, as with self-directed learning, the focus is on the student, but here, the emphasis is on active communal participation. Collis and Moonen (2009, p. 327) observe that a contribution-oriented pedagogical approach where "students find, create, submit and/or share resources using a Web-based course-support environment is identified as a model particularly valuable for forms of online and computer-based learning." The important role of technology and the multimodal environment is, therefore, evident in terms of contribution-oriented pedagogy. Moreover, Collis and Moonen (2009, pp. 330–331) provide some highly relevant typical activities for contribution-oriented pedagogy in terms of different factual and reflective contributions.

Microlearning and the importance of a communal contribution-oriented approach also seems highly relevant in an online context where the ability to create knowledge has been democratized and made more open. The increase in the importance of so-called micro-content is attributed to an increase of online publishing by individuals (Mosel, 2005). However, "[w]ith personal publishing, it becomes more and more easy to generate and publish microcontent, based on one's personal, subjective view of the world" (Mosel, 2005, p. 2). In turn, this subjectivity emphasizes: the need for consumers of online content to be critical; the importance of information literacy; and by implication, the importance of metaliteracy (Mackey & Jacobson, 2011).

The focus on the learner as the content generator can be associated with Kress and Pachler's (2007, p. 141) view of the "fundamental shift in agency from broadcast to content generation." This view implies the importance of two-way or even polydirectional – or multidirectional – communication and learning. Consequently, in the approach to the learning environment and the broader pedagogy, a contribution-oriented view can potentially facilitate self-directed learning effectively in a multimodal context.

Self-Directed Multimodal Learning

In order to clarify the role of self-directed learning within the context of self-directed multimodal learning, the concept of self-directed learning needs to be more fully understood. Self-directed learning is defined by Knowles (1975, p. 18) as:

> a process in which individuals take the initiative, with or without the help of others, in diagnosing their learning needs, formulating learning goals, identifying human and material resources for learning, choosing and implementing appropriate learning strategies and evaluating learning outcomes.

Consequently, self-directed multimodal learning relates to the process where individuals are responsible for their own learning within the context and through the use of different modes of communication and learning.

The key to self-directed multimodal learning is the centrality and learning responsibility of the learner, but also the importance of resources. Mentz et al. (2018, p. 152) highlight the importance of self-directed learning within a context where there are constant and quick changes in technology, as well as information being available. Hence, in terms of self-directed learning, the multimodal learning context also requires availability of information and resources.

Self-directed learning has a long history (cf. Bosch et al., 2019, pp. 3–5), and several models have been constructed to explain this concept (cf. Bosch et al., 2019, pp. 6–21; Şentürk & Zeybek, 2019, pp. 153–157). Furthermore, research has shown that some teaching methods can foster self-directed learning, and this includes cooperative learning (cf. Bosch et al., 2019, pp. 25–26; Johnson &

Johnson, 2019), problem-based learning (cf. Bosch et al., 2019, p. 26), and process-oriented learning (cf. Bosch et al., 2019, pp. 27–28). Such methods can also be used to effectively employ microlearning objects. According to Buchem and Hamelmann (2010), microlearning can be supportive of self-directed lifelong learning in terms of the integration of short activities into a person's everyday activities.

The importance of self-directed learning in a microlearning context is clarified by Hug and Friesen (2007, p. 27), while building on Stephen Downes's views regarding self-directed learning (SDL). Insofar as with microlearning, "[t]he learner directs and decides the affiliations, links, contents, forms of guidance and direction (if any) that will be constitutive of the learning process – in some cases creating these him or herself," there might be "no pre-ordained structure, curricular, sequential or otherwise." Furthermore, Mosel (2005, p. 3) acknowledges that self-direction is emphasized through a view of learning where "[h]umans are not seen as recipients without any self-activity which could be determined by changes of their environment, inscribing cognitions into them" and where in fact, "they are seen as inventively active subjects (autopoietic) who create (the perception of) their environments through self-activity and the resulting constructions." Deniozou (2016) also showed how microlearning, by means of learning through games on mobile devices, can support self-directed learning.

Central to self-directed learning and resources is the fact that learners must be able to identify material resources to be used in the learning process. This aspect ties in well with microlearning as it facilitates greater content choices and flexibility for learners in terms of when it can be accessed (Burton-MacLeod, 2019, p. 7). Moreover, Burton-MacLeod (2019, p. 7) importantly notes, "[g]iving such agency to learners can help them personalize their learning and support their individual transfer experiences." For Buchem and Hamelmann (2010, p. 7), it is also significant that "[l]earning materials can be used as attachments or links to micro-content units to direct learners' attention to key topics and allow further exploration of the subject matter."

As the learner, within a self-directed learning context, is able to set specific learning goals, so too can the development of microlearning objects support specific goals. In this context, Burton-MacLeod (2019) highlights not only the affordances in terms of cognitive load, but also the focus in terms of setting a specific objective, that "microlearning design must be efficient and stream-lined for the chosen objective which can help to limit extraneous load" (p. 6). Yet, it should be noted, this object setting can also be facilitated throughout the self-directed learning process and not be necessarily connected with the specific microlearning object itself.

Multimodal Learning

The prominence of technology in learning contexts prompt learning facilitators to be aware of the opportunities and challenges of the multimodal environment.

In this chapter, self-directed learning is approached in the ubiquitous context of multimodal learning. In the context of microlearning, Kress and Pachler (2007, p. 143) observe that multimodality relates to the fact that "digital technologies allow content to be presented using a diverse range of systems of representation and a combination of different semiotic means of meaning-making." Freeman (2016, p. 7) also observes that "microlearning and technology are connected," and therefore, the different modes of delivery in the educational context play into the way learning, and specifically microlearning, is approached.

The type of mode, whether it relates to communication or the learning process, depends on the context, and in this regard, Jewitt (2013) is of the opinion that the way in which knowledge is represented, and can be experienced, is essential to enable understanding the process of knowledge construction. This aspect also relates to the choices regarding communicational modes, as well as the relevant technology. In terms of multimodal learning, microlearning is influenced by different modes of communication in terms of interactional multimodality and learning modes of delivery regarding instructional multimodality.

An essential element of self-directed learning is real-world relevance. In this regard, Bair and Bair (2018, p. 15) propose that "a key to the microlearning design is to engage the learners with a meaningful experience that implements some critical thinking elements." According to Burton-MacLeod (2019), microlearning allows for replicating reality and can make it possible to counter theoretical and passive learning through hands-on practices. Consequently, learners need to situate microlearning objects within specific real-world and practical contexts.

The multimodal nature of microlearning is emphasized by Hug and Friesen (2007) as they acknowledge the role of different media technologies for microlearning. Contribution-oriented pedagogy is also highly relevant in multimodal contexts as Collis and Moonen (2009, p. 329) note that, "[t]echnology is a critical tool in contribution-oriented activities in that it provides the affordances for contributing, sharing and reusing contributions so they are accessible to others over time or distance." Building on these affordances, the chapter now turns to the theoretical background of microlearning.

Microlearning

Different views exist in terms of what microlearning involves (Freeman, 2016; Hug & Friesen, 2007, p. 17; Zhang & Ren, 2011, p. 2024). Hanshaw and Hanson (2019, p. 150) further describe microlearning as, "a 'catchphrase' for a variety of new technologies and web applications used for learning using 'digital micro content.'" With sources associating it with informal learning (Buchem & Hamelmann, 2010; Deniozou, 2016; Giurgiu, 2017; Kapp & Defelice, 2019; Zhang & Ren, 2011), learning objects (Bair & Bair, 2018), and chunking (Bair & Bair, 2018), Kapp and Defelice (2019, p. 21) define microlearning as "an instructional unit that provides a short engagement in an activity intentionally designed to elicit a specific outcome from the participant." In addition, Hug and Friesen (2007, p. 18) refer to "microlearning in terms of special moments or episodes of learning while dealing with specific tasks or content, and engaging in small but conscious steps." Furthermore, such moments, processes or episodes may be different based on the specific pedagogy or media used (Hug & Friesen, 2007). Despite some differences in emphasis, there seem to be some common elements among the various definitions of microlearning which involve small learning objects, student engagement, and cohesion in terms of outcome and semantic content.

Furthermore, Emerson and Berge (2018, p. 126) define microlearning as "learning in short, focused bursts designed to meet specific knowledge outcomes," and they acknowledge that it is prevalent around us. While Göschlberger (2016, p. 514) describes microlearning as "short-term and informal learning activities using small, but self-explanatory learning resources that are available via Internet," Burton-MacLeod (2019, p. 6) defines the concept as "temporally short, stand-alone learning experiences that are designed to cover one to two actionable learning objectives." All three of these definitions emphasize the shortness of the learning unit, and in this regard, Kapp and Defelice (2019) provide an overview of the ideal duration for microlearning. Garbers (2018, p. 34) notes that in this context, "[l]earning content is presented in smaller digestible 'chunks' (micro-content) and displayed as steps." Interestingly, this definition also includes a reference to some processes within the microlearning objects.

Different terms are used to refer to the resources employed in microlearning. This includes: *microlearning objects* (Kapp & Defelice, 2019; Skalka & Drlík, 2017), *snippets* (Khan, 2019), *microlearning units* (Bair & Bair, 2018; Deniozou, 2016), *bite-sized content* (De Gagne et al., 2019), *instructional units* (Kapp & Defelice, 2019), and *microcontent* (Buchem & Hamelmann, 2010; De Gagne et al., 2019; Deniozou, 2016; Freeman, 2016; Garbers, 2018; Giurgiu, 2017; Zhang & Ren, 2011). Central to microlearning is the concept of *snippets,* and Khan (2019, p. 278) describes this as "quick and meaningful solutions to training environments." Furthermore, Khan distinguishes between informational and instructional snippets. In this context, *informational snippets* can be utilized to share quick bits of information with a group," while instructional snippets pertain to learning objects that could be employed to specifically teach something (Khan, 2019, p. 278). Despite these definitions emphasizing a teaching-centered approach, microlearning objects can also have potential within a learner and learning-centered context. In a contribution-oriented pedagogy context, the term "product" is also used (Collis & Moonen, 2009, p. 329). For the sake of consistency, this chapter will use the term *microlearning objects.*

Microlearning has also been researched in different contexts including mobile learning (Deniozou, 2016; Garbers, 2018; Kress & Pachler, 2007), online learning (De Gagne et al., 2019; Hanshaw & Hanson, 2019), through social media such as

Twitter (Aitchanov et al., 2013), and even learning by means of videos (Ahmad, 2017; Dessì, Fenu, Marras, & Recupero, 2019; Olivier, 2019). The use of microlearning objects can also be influenced through learning analytics (Dessì et al., 2019).

Despite some functional overlap, it is essential to distinguish between what can be considered a microlearning object and a learning object. Specific sources, such as Hanshaw and Hanson (2019), use learning objects within the context of microlearning. According to Bennett and McGee (2005, p. 15), learning objects "are designed to function as asynchronous learning resources delivered through distributed learning environments such as Learning/Course Management Systems," while Wiley (2002, p. 6) uses the broader definition of "any digital resource that can be reused to support learning." Consequently, the particular size of a microlearning object distinguishes it clearly from a generic learning object. Kapp and Defelice (2019) even consider sharable content objects (SCO) in the context of microlearning. Emerson and Berge (2018, p. 128) describe microlearning "as a strategy that can help deliver the right information to the right learners, at the right level of detail and at the precise moment they need it." This view of microlearning suggests that it can take on many different guises. In this regard, Burton-MacLeod (2019, p. 6) that microlearning can take the form of "short videos, to job aids, quizzes with feedback or case studies." Importantly, microlearning not only relates to content but also micro-interactions (cf. Garbers, 2018, p. 82).

Promoting Self-Directed Multimodal Learning Through Microlearning Object Creation

As mentioned above, the focus of this chapter is not merely on microlearning but specifically on the use of microlearning objects within the context of self-directed multimodal learning. With the aforementioned literature overview in mind, this section proposes practical recommendations for effective microlearning object creation designed to promote learner engagement through self-directed multimodal learning. To facilitate self-directed learning in multimodal contexts, the use of microlearning objects can create potential opportunities for learners to choose resources themselves in the process of taking charge of their own learning. For example, for facilitators of learning, this may imply packing and subdividing resources into thematically cohesive ways in the learning management system. From this perspective, Hug and Friesen (2007) are of the opinion that microlearning is limited to small or very small units of topics with a narrow scope. Apart from being able to create new learning objects, students should also be able to determine whether existing learning objects cannot perhaps be reused and adapted with adequate acknowledgement and when licensing allows. In this regard, learners need to take charge, in a self-directed manner, of creating resources or selecting from existing resources. In addition, on a semantic level, complex content can be reduced to smaller objects that share semantic content and has coherence and cohesion. In terms of reuse, the modes of delivery also need to be considered and the creation of a new microlearning object may require a form of intersemiotic translation where, for example, written content is converted to visual material.

Some sources on microlearning assume an approach that is very teacher and teaching centered. This approach may imply that learners should gain knowledge from the microlearning objects passively. This view is described by Baumgartner (2013, p. 6) as Learning I or "to absorb knowledge" as in this context, it is "the teachers' responsibility to transfer this knowledge into the student's mind as easily as possible providing and helping the student to use well known cognitive strategies." Learning is contrasted with Learning II or "to acquire knowledge," where learning is regarded as an active process, and Learning III where the aim is "to construct knowledge." It is the active engagement by learners with learning objects that is supported in this chapter. Bair and Bair (2018, p. 15) state that "[t]he learner should acquire a concept from the program and perform or simulate a simple task using what they just learned" and that microlearning can employ a "taster effect" in order to be "filling knowledge gaps" (Bair & Bair, 2018, p. 14). This implies active engagement on behalf of the learner. Consequently, the use of microlearning objects must, as much as possible, be considered part of an active learning process where learners not only use microlearning objects, but also critically engage with such objects in order to determine the relevance and reliability of the content.

How microlearning objects are stored and curated is also important as it would determine how easily resources can be accessed. Emerson and Berge (2018, p. 128) link microlearning with knowledge management. They observe, "storing micro-learning interventions in an indexed and searchable information repository, such as a learning management system or Intranet, is an obvious connection to knowledge management …" They warn however, that if users "… cannot efficiently and effectively locate the required bits and bytes of information that microlearning can offer, then microlearning falls short as a successful learning strategy." Collis and Moonen (2009, p. 329) highlight the importance of using a repository by stating:

> Given the outcomes of the collaborative work of students, and the storage capacity of the Web-based system used as the communal repository, the results of collaborative work can be used to expand the original learning resources not only directly for the other students in a course, but also for students in other circumstances and in other time frames.

Kapp and Defelice (2019, p. 25) also note the importance of using a resource library. Facilitators of learning, therefore, need to carefully plan the storage and curation of microlearning objects. In fact, this is actually something that should be considered at an institutional level in order to ensure quality and consistency. In addition, when it comes to learner-generated content, there might also be copy-right or even confidentiality issues when context-specific details are included in content. In such cases, storage of microlearning content might have to be maintained securely. As a result, another important aspect to consider in terms of microlearning objects is that learners and facilitators need to be aware of the copyright implications when reusing existing resources combined with how licensing can be used to determine the future use and limitations of created objects. Subsequently, the *Creative Commons* licensing is one tool that provides a universally acceptable and fairly easy way of indicating restrictions and possibilities with objects. Therefore, it is essential that both facilitators of learning and learners be aware of licensing and how it can be used by them in the creation of micro-learning objects.

Building on the research by Dessì et al. (2019), learning analytics can provide data towards constructing adaptive systems where appropriate microlearning objects can be suggested to students to support their self-directed multimodal learning process. The approach by Dessì et al. (2019) has demonstrated that there is potential in a system where a large number of videos can be indexed through a data mining process and informed recommendations be made to learners. Burton-MacLeod (2019, p. 61) also successfully employed microlearning in a manner which allowed for interaction and learner-led decision-making, which included responsive aspects, as well as elements of cueing and feedback. Therefore, as much as possible, when employing self-directed multimodal learning with the use of microlearning objects, the learning should be customized to learners' needs. Ideally, adaptive learning systems can be employed in this regard, as dividing learning content into smaller objects allows for easier access to more manageable parts in terms of revision or extension as the learners' needs arise.

Additionally, microlearning is often associated with personal learning environments (PLEs) (cf. Buchem & Hamelmann, 2010; Giurgiu, 2017). In this regard, Buchem and Hamelmann (2010) note that microlearning can be included in PLEs. Yet, it is essential to regard microlearning not in isolation, but also as being a part of a wider learning ecosystem (Kapp & Defelice, 2019). So microlearning can be useful in informal learning contexts where microlearning object repositories are made openly available. However, the affordances in more structured activities in the learning ecosystem are also evident. Therefore, the process around microlearning is important as will become evident in the next section.

Microlearning Object Creation

The use and creation of microlearning objects do not only require the development of the microlearning objects themselves, but also the addition of a supportive context and learning process. To this end, Mosel (2005, p. 8) observes, it is, "not only microcontent itself, but also its contextualization through learner-centered approaches, discussion through trackbacks or commentaries, and 'soft' object metadata which contribute to an understanding of microlearning and provide insights for implementing personal publishing systems in (educational) institutions." The competence spiral by Baumgartner (2013) also provides a useful educational taxonomy for planning and designing interactions in an educational setting. Buchem and Hamelmann (2010, p. 6) state, "[d]idactical design of microlearning is not only about design of microcontent but it is also about designing microlearning activities based on microcontent and resulting in microcontent." While Buchem and Hamelmann (2010, pp. 6–7) list five important design principles for microcontent that include format, focus, autonomy, structure, and addressability, Kapp and Defelice (2019, pp. 84–152) also provide detailed information regarding how a microlearning strategy can be created, as well as how microlearning can be planned, designed, and implemented.

To achieve self-directed multimodal learning through microlearning and object creation, collaboration among learners is important. Therefore, opportunities for learners to work together must be created. However, collaboration in itself might not be sufficient and learners still need to contribute effectively. In this regard, Collis and Moonen (2009) note that through collaboration learners can relate with each other to create and develop content that is meaningful, not only to themselves, but also authentically to others. In this regard, learners can collaborate in the process of creating microlearning objects. However, on another level a form of peer review can also be useful in ensuring good quality in terms of the created objects. Online collaborative spaces such as wikis or Google Docs can be useful in this context, unless the particular learning management system used has a sufficient collaboration space available.

In considering the recommendations from this chapter as described in this section, the main tenets are summarized in Figure 11.1 (see p. 000).

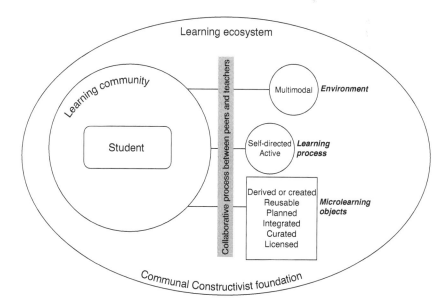

FIGURE 11.1 Self-directed multimodal learning through microlearning object creation

When developing self-directed multimodal learning opportunities, facilitators of learning need to be aware of three important variables: (1) the environment, (2) the learning process, and (3) the microlearning objects themselves. As the environment can be multimodal in terms of individual preferences, interaction, instruction, and the institution, the microlearning objects and learning processes need to be adapted to the specific modal needs of the learners. The learning process should ideally be driven by the requirements of self-directed learning where the learners take charge in terms of the goals, resources, and processes, as well as evaluating the learning that has taken place. Finally, the microlearning objects themselves may be different depending on the wider learning ecosystem and the needs of the learning community and learners involved. Importantly, with the aim of creating a communal constructivist learning flow, facilitators of learning should plan for context to be reused and this would involve a long-term commitment to the creation and use of microlearning objects. Consequently, a longitudinal view of learning communities should be observed.

Therefore, learners must be able to review, select, and/or create learning objects. It is important that they also be actively engaged with the learning objects. The storing of learning objects should be planned and systematic. It is helpful for learners and facilitators of learning to be aware of, and actively use, appropriate licenses. Learning analytics, if available, could be used to employ microlearning objects in the self-directed multimodal learning process successfully. The place of microlearning within the wider learning ecosystem should be recognized, and this must form part of the overall supportive context and learning process. Finally, the collaborative process should be actively encouraged and managed towards the creation and review of microlearning objects. To illustrate the aforementioned aspects in practice, a brief case study is presented in the next section.

Illustrative Case Study

This case study relates to the use of short videos and animations as microlearning objects. The focus of the case study in this chapter relates specifically to the process that was followed for the implementation of microlearning, as well as to illustrate how self-directed multimodal learning can be fostered through microlearning object creation. For this specific case, students in an Afrikaans linguistics class were required to create short videos or animations on selected terms or topics relevant to a specific unit. The education students who participated in this case study were all first-year students studying an introductory module to linguistics for teachers. For more on the context and students' perceptions, see Olivier (2019).

In this case, although the topics were selected by the instructor, there was some room for adaptation by the students. Depending of course on the pre-existing knowledge of students regarding the content, learners could be encouraged to come up with topics themselves. For a true student-centered approach, the ideal would be for the learners to be involved in the process even before topics are selected. Hence, it is suggested that learners collaborate with the facilitator of learning in setting the parameters for the microlearning task. Such pre-activity interactions can contribute towards gauging students' technical capabilities, interests, and even content knowledge. This collaborative planning process not only gives agency to the learners, but also provides useful opportunities for additional assessments.

It is important that students be prompted to identify their specific needs and outcomes in order to create a microlearning object within the parameters that were set collaboratively. Only then can they create the microlearning objects based on their own set outcomes and selection of resources. In this context, students should be supported in order to be made aware not only of the opportunities of the reusability and adaptation of Open Educational Resources (OER), but also regarding how they can license their own microlearning objects, for example by means of Creative Commons licenses, for future reuse by others.

An essential aspect of collaboration in this particular case was to give students flexibility in the manner in which they collaborated with others. As a result, students had a choice to work individually in pairs or groups of three. Spontaneously, students opted to also consult individually or as groups in order to gain further expertise or engage with others in the class to plan and create the videos or animations. However, learning facilitators might also opt to structure this collaboration in finer detail to assign specific roles.

In terms of the nature of the microlearning objects, students were also allowed to create either videos or animations using different platforms. Therefore, a requirement for self-directed multimodal learning is offering learners choices. In formal learning environments, learners can more effectively take charge of their learning and choose appropriate human and material resources if options are presented and an atmosphere is created that is supportive and conducive to them being self-directed.

In this case study, students encountered many challenges in terms of content, collaboration, access to technology, and technical issues. This revealed the value of employing pre-activity discussions, as well as providing ongoing support throughout the process of creating the microlearning objects. Learners' needs and capabilities vary tremendously, and hence flexibility on the side of the learning facilitator in terms of possible processes and formats is also necessary. It may also be useful for the learning facilitator to build a bank of microlearning objects (on certain content-specific, technical, or even licensing issues) to address specific student needs in order to empower them to effectively create their own microlearning objects.

A final step before a microlearning object can be submitted for assessment or be included in a repository is self-evaluation and quality control. Therefore, learners must evaluate whether they have actually reached the learning outcomes they set forth and also evaluate the microlearning object itself. A further step could be to have the microlearning objects undergo some form of peer evaluation. This would allow for further improvement and refinement based on the feedback from other learners. This can take the form of open-ended or structured feedback facilitated through the use of a rubric. From the language and technical errors observed in the microlearning objects created by the learner in this case study, additional peer evaluation steps could have eliminated many of the challenges. In addition, the way a task is structured should also help students with time management in order to avoid rushing the microlearning development process.

The final step in the process is assessment and curation of microlearning objects for reuse. The fact that such student-created microlearning objects are reusable, can be an incentive for learners as their work will not only be seen by the facilitator of learning, but could also be of value for others. Finally, effective feedback from the assessment process could identify areas for further development for students in order to support their future microlearning objects' endeavors. This is especially appropriate for student teachers, as is relevant in this specific case study, where their job would one day require them to be active creators of learning content.

In retrospect, students found this approach very positive and many advantages were evident. However, the use of different formats, some stored online and others submitted through the learning management system or e-mail, made the administration on the side of the instructor quite daunting. In addition, assessments are made quite difficult as an animation created by means of a PowerPoint presentation requires different skills than a multimedia video. The case study revealed the need to adjust the assessment criteria and negotiate the parameters with the learners to improve the process even further. Especially for student teachers, this kind of approach to learning holds value in terms of covering certain content, addressing certain pedagogical concepts, as well as promoting responsible online content creation.

Summary

In summary, it is evident that through a communal constructivist approach and contribution-oriented pedagogy, students can become active producers of content for reuse. To this end, the role of learning facilitators is not diminished, as they can fulfill a supportive role of the learners throughout the process. This is particularly relevant in a context of learner self-directed multimodal learning through microlearning object creation where learning is learner-centered and responsive to the needs of 21st century learning environments and society. This is particularly relevant as Mentz et al. (2018, p. 156) observe, "[f]or an individual to cope in the 21st century, self-directed learning is needed as it prepares one to keep up with changes and be a lifelong learner – most importantly, it enables one to take responsibility for one's own learning."

Microlearning provides a solution for promoting lifelong learning, which is also important in terms of self-directed learning's aims. In this regard, Buchem and Hamelmann (2010) conclude:

> Microcontent and microlearning enhanced by Web 2.0 provide a viable solution to fast-paced and multitask-oriented patterns of learning and working today, enabling learning in small steps and with small units of content through social interaction. Microlearning aligned with formal learning and embedded in online communities has a potential to support ongoing professional development.
>
> *(p. 12)*

In essence, the future context of learning in the classroom and the workplace needs to be adaptable and open for increased microlearning, especially in relation to a communal constructivist approach. In this regard, Holmes et al. (2001, p. 4) noted that learning experiences need to be dynamic and adaptable as the wider technologically enhanced context is

> so dynamic it is necessary that both the course content, and more importantly the method of delivery, be capable of adapting to new information and new techniques as they emerge from within the course itself and from the discipline at large.

Central to this dynamic context is creating a space where learners can become co-creators and not just users of microlearning objects in the process of becoming more self-directed lifelong learners.

This chapter provided an overview of communal constructivism, contribution-oriented pedagogy, self-directed multimodal learning, and microlearning to provide a theoretical framework for self-directed multimodal learning by creating microlearning objects for facilitating learning. Finally, this chapter presented practical recommendations towards creating a context where self-directed multimodal learning can be supported through the creation of microlearning objects by learners.

Discussion Questions

1. How can microlearning objects be employed to support self-directed learning?
2. If learning is considered as communication, what role could microlearning play in a multimodal context?
3. How can quality be assured in the collaborative creation of microlearning objects?
4. What requirements would reusable microlearning objects entail within the context of communal constructivist learning?

References

Ahmad, N. (2017). Video podcast as a micro-learning tool in a blended learning environment. *E-Leader International Journal*, 12(1). www.g-casa.com/conferences/macau/pdf_paper/Ahmad%20-%20Video%20Podcasts.pdf.

Aitchanov, B. H., Satabaldiyev, A. B., & Latuta, K. N. (2013). Application of micro-learning technique and Twitter for educational purposes. *Journal of Physics: Conference Series*. 423(1), 012044.

Bair, R. & Bair, B. (2018). A creation education avenue for microlearning. *Training & Development*, 45(4), 14–15.

Baumgartner, P. (2013). Educational Dimensions of MicroLearning – Towards a Taxonomy for MicroLearning. In Roth, M., Bruck, P. A., & Sedlaczek, M. (Eds.) *Designing MicroLearning Experiences – Building up Knowledge in Organisations and Companies*. Pre-print version. Innsbruck: Innsbruck University Press. https://portfolio.peter-baumgartner.net/files/pdf/2013/Baumgartner_2013_Educational%20Dimensions%20for%20MicroLearning.pdf.

Bennett, K. & McGee, P. (2005). Transformative power of the learning object debate. *Open Learning: The Journal of Open, Distance and e-Learning*, 20(1), 15–30.

Bosch, C., Mentz, E., & Goede, R. (2019). Self-Directed Learning: A Conceptual Overview. In E. Mentz, J. De Beer, & R. Bailey (Eds.), *Self-Directed Learning for the 21st Century: Implications for Higher Education* (NWU Self-Directed Learning Series Volume 1), pp. 1–36. Cape Town: AOSIS. https://doi.org/10.4102/aosis.2019.BK134.01.

Buchem, I. & Hamelmann, H. (2010). Microlearning: A strategy for ongoing professional development. *eLearning Papers*, 21(7), 1–15.

Burton-MacLeod, N. (2019). A case study of a microlearning follow-up initiative to support training transfer. (Master of Arts (Educational Technology) thesis, Concordia University).

Collis, B. & Moonen, J. (2009). Collaborative Learning in a Contribution-Oriented Pedagogy. In P. Rogers, G. Berg, J. Boettcher, C. Howard, L. Justice, & K. Schenk (Eds.), *Encyclopedia of Distance Learning* (pp. 327–333). Hershey, PA: IGI Global Information Science Reference.

De Gagne, J. C., Park, H. K., Hall, K., Woodward, A., Yamane, S., & Kim, S. S. (2019). Microlearning in health professions education: Scoping review. *JMIR Medical Education*, 5(2), p.e13997.

Deniozou, T. (2016). Investigating the potential of mobile games as learning environments for independent adult skill development. (Ph.D. thesis, The University of Edinburgh).

Dessì, D., Fenu, G., Marras, M., & Recupero, D. R., (2019). Bridging learning analytics and cognitive computing for big data classification in micro-learning video collections. *Computers in Human Behavior*, 92, 468–477.

Emerson, L. C. & Berge, Z. L., (2018). Microlearning: Knowledge management applications and competency-based training in the workplace. *Knowledge Management & E-Learning: An International Journal*, 10(2), 125–132.

Ershler, J. & Stabile, C. (2015). The Learning Virus: An Affective, Constructivist Movement Shaped by Ultrasociality in the Age of Social Media. In C. Stabile and J. Ershlereds. *Constructivism Reconsidered in the Age of Social Media.: New Directions for Teaching and Learning*, Number 144. San Francisco, CA: John Wiley & Sons.

Freeman, L. E. (2016). Microlearning, a video series: a sequence of videos exploring the definition, affordances, and history of microlearning (Master of Arts Report, The University of Texas at Austin).

Garbers, R. (2018). An e-learning instructional design framework for mobile devices in Africa (M.Ed. dissertation, UNISA).

Giurgiu, L. (2017). Microlearning an evolving elearning trend. *Scientific Bulletin*, 22(1), 18–23.

Göschlberger, B., (2016). A Platform for Social Microlearning. In *European Conference on Technology Enhanced Learning* (pp. 513–516). Springer, Cham. https://link.springer.com/chapter/10.1007/978-3-319-45153-4_52.

Hanshaw, G. & Hanson, J. (2019). Using microlearning and social learning to improve teachers' instructional design skills: A mixed methods study of technology integration in teacher professional development. *International Journal of Learning and Development*, 9(1), 145–173.

Holmes, B., Tangney, B., FitzGibbon, A., Savage, T., & Mehan, S. (2001). *Communal constructivism: Students constructing learning for as well as with others*. In Society for Information Technology & Teacher Education International Conference (pp. 3114–3119). Association for the Advancement of Computing in Education (AACE).

Hug, T. & Friesen, N. (2007). Outline of a Microlearning Agenda. In Hug, T. (Ed.) *Didactics of Microlearning. Concepts, Discourses and Examples*, pp. 15–31. New York, NY, Waxmann Verlag.

Jewitt, C. (2013). Learning and communication in digital multimodal landscapes, Inaugural Professorial Lecture delivered at the Institute of Education, University of London, on 1 November2012, Institute of Education Press, London.

Johnson, D. W. & Johnson, R. T. (2019). The Impact of Cooperative Learning on Self-Directed Learning. In E. Mentz, J. De Beer, & R. Bailey (Eds.), *Self-Directed Learning for the 21st Century: Implications for Higher Education* (NWU Self-Directed Learning Series Volume 1), pp. 37–66, Cape Town, AOSIS. https://doi.org/10.4102/aosis.2019.BK134.02.

Jones, T. L. (2017). Building communities of practice: Experiences in a social and communal constructivist environment. *Canadian Journal of Action Research*, 18(3), 34–43.

Kapp, K. M. & Defelice, R. A. (2019). *Microlearning: Short and Sweet*. Alexandria, VA: American Society for Training and Development.

Khan, B. H. (2019). Microlearning: Quick and meaningful snippets for training solutions. *International Journal of Research in Educational Sciences (IJRES)*, 2(2), 275–284.

Knowles, M. S. (1975). *Self-Directed Learning: A Guide for Learners and Teachers*. Chicago, IL: Follett.

Kress, G. & Pachler, N. (2007). Thinking about the 'm-'in mobile learning. In Hug, T. (Ed.), *Didactics of Microlearning: Concepts, Discourse, and Examples*, pp. 139–154. New York, NY: Waxmann Verlag.

Mackey, T. P. & Jacobson, T. E. (2011). Reframing information literacy as a metaliteracy. *College & Research Libraries*, 72(1), 62–78.

Mentz, E., Bailey, R., Verster, M., & Breed, B. (2018). Incorporating Active Teaching–Learning Strategies to Enhance Self-Directed Learning within the Curriculum as Praxis: An Imperative for the 21st Century. In C. C. Wolhuter (Ed.), *Raising the Impact of Education Research in Africa*, pp. 151–180, Cape Town, AOSIS. https://doi.org/10.4102/aosis.2018.BK53.08.

Mosel, S. (2005). *Self directed learning with personal publishing and microcontent*. In Microlearning 2005 conference, Innsbruck. http://citeseerx.ist.psu.edu/viewdoc/download?doi=10.1.1.167.4378&rep=rep1&type=pdf.

Olivier, J. (2019). Short instructional videos as multimodal open educational resources in a language classroom. *Journal of Educational Multimedia and Hypermedia*, 28(4), 381–409.

Rothkrantz, L. J. M. (2016). *New didactical models in open and online learning based on social media*. In International Conference on e-Learning: e-learning'14, La Laguna (Spain) Sept. 12, 2014. University of Ruse.

Şentürk, C. & Zeybek, G. (2019). Overview of Learning From Past to Present and Self-Directed Learning. In F. G. Giuseffi (Ed.), *Self-Directed Learning Strategies in Adult Educational Contexts*, pp. 138–182, Hershey, PA, IGI Global.

Skalka, J. & Drlík, M., (2017). November. Conceptual Framework of Microlearning-Based Training Mobile Application for Improving Programming Skills. In *Interactive Mobile Communication, Technologies and Learning*, (pp. 213–224). Springer, Cham.

Wiley, D. A. (2002). Connecting Learning Objects to Instructional Design Theory: A Definition, a Metaphor, and a Taxonomy. In D. A. Wiley (Ed.) *The Instructional Use of Learning Objects*, pp. 3–24. Bloomington, IN: AIT & AECT.

Zhang, X. & Ren, L. (2011). August. *Design for application of micro learning to informal training in enterprise*. In 2011 2nd International Conference on Artificial Intelligence, Management Science and Electronic Commerce (AIMSEC). (pp. 2024–2027). IEEE.

12

GAMIFYING MICROLEARNING ELEMENTS

Alexander Salas

Introduction

So far, it can be assumed that anyone who has been reading this book from the beginning, now has a clear idea of the value of microlearning and its potential to make learning and education programs effective. However, what if microlearning strategies could be enhanced with the behavior-altering and motivational powers of gamification? Sounds interesting, right? First, there is a need to define gamification as a concept because it has been applied in several and diverse contexts. Often, gamification is confused with game design and although these are very interrelated concepts, they are not the same. In his book, *The Gamification of Learning and Instruction*, Karl Kapp (2012) provides the following definition: "Gamification is using game-based mechanics, aesthetics and game thinking to engage people, motivate action, promote learning, and solve problems" (p. 13). Following Kapp's definition, gamification applies the engaging, and sometimes addicting, features of game design to get users to do something. A prime example of the success of gamification strategies is marketing campaigns. The marketing industry has been one of its main practitioners, such as in the use of reward systems where customers are encouraged to purchase a brand as they collect points toward future purchases. But how does gamification apply in the context of learning? In the book, *Gamification in Learning and Education: Enjoy Learning Like Gaming*, Kim et. al. (2018, p. 27) define gamification for learning and education as a "set of activities and processes to solve problems related to learning and education by using or applying game mechanics." *What are game mechanics?* The simple answer is, game mechanics are the rules of the game. This chapter will get into the finite details of game mechanics. Second, it is hard to ignore how gamification influences our daily lives. As a customer, one may repeatedly use a brand because of its loyalty rewards program in addition to the quality of its products or services. For example, the Starbucks app grants customers points with each purchase and allows them to redeem a free drink or meal once they have met a set point quantity. According to a 2018 loyalty reward app case study conducted by The Manifest, "48% of smartphone owners who regularly use restaurant loyalty apps, use the Starbucks app" (Panko, 2018, paras. 3–4). It is time to think about the behavioral implications of the success of the Starbucks app. The more customers who use it, the more revenue Starbucks gets, but whether they realize it or not, customers are being conditioned to: (1) use the app, and (2) think of Starbucks as the brand to use every time they want a coffee, tea, or tasty treat. Therefore, what if an organization's microlearning strategies could incite a sort of "learning loyalty" and influence learner behavior through gamification? Implications of the gamification of microlearning are discussed in this chapter, regarding learner engagement, game mechanics, game dynamics, and aesthetics. These are all elements that would influence the design and delivery of gamified microlearning solutions. Additionally, several gamification technologies and analytics tools are also discussed to reinforce the attributes of real-time feedback and personalization, which are important for the success of any gamification intervention.

Why Gamify Microlearning?

In most instances, the way microlearning is applied involves a very concise, highly targeted, and packaged learning intervention. Regardless of its format and duration, microlearning efforts may be met with the same lack of enthusiasm as a full-fledged course or performance support initiative. The basics of effective instructional design must be present, and gamification would only enhance the effects of good learning design. Gamifying microlearning can help engage audiences by finding the sweet balance between things that must be done and things that are fun to do. In other words, gamification can make content and learning experiences more enjoyable and therefore, increase learner retention. Gamification design benefits from several creative outlets not often experienced in non-gamified educational content. Storytelling, mission objectives, constant feedback, trial and error opportunities, and real-world simulations are some of these creative expressions often found in gamified learning experiences. "Gamification focuses on engaging trainees in learning with same intensity that games engage players on playing. The aim is to get people engaged in serious or important work with the same intrinsic motivation than in games" (Gallego-Durán et al., 2019, p. 2). Gamifying microlearning content can also help developers become more attentive to the needs of the learner audience as gamification for gamification sake can yield unsatisfactory results. The last thing designers want as part of their learning strategy is to give learners a reason to disengage from their content. On the flip side, a well-crafted set of game mechanics can keep learners engaged and reinforce new desired behavioral patterns.

Gamification and Game Design Frameworks

Just as the proper design of learning experiences requires a foundational knowledge of learning theories and design frameworks, gamification strategies are more likely to achieve their goals by incorporating the basics of good game design. The realm of game design and gamification for learning purposes is rapidly evolving with its own guiding design frameworks. For instance, serious games, which are "electronic/computer-access games that are not designed for commercial purposes, but rather for training users on a specific skill set" (Annetta, 2010, p. 105), tend to rely heavily on simulation-based approaches to design. Serious Educational Games or SEGs are more focused on academic settings and use models such as the *Identity, Immersion, Interactivity, Increasing Complexity, Informed Teaching, and Instructional* or six "I's" model. According to Annetta (2010, p. 107), "this model functions as a hierarchy with identity as the basic foundational element. Yet, this model is different from other models with the inclusion of the idea of informed learning." The six "I's" model seems to offer a sound set of structures to develop educational games.

As Annetta (2010) also mentions, "[t]he six elements of the model are derived from over a decade of developing and testing educational games and using research from commercial video games to inform SEG research" (p. 106). It is fair to say that the six "I's" model may be the ideal choice for learning designers looking to develop full functional educational games. However, microlearning gamification calls for a simpler approach, a more manageable method that fits the requirements of a microlearning experience. That approach may be a framework known as the *Mechanics, Dynamics,* and *Aesthetics* or *MDA framework.* The *MDA framework* is one of the most recognized frameworks in use by game developers and gamification experts, and makes developers think about the essentials of any effective game or gamification experience. Keep in mind that although the MDA framework was selected for this chapter, the research in this field is very active as of late. As such, there is a significant chance that there will be several other influential frameworks worth looking into by the time this book is published. The next section will take a deeper dive in each of the three stages of the MDA framework (*Game Mechanics, Game Dynamics,* and *Game Aesthetics*) and how each impacts the design of effective microlearning gamification.

Game Mechanics

The first stage of the MDA framework is *Mechanics.* Game mechanics are often referred to as the *rules* of the game. If you think of it, all games have a set of conventions by which the game is played. "Mechanics are the various actions, behaviors and control mechanisms afforded to the player within a game context. Together with the game's content (levels, assets, and so on) the mechanics support overall gameplay dynamics" (Hunicke, LeBlanc, & Zubek, 2004, p. 3).

Examples of mechanics would be sport games like baseball or American football. In baseball, a ball hit within the foul lines of a diamond-shaped field is a fair ball. In American football, teams must get the ball across their opponent's endzone to score six points. The classic phrase "Collect $200 as you pass GO" is perhaps the most famous mechanic pertaining to the board game of Monopoly, which rewards each player by rolling dice with the sufficient number values to complete a turn around the board. Game mechanics can also incentivize players to be highly engaged by aligning to their player type needs. While researching Multi-User Dungeon games or MUDs with virtual worlds, Richard Bartle identified four player types: *Achievers, Explorers, Socializers,* and *Killers.* Bartle (1996, pp. 2–4) described each player type as follows:

- *Achievers* regard points-gathering and rising in levels as their main goal, and all is ultimately subservient to this.
- *Explorers* delight in having the game expose its internal machinations to them.
- *Socializers* are interested in people, and what they have to say. Inter-player relationships are important to them.
- *Killers* get their kicks from imposing themselves on others. Much more commonly, people attack other players with a view to killing off their personae.

Gamified microlearning can be designed with these player types in mind, especially when virtual world environments are involved. For example, gamification mechanics for achiever-type players would include point collection, treasures, badges, and any other symbol of achievement. Exploring game mechanics can be supported with escape room-like situations where players must find clues and solve problems by searching the gamified environment. Socializing gamification mechanics should offer communication tools, inter-player interaction, and even the involvement of social media channels. Killing gamification mechanics can be engaged with competitive scenarios, leaderboards, and a clear definition of success over others. By now, it should be clear that without mechanics there may not be much of a gamified experience or at least the incentivizing of players to engage.

Game Dynamics

Once the game mechanics are in place, learning designers need to consider the dynamics involved. *Game Dynamics* are the inherent effect certain mechanics have on learners/players. "Dynamics in the MDA model are the game design principles that create and support aesthetic experience. For example, time pressure and opponent play are two game dynamics that create and support the aesthetic of challenge" (Kim, 2015, p.19). The time pressure dynamic relates to time-sensitive tasks. Time pressure may not be welcome by many learners but, there are instances where a job or skill must be performed within time constraints. For time pressure, think of drive-thru cashiers in fast-food restaurants whose performance is measured by the duration of seconds spent per vehicle. This real-life scenario is a good example where mechanics, dynamics, and aesthetics transcend into real life outcomes. In this example, consider the drive-thru cashier to be a player; he or she wins by meeting the performance metric aka mechanics of dispatching of a customer within 30 seconds. In this time pressure dynamic, the player will: (a) meet or not meet the 30-second standard, and (b) find a way to beat the system. Customers experience the latter when they are asked to pull forward out of the drive-thru to have their meal hand-delivered a few minutes later. There are several other dynamics that can be discerned from observing real life because dynamics are all about the interaction between players and the mechanics involved.

Game Aesthetics

The last stage of the MDA framework is *Aesthetics* and it is perhaps one of the most important parts of it all. Believe it or not, game aesthetics are not so much about looks as they are about player emotions. "Aesthetics are the desirable emotional responses evoked in the player when interacting with the game system" (Mora et al., 2015, p. 101). Game elements like points and badges can incite the right emotions of engagement in learners who enjoy the aesthetics of expression and challenge. "The aesthetic of expression is created and supported by the dynamics that encourage individual users to leave their mark, such as systems for purchasing, building, or earning game items" (Kim, 2015, p.18). However, designers can run the risk of creating superficial rewards thus disengaging learners. For example, consider the implementation of badges with little to no meaning for those trying to attain them. What is the point of earning the badge? What is the symbolism of the badge? Is there an emotional connection to earning the badge? Organizations like the military and the Boy Scouts of America have been using badging for decades and the reason why badging is relevant in these organizations is because there is significant symbolism behind each badge. Military ribbons and medals are awarded based on observed achievements and real-life experiences. By looking at a military uniform, members of that community can estimate how long a person has been in service, where have they been, or whether he or she has experienced combat. So, whether you use leaderboards, narratives, badges, points or levels, considering the impact of gamification mechanics on the dynamics and aesthetics needs to be paramount in the context of relevancy to learners.

Ready. Set. Microplay.

Microlearning, as well as gamification, can be implemented at the authoring tool and delivery-method level. Full-fledged games are best created using game engines only because these software tools were designed to create gaming environments.

Although game engines are the most robust solution for games, gamification can be achieved through easier-to-use applications and some custom designs in e-learning authoring tools. "Gamification and microlearning have been used successfully in several workplace environments with favorable results" (Orwoll et al., 2018; Göschlberger & Bruck, 2017, p. 8). The following are some suggested strategies combining MDA gamified approaches with microlearning.

Desktop Implementations

One scenario where the use of spaced repetition microlearning is combined with gamification is that of desk-based employees. This type of worker can be best served with specialized microlearning platforms that can provide daily challenges directly to their computers via desktop notifications. Such an approach would not disrupt their workflow as much as having to walk to a training center or stop working to log into the organization's Learning Management System (LMS). Microlearning technology platforms vary from LMSs in that they often provide better web analytics with the ability to indicate watch time on videos, click interactions engaged, and even the device used. Some of these aspects may or may not be important for the organization but, what is measured thoroughly depends on the project and the expected outcomes. For example, in call centers, watch time metrics may be of high relevance because personnel may not be making the best use of their allotted training time causing potential monetary losses in make-up time during operational hours. Other solutions that are not solely for microlearning may also be useful as in the case of Freshdesk, a helpdesk software program that uses gamification for performance support. "The Freshdesk solution involves transforming customer inquiries (e.g., telephone questions, comments posted on Twitter and Facebook) into virtual tickets that are then randomly assigned to players (i.e., customer service employees)" (Robson et al., 2016, p. 32). This is an innovating approach that combines social mechanics and dynamics with real-world applications.

Desktop Design Considerations for Gamified Microlearning

There are various advantages and limitations to face according to the design environment, screen size, and player interface involved in game play. Desktop design considerations for microlearning games include keyboard navigation, mouse movements, left or right-click interactions, multiple browser tab or screen play. None of these would be feasible, or even an enjoyable experience, on mobile devices. Also, desktop players can only be engaged in game interactions while sitting at their desks. Therefore, as it does in anything else, context matters in how the microlearning gamified experience is delivered. Once it has been determined the microlearning experience will be desktop based, designers can focus on maximizing the environmental, player interface, and navigation features of desktop play.

Hotkeys

A desktop gamified experience that can take advantage of enabling keystroke interactions known as *hotkeys* can align well with several of the aforementioned player types such as explorers, achievers, and killers. By using hotkeys, a player can perform a designated action by one, two or a combined set of keyboard strokes. An explorer-type player is likely to find the act of discovering hotkey interactions as rewarding. The use of hotkeys may be seen as an efficiency and speed advantage by killer-type players and a symbol of skill attainment by achievers. Although, hotkey interactions can align well with gamified desktop experiences, there are some limitations and challenges to their use. Table 12.1 (see p. 000) shows some of the limitations and the best practices to mitigate their impact.

Multiple Browser Tabs or Screens

Desktop users traditionally sit at a desk, but many users can have multiple screens, and all have the ability to support multiple browser tabs. Designers also have to consider laptop users as having some of the same capabilities as desktop users. This will become a bit more challenging as many laptop devices offer a mobile or tablet view of their operating systems. Therefore, if the gamified event is intended for desktop users and their intended play features, then, designers would need to account for clear communication of game navigation and interaction to account for devices that can display in mobile and desktop versions.

Mobile Design Considerations for Gamified Microlearning

Mobile microlearning can be expected to be more prevalent in the next few years as most humans have adapted to the daily use of mobile devices. Microlearning

TABLE 12.1 Hotkey limitations and design mitigation best practices

Hotkey limitation	Details	Design best practice
Difficult to learn	Grossman, Dragicevic, and Balakrishnan (2007) noted that each individual or combination stroke requires memorization.	Associate the use of hotkeys with the action as it takes place, i.e., display information about the hotkey when the player performs the action with the mouse *Press CTRL + to zoom in.*
Lack of visibility	Grossman, Dragicevic, and Balakrishnan (2007) suggest using marked menus can increase the likelihood of users adopting a hotkey option.	Include a side-by-side reference of the game action and corresponding hotkey in menus and other player information elements.

platforms offer their interactions on web-based responsive applications. The term *responsive* applies to the automatic resizing of content to fit phone, tablet, and desktop screens, thus providing a better viewing experience. Popular e-learning authoring tools like Articulate Storyline 360 and Adobe Captivate already support mobile viewing without the requirement of other dedicated applications. The convenience of mobile learning cannot be overstated as learners can engage in microlearning sessions of five to seven minutes anytime, anywhere. For example, a microlearning game built for mobile first, allows players the autonomy of playing while commuting to and from work. The use of mobile devices opens some designs dynamics like text messaging and encouraging the aesthetics of social players. The game *Thug Life*, developed by Chobolabs, LLC, is one of the biggest successes of strategic marketing seen in the mobile game landscape. The game leverages the use of Facebook profiles and the Facebook messenger app. Players are rewarded with points when they promote the games to their Facebook friends or connections. This game clearly appeals to killer-type players with the tagline, "Build up your territory by attacking and raiding other players! Spin to win big and grow your wealth. Will you be the next ultimate gang boss?" (apps.apple.com, 2020). Mobile games like *Thug Life* can also benefit from the multimedia features available in most smartphones today. For example, player challenges can be based using geolocation and users can be encouraged to use their cameras to snap pictures of landmarks in their worksite as an onboarding game. Social dynamics have a major influence in game play when players are able to communicate through in-game chats or know the proximity of other players to their location. It is good to know that microlearning platforms also offer quizzes, built-in games, and progress and ranking leaderboards, which enable designers to align to various player types. Whenever possible, organizations should strive to make their microlearning campaigns mobile ready by designing for mobile first.

Foundational Design Elements of Gamified Microlearning

This section of the chapter assumes that the basics of sound instructional design have taken place prior to developing a microlearning game. Primarily, that the designer already knows: the target audience involved; a learning intervention is needed as part of the business solution; and the delivery platform to use. There are foundational design elements every game has that makes it engaging and contributes to its success. These elements are personalization, feedback, and storytelling.

Personalization

Personalization is about giving the player agency in the game. Agency can be easily provided with the autonomy of choice. Allowing players to choose their name, their avatar, and their set of tools can support a player's sense of control in the game. "Gamification techniques should try to understand users, their personality, feelings, behaviors and actions. Big data, behavioral insights and elements of psychology can be used in gamification to provide a better end-user experience" (Gonzalez, Toledo, & Muñoz, 2016, p. 535). Some basic practices of personalization are capturing player data, like name and email address, and using it to interact with the player. For example, a microlearning game interface may start by having a character welcome the players and ask for their names and job titles. Then, that character can address the players by their names for the rest of the game. Personalization is the aim to engage players as they create their identity within the game. Allowing the player to have agency over the game and how it is played can contribute to higher levels of engagement.

Feedback

Feedback is one of the main advantages game design offers as it often seems to be a continual presence. Educational interventions often give the user corrective feedback after the fact or as the result of an examination. However, most players encounter feedback each time they interact daily with non-game objects like doorknobs, computer screens, smart phones, etc. Games provide custom feedback through their *Heads Up Displays* (*HUDs*), which show number of points, progress meters, health levels, badges, time markers, and anything else players can use to stay informed about how they are performing in the game. For example, when applying survival game mechanics, a HUD may display a certain number of lives within the game signaling the player the number of times mistakes are permitted before losing. Another good example of feedback can be progress meters indicating to the players how close they are from achieving the next level or end goal.

Storytelling

Storytelling is a foundational element of impactful games. "There are two perspectives on storytelling in games, the designer's story and the player's story" (Rouse as cited in Winn, 2009). In an organizational context, the designer's story is closely related to what the organization needs the user to do or achieve, as a result of the learning intervention. Winn (2009) explains the designer's story as a way to set the stage and purpose of the game for the player. The player's story in turn, is created as the player experiences the game. This dichotomy can be helpful to quickly give learners context in gamified microlearning events. It is recommended to remain relevant to the user's role in the organization to prevent the learner interaction from being gimmicky. Fantasy stories of unrelatable fiction may deter busy professionals from engaging. For example, consider introducing pirate stories in a setting of medical professionals who do not share this creative affinity. It is recommended to quickly provide a relevant story setting which is already familiar to the user. Referring to the previous example, present the medical professional with a patient-related problem and ask him or her to solve it with the tools provided in the game.

Summary and Next Steps

In summary, the gamification of microlearning shows substantial value as the assumption of shorter content duration does not guarantee greater engagement. Gamification has the power to engage learners because game mechanics have an impact on learner interaction, and therefore, behavior. Bartle's player types can help designers align their game design and mechanics to engage players. There are a growing number of game and gamification design frameworks, such as the six "I's" but, the most recognizable one is the MDA framework. Mechanics are often thought of as the rules of the games and game elements affecting dynamics. Game dynamics are categorized as design principles that support aesthetics. Time pressure is a common example for dynamics, as well as opponent play. Game aesthetics is more related to player/learner emotions, as it is about the look of the game. As a designer, it is critical to understand the interdependencies among the three stages of the MDA framework. The use of gamification and microlearning has been well documented with favorable results. The most robust game elements are built with game engine software. However, platforms dedicated to microlearning offer many gamification elements that are also found in industry-specific software like helpdesk support. The implementation of gamified microlearning needs to consider the variances between desktop and mobile implementations. Desktop-based experiences have certain advantages as designers can enable hotkey navigation and learners can benefit from multiple screen use. Mobile designs can maximize on social and exploration dynamics by enabling a device's ability to share location and messages. Foundational elements of game design, such as personalization, feedback, and storytelling, enrich gamified microlearning experiences and therefore, user engagement. Personalization allows players to create their identity and have agency in the game. Feedback in game design offers a constant status check for users to identify their level of success in the game. Storytelling quickly ramps users up into a specific situation, providing relevant context and meaning. Finally, although the research continues to evolve, instructional designers today can develop effective and engaging gamification solutions with the implementation of appropriate microlearning platforms while following the MDA framework.

Discussion Questions

1. How would you incorporate the MDA framework in the development of your microlearning solutions? Please provide specific examples.
2. What barriers should be considered before deciding to gamify microlearning?
3. How can you ensure the mechanics of a game do not cause undesired dynamics?

4. What are at least three considerations designers should have about mobile vs. desktop design of gamified microlearning?
5. What are the foundational design elements of gamified microlearning?

References

Annetta, L. A. (2010). The "I's" have it: A framework for serious educational game design. *Review of General Psychology*, 14(2), 105–113.

apps.apple.com (2020, August 7). *Thug Life Game*. Apple App Store. https://apps.apple.com/us/app/thug-life-game/id1498408706?mt=8.

Bartle, R. (1996). Hearts, clubs, diamonds, spades: Players who suit MUDs. *Journal of MUD research*, 1(1), 19.

Gallego-Durán, F. J., Villagrá-Arnedo, C. J., Satorre-Cuerda, R., Compañ-Rosique, P., Molina-Carmona, R., & Llorens-Largo, F. (2019, December). A guide for game-design-based gamification. *Informatics*, 6(4), 49. Multidisciplinary Digital Publishing Institute.

González, C. S., Toledo, P., & Muñoz, V. (2016). Enhancing the engagement of intelligent tutorial systems through personalization of gamification. *International Journal of Engineering Education*, 32(1), 532–541.

Göschlberger, B., & Bruck, P. A. (2017, December). *Gamification in mobile and workplace integrated microlearning*. In Proceedings of the 19th International Conference on Information Integration and Web-based Applications & Services (pp. 545–552). ACM.

Grossman, T., Dragicevic, P., & Balakrishnan, R. (2007, April). *Strategies for accelerating on-line learning of hotkeys*. In Proceedings of the SIGCHI conference on Human factors in computing systems (pp. 1591–1600).

Hunicke, R., LeBlanc, M., & Zubek, R. (2004, July). *MDA: A formal approach to game design and game research*. In Proceedings of the AAAI Workshop on Challenges in Game AI, 4(1), 1722.

Kapp, K. M. (2012). *The Gamification of Learning and Instruction: Game-Based Methods and Strategies for Training and Education*. John Wiley & Sons.

Kim, B. (2015). Understanding gamification. *ALA TechSource*.

Kim, S., Song, K., Lockee, B., & Burton, J. (2018). What is Gamification in Learning and Education? In *Gamification in Learning and Education* (pp. 25–38). Springer, Cham.

Mora, A., Riera, D., González, C., & Arnedo-Moreno, J. (2017). Gamification: A systematic review of design frameworks. *Journal of Computing in Higher Education*, 29(3), 516–548.

Panko, R. (2018, May 15). How customers use food delivery and restaurant loyalty apps. *The Manifest*. https://themanifest.com/mobile-apps/how-customers-use-food-delivery-restaurant-loyalty-apps.

Orwoll, B., Diane, S., Henry, D., Tsang, L., Chu, K., Meer, C., & Roy-Burman, A. (2018). Gamification and microlearning for engagement with quality improvement (GAMEQI): A bundled digital intervention for the prevention of central line–associated bloodstream infection. *American Journal of Medical Quality*, 33(1), 21–29.

Robson, K., Plangger, K., Kietzmann, J. H., McCarthy, I., & Pitt, L. (2016). Game on: Engaging customers and employees through gamification. *Business Horizons*, 59(1), 29–36.

Winn, B. M. (2009). The Design, Play, and Experience Framework. In *Handbook of Research on Effective Electronic Gaming in Education* (pp. 1010–1024). IGI Global.

13

SHARING MICROLEARNING MATERIALS AS OPEN EDUCATIONAL RESOURCES (OER)

Kari Word and Vanessa P. Dennen

Introduction

In contemporary life, information and learning needs arise continuously and are diverse in their scope, urgency, and timeliness. People tend to use Google to satisfy their smaller and more immediate needs, with a reasonable belief that the answer to their question or a demonstration or tutorial for the needed skill has been shared online by someone else. The Internet also helps with more substantive knowledge needs – the kind of needs that one cannot reasonably expect to satisfy with a simple Internet search and an hour or two of attention. However, a search query remains valuable, and may yield network connections or resources that over time can be used for professional development or personal learning. The Internet excels as a starting point for solving learning problems and satisfying knowledge needs, helping people who seek targeted learning materials or experiences that balance efficiency with effectiveness.

The developing market for small scope, Internet-distributed, just-in-time learning experiences potentially changes the locus and economics of learning design, development, and distribution activities from larger institutions to smaller ones, or even individuals. The traditional landscape of educational content and learning experiences has educational institutions, such as universities and school systems, shaping the mission through the degree programs and curricula that they develop and support. Educational publishing companies form another large part of the foundation, providing learning materials that are aligned with the curricula for purchase. In the workplace learning sphere, companies develop in-house training programs, or outsource the development to educational companies. Professional organizations serve individuals at all levels, providing professional development opportunities.

Smaller-scale, informal learning experiences, such as those we would consider to be examples of microlearning, are nothing new. They have long been the domain of community organizations and personal networks, in which people share their knowledge and expertise with each other, often at no cost to the learner and in ways that are directly tailored to meet a specific need. However, this approach can be limited to people with pre-existing relationships or who are within geographic proximity of each other. The Internet serves to extend the reach of personal networks and makes it easier for individuals with mutual interests, who might not otherwise meet, to find each other and share their knowledge and expertise. In this chapter, we explore the convergence of microlearning and open educational resources (OER), which are complementary emerging technologies that facilitate informal learning processes.

The Convergence of Microlearning and OER

Conceptually, both microlearning and open educational resources have existed for a long time and their paths have crossed in practice as well. Microlearning has roots in just-in-time training, which became popular in the 1990s. Situated in a job-based learning context, just-in-time training meant that learning options for employees could be timely and focused on knowledge and skills that were going to be immediately used (Jones, 2001). Emerging technologies allowed knowledge support to be provided on the job with even greater ease, so employees could better perform their jobs without leaving their workspaces (Dorsey, Goodrum, & Schwen, 1993). The idea is simple: rather than require someone to complete an entire course in order to learn a small concept or skill, why not enable them to learn precisely and only what they need in the moment that they need it? Many employees already engaged in microlearning locally and informally, asking more experienced colleagues to provide assistance when a need arose. The Internet simply expanded microlearning options by providing a place to both search for information and network with others who have shared interests. When learning professionals share their microlearning resources, they are often leveraging the power of open educational resources (OER).

Open Educational Resources

The underlying concept behind open educational resources (OER) is open access. In other words, they are educational resources that learning professionals can find and use without any cost or copyright-related barriers (Butcher, 2015). Wiley (Wiley, n.d.; Wiley & Hilton, 2018) expands this definition to specify that end users should have the ability to engage in the *Five Rs* of open: retain, reuse, revise, remix, and redistribute. These five conditions provide a wide berth for OER users to engage in flexible and creative use of microlearning materials. In particular, the ability to revise or remix and then redistribute a substantively altered version of learning materials is something that traditional copyright would not support, but that learning professionals and learners both benefit from.

Although OER is a relatively new term, coined in the digital era, the concept has been practiced by teachers for decades. Before they could share course materials online, teachers shared hard copies of materials they created or acquired. It was typical to see photocopies of photocopies shared from teacher to teacher. This typically was done without the expectation of financial gain by either party; they were just people helping each other do their job. The same type of sharing occurs now, only online and with a greater potential reach. For example, a teacher who created a lesson plan might post it online to be used free of charge in hopes that teachers elsewhere may be able to use it in their classroom. Another teacher might locate that lesson plan through an Internet search, make a few modifications so it best meets their individual needs, and implement it. There is a monetized version of this teacher sharing economy on sites like *Teachers Pay Teachers*, which connects parties with curricular items for sale to paying customers, often funneled through Pinterest (Pittard, 2017; Shelton & Archambault, 2019). This practice has expanded to other professions, such as business, IT, and healthcare, where professional development through a combination of formal and informal learning activities has become an integrated component of the operations of daily work.

Reusable Learning Objects

The OER movement brings to mind an earlier trend, reusable learning objects (RLO). The concept behind reusable learning objects was that if Person A developed a course on Topic X, and Persons B and C also needed to develop a course on Topic X, rather than have all three of them separately build courses and likely duplicate labor in the process, they could share their materials and efforts. Recognizing that each could have a high degree of course similarity due to common content, as well as some needs for personalization due to local needs or organizational personalization, the RLO movement encouraged people to think about course development in terms of each discrete component, or learning object, being built. A learning object could be as small as an image or a paragraph of text; granularity is among the concerns for learning objects in order to maximize usability (Nash, 2005). Essentially, the more granular the object, the more functional it is for different users.

Three criteria define the functionality of RLOs. They need to: (1) be tagged with metadata so they can be stored and searched in a database; (2) be functional in different educational contexts; and (3) exist as units unto themselves, and not be tethered to other media or a learning management system (Polsani, 2006). Other factors that determine whether they are actually usable by others include instructional alignment, accessibility, and quality (Yassine, Kadry, & Sicilia, 2016). Standards are necessary for success in this realm (Polsani, 2006), and have transitioned from the *Sharable Content Object Reference Model* to the *Experience API,* also known as xAPI (Yassine et al., 2016).

The conversation about RLOs typically occurs among instructional design teams who are developing large scale learning experiences. However, the idea that learning objects could be used to support individual learning needs has been raised previously as well. For example, learning objects can be used as the foundation of constructivist learning experiences when learners access them on an as-needed basis to solve authentic problems (Bannan-Ritland, Dabbagh, & Murphy, 2002). In short, small chunks of information or instruction, such as microlearning objects, can be useful for learning in any context or setting.

Repositories and OER Sharing

In order for effective sharing and use to occur, microlearning objects need to be widely accessible to potential end-users. If we were to create a learning resource and store it on a local computer, few people will benefit from it. Online sharing is the key to widespread use, and repositories facilitate this sharing process. Repositories, which are akin to digital libraries, allow people to share, store, and find learning objects (Richards, McGreal, Hatala, & Friesen, 2002). Metadata is a critical part of their functionality (Zschocke & Beniest, 2011), facilitating the end-user's ability to find relevant learning objectives. OER repositories typically offer some sort of quality indicators (Atenas & Havemann, 2014; Clements, Paw-lowski, & Manouselis, 2015), so end-users can easily learn more about an item's content and strengths, and read reviews from authentic users.

Some repositories serve users at the institutional level (Chapman, Reynolds, & Shreeves, 2009), whereas others are open to the public. Popular public repositories for OER include MERLOT, OER Commons, and Teaching Commons. Although repositories are considered a helpful innovation, they are only as useful as the metadata they record (Zschocke & Beniest, 2011), which raises issues about who gets to input and classify learning objects in a repository. Additionally, repository interfaces may not clearly supply information about intellectual property ownership and allowable learning object use (Amiel & Soares, 2016), which can lead to confusion or inappropriate use among end-users.

OER are not always shared via repositories. Sometimes individuals host their creations on servers or in spaces that they control, and then these learning objects get further shared via social media platforms like blogs, wikis, Twitter, and Pinterest. Again, metadata and tags can support people as they share and search for relevant resources. This type of hosting and sharing has also made possible a new role to emerge, one that blurs the lines between the producer and the consumer. Anyone can become what Bruns (2008) terms a *produser* or one who alternates between the producer and consumer roles online depending on the situation. Further, by engaging in processes like curation, a person might assemble existing microlearning objects into a collection, thereby creating new meaning and learning opportunities for others.

OER and Intellectual Property

Intellectual property is an issue that sits at the heart of the OER movement. Intellectual property refers to the ownership rights for intangible items that are protected by law usually in the form of copyrights, patents, and trademarks. Traditionally, the ownership of educational intellectual property (e.g., textbooks, videos, graphics, worksheets) has been designated via the application of copyright. The copyright holder may or may not be the author of the work. Instead, the copyright holder could be a publishing company or other institution, the result of either work-for-hire or an author formally giving the institution ownership rights in exchange for publishing and perhaps royalties.

Historically, the education world has used formally published and purchased resources with copyright restrictions. For example, textbooks are not supposed to be photocopied, and videos or DVDs are not meant to be duplicated or shared with a public audience. This approach to learning materials is restrictive. It promotes large-scale adoption of proprietary materials that present an educational narrative and follow standards determined by those in power (e.g., states), even when that narrative is racist or runs counter to social and pedagogical trends and the needs of learners (Díaz & Deroo, 2020; Hunt, Locklear, Bullard, & Pacheco, 2020). There is an economic side to this story as well. Curricular materials are sold on a per-teacher or per-student basis. The traditional textbook publishing industry in the United States has seen a steady decline amid the increased popularity of textbook rentals and used sales, largely enabled by the Internet (Carbaugh, 2020). Once they have purchased or required students to purchase an educational product, teachers are often reluctant or unable to require additional materials due to cost. Additionally, purchasing decisions tend be largely out of the hands of the average teacher (Polikoff et al., 2020). To synthesize what is happening here: the people who own the materials profit from them, and tend to sell them in bulk and in large units (e.g., whole books or collections), which makes them impractical for individuals who want to use just a small portion of an item for instructional purposes.

OER takes a different approach. Rather than suggesting individuals should own knowledge, the underlying philosophy is that knowledge exists to be shared with the commons for the greater good (Bernstein-Sierra, 2017). Although authorship may be important to individuals for a variety of personal and institutional reasons, open approaches to knowledge objects removes various sharing restrictions that are at play when corporations and financial gain are part of the intellectual property conversation. An OER approach offers alternative ways to designate intellectual property and, as a result, may facilitate more granular adoption and use of knowledge objects. Conceptually, it promotes the ability for individuals to use an item in whatever way best suits their needs.

In concrete terms, an item can have a Creative Commons license applied (discussed in more detail later in this chapter) to help end users identify the original creator and use the item in the ways that they permit. Sharing venues also become more diverse, to include social networking sites such as Twitter, You-Tube, Facebook, and LinkedIn (Abbasi, 2016), while others decide to use open education resource repositories created by various U.S. government agencies, educational institutions, organizations, statewide, or by scholarly journals.

There is one final area in which intellectual property might be considered. Whereas in traditional educational publishing, formal contracts and copyright agreements are used, in an OER context the agreements may be less formal. Collaborative ownership may become an issue when intellectual property is developed by a group (Dennen, 2016), and individual contributors will need to agree upon a specific license and approach to sharing before making an item available for others to use.

The OER Mindset

The OER mindset requires different considerations for both the creators of microlearning objects and the users of them, as well as the people whose role sits somewhere between (e.g., individuals who modified an existing resource, and then shared it with others). The OER mindset shifts the focus from who owns a resource to how a resource can best be shared with, used by, and improved upon by others. With that in mind, people engaged in various aspects of OER creation and use may find themselves asking the following questions:

- Is there a cost associated with using this object?
- Does it matter where, how, or with whom I use it?
- Am I free to share it with other people who are interested?
- When I share it, do I have to share all of it, or can I just share parts of it?
- Can I add to it? If so, what is my role (and credit) in terms of authorship and intellectual property?
- Can I share it by giving the other person an actual copy, or am I only allowed to provide a link to it?
- Do I need to provide attribution when I use it or when I share it with others?

Alternately, people may not ask these questions because they are not fully in the OER mindset. To get into the OER mindset, it can be helpful to envision a familiar setting:

Imagine you are invited to a potluck style event where everyone brings a dish to share. You have been asked to bring a dessert. You look on Pinterest and find a recipe for red velvet cookies. The web page with the recipe includes the ingredients and the instructions, as well as reviews from others who have made the recipe. After reading it all carefully, you make a plan. Taking other people's recommendations and your experience into consideration, you decide to make a few changes to the recipe. You add a little more almond than the recipe calls for and you substitute the milk for heavy cream. Your oven runs a little hot and you read that the cookies burn easily, so you decrease the oven temperature from 350 to 325 degrees Fahrenheit. At the potluck party, several people ask you for your recipe. You're happy to share, but you also realize that you need to make sure you remember what changes you made to your version so you can share it and also replicate it for yourself. You even had a few more ideas for ways to tweak the recipe that you want to make note of. Should you return to the website and share your experience with the people who comment there? Perhaps. You also realize that you should be sure to give credit to the original source of the recipe when you pass it along to others, even if you give them the version with your modifications.

This example refers to a recipe found online, modified, and then shared with others, but can readily envision the same happening in a learning context. An instructor could find a lesson plan, adjust it, and share it with colleagues. A professional development leader could find an activity to carry out at the next meeting to emphasize a point. Alternately, a learner could find a microlearning object, use it in a specific way or embed it into their own learning plan, and then share it with friends or co-learners.

Returning to the recipe example, a person who was asked to share a recipe might consider some of the following options:

1. Write out the recipe by hand and mail it to someone. Repeat as many times as necessary to fulfill requests.
2. Take a photo of the recipe and email or text it to all who requested it.
3. Send a link to the original recipe along with notes about personal modifications to all who requested it.
4. Type out the recipe, with modifications and either share the file privately to all who requested it or post it online.

Of these options, the first two are the most restrictive. They involve file types that cannot be easily modified by others. The fourth is the most flexible, especially if the file is posted online in a way that allows other people to share (or stumble upon) the link, save a copy for themselves, and even easily edit that saved copy.

Here are some of the questions related to content, format, and authorship and attribution that a person could grapple with when preparing the recipe file:

- **Content**: Is the recipe sufficiently detailed that someone else can follow it? Does it include an accurate ingredient list and set-by-step instructions? What other details about the recipe might people need or want?
- **Format**: How do I share the recipe so that other people can easily store, reuse, and revise it in ways that makes sense for them? How might they want to save it? What format is most useful and flexible to them? Should I share an editable copy of it?

- **Authorship and attribution**: Do I create a new version of the recipe to share? If so, do I take credit for the recipe or share where it originated? Do I share it with my name on it, too? Do I request that if it is shared further that credit continue to be given to me and to earlier authors/contributors?

Distributing the recipe may lead to additional questions related to local and global sharing:

- Assuming the recipe is contained in a digital file of some sort, is it hosted and shared online? Can it be shared via a link, or must it be sent to someone as an attachment?
- Can people beyond the original requesters see and access it? How?
- If online, has it been tagged or has metadata been added to help it show up effectively in searches?
- Is there any way to find out who has viewed or downloaded the recipe? How about to get feedback from people who have tried it?

Admittedly, these questions extend beyond the thought process of the typical recipe sharing activity. Still, all of these questions relate to how the recipe will be used by other people. Certain decisions might make the sharing process easier for the sharer, but difficult for end users. Sending a paper copy or image of the recipe would offer low flexibility for future bakers, whereas a word-processed file of some sort, perhaps hosted on a website, would offer greatest flexibility. People might think it odd or fussy if I specified that I require attribution to be provided on an ongoing basis, although if we titled it *Kari's Cookies* the recipe might be shared broadly under that name. If hosted on the Internet, people might be further inclined to share by providing the URL, which would consistently point back to the original recipe. Regardless, the easier it is for other people to access the recipe and save it in their own preferred format, the more likely they will be to try and save it.

These same ideas apply to learning objects when the OER mindset is invoked. When one is the producer of microlearning content, additional focus is placed on making that content easily available to others for flexible use. For consumers, in turn, OER provides new options for accessing and acquiring learning content and the opportunity to use that content in diverse ways. The flexibility afforded to OER users, whether consumers or producers, can be described through a set of five affordances or activities offered to the users of a learning resource (Wiley, n. d.). These five activities, referred to as the 5Rs – *retain, reuse, revise, remix,* and *redistribute* – describe the different ways that a person might want to interact with and make use of a microlearning object. Table 13.1 provides a description of how the 5Rs might apply in the recipe sharing example used in this chapter and compares the open condition with the not open condition.

TABLE 13.1 The 5Rs of open (Wiley, n.d.) applied to the recipe example

	Not Open	Open
Retain	Others have no right to your recipe. It is proprietary.	Others have the right to your recipe.
	If someone gets a glimpse of the recipe or helps you bake the cookies, they may not write it down or otherwise make a copy of it.	Other people can have and keep a copy of your recipe.
Reuse	Others have no right to use your recipe for their guests.	Others have the right to use your recipe when baking for their own guests.
	Anyone who wants to serve your cookies must get you to bake them.	Your recipe will be used over and over, allowing many people to try the cookies.
Revise	Others have no right to try to recreate and adjust your recipe.	Others have the right to recreate your recipe and adjust as needed.
	Only one version of your recipe exists, and it is the only way the recipe can be made.	Fellow bakers can experiment with the directions and ingredients, making their own variations of the recipe.
Remix	Others may have no right to combine your recipe with another to create a mashup.	Others have the right to combine your recipe with another recipe to create something entirely new.
	Only one version of your recipe exists, and it is the only way the recipe can be made.	Fellow bakers may morph the title, ingredients, and overall recipe into a totally new recipe.
Redistribute	Others have no right to share your recipe with others.	Others have the right to share your original recipe or any revised or remixed version of your recipe.
	You are the gatekeeper and the only one who is allowed to give a copy of the recipe to anyone else.	Anyone who has a copy of the recipe (or the variants, if they are permitted) can share it freely with other people.

To best understand the value of the 5Rs, it is useful to consider several learning scenarios where these activities are restricted. For example, a person who views a *how-to* video at the local hardware store may feel lost trying to replicate the technique or procedure from memory at home. A sample resume is of little use to job seekers if they do not have permission to rework them to suit their own purposes. Learning professionals will find an infographic most useful when they have permission to share them with their learners. A person cooking dinner will appreciate the ability to freely substitute shallots for garlic in a recipe to avoid a trip to the store for one ingredient. Through these examples, it becomes apparent the degree to which the open mindset has supported learning and performance throughout history. However, contemporary copyright laws and an economy dependent on selling proprietary items has stifled openness at the same time that technology has facilitated widespread sharing, mixing, and editing of creative and scholarly works.

Designing for OER

Any item that someone has created potentially could be shared as OER. However, not every item is designed in a way that maximizes its usefulness to others as OER. Casting aside the corporate learning marketplace that includes educational publishing companies and institutional learning departments designing and developing materials for profit, there are many people who design learning materials to suit their own needs. These designers may not be thinking about profits or widespread adoption of their creations, but rather how they can help teach something to other people. Even when they are designing for a specific and perhaps narrow group of learners, their learning designs may nonetheless be of value to a much wider group of others if shared as OER. However, these designers can maximize the usefulness of their creations by attending purposefully to elements of the 5Rs during their design process (Dennen & Bagdy, 2019), which entails considerations such as granularity, sharing source files, and Creative Commons licensing. Additionally, designers' decisions about where and how to share their work affects the likelihood it will be found and used by others.

Granularity and Sharing Source Files

Granularity refers to the size of an OER. Some OER are quite large. For example, an open access textbook might easily exceed 100 pages. Others are quite small, such as a simple graphic that conveys a single concept. From the perspective of the designer, a learning product might be a single large item. The component parts may be intended to be bound and used as a collective whole. Consequently, the designer may be inclined to share the final, compiled version of a learning product. However, from the consumer's perspective, that compiled version might be much larger than is needed and could include content that is irrelevant or extraneous to the learning context. Again, using a book as the example, whereas the author might write eight chapters that constitute 200 pages in total, the reader may only be interested in one of those chapters, or less. That selection may represent the entirety of the reader's interests or needs on that topic, or the reader may wish to combine a selection from one book with a small selection from another, or even some other type of learning media such as a video.

With this in mind, designers make it easier for end users when they consider granularity and perhaps even offer source files to others. Returning to the book example, sharing individual chapters in addition to a fully compiled version should not be substantially more difficult. Offering editable text and individual image files to others encourages flexible reuse and remixing.

Creative Commons Licensing

Open educational resources are not items shared without any attention to copyright. Instead, licensing through Creative Commons (https://creativecommons.org) helps provide information about how an item's copyright should govern its use. Creative Commons is not the antithesis of copyright, but rather a component of or addendum to copyright (Gumb, 2019). By providing a variety of intellectual property licenses that a creator can choose among and apply to a given item, Creative Commons facilitates the open use of intellectual property. Whereas copyright on its own suggests restrictions on how an item may be used, Creative Commons licenses open up some of those restrictions. Specifically, the six types of Creative Commons licenses allow creators to specify if others can "distribute, remix, adapt, and build on an item" (Creative Commons, n.d., para. 1), and whether attribution must be given to the original author when an item is used, whether users can use an item for commercial purposes, and whether any derivative works can be further shared.

Creative Commons licenses include visual indicators, similar to the familiar copyright symbol, that communicate allowable use and provide attribution information when relevant to the license. They also include digital metadata when that functionality is compatible with the file type. The metadata allows search engines to identify items by license type. For example, Google image searches can be conducted with the option to search by image license. In the end, Creative Commons licenses work in concert with producers' decisions about granularity and file sharing.

A Recipe for Success: OER and Microlearning

Instructional designers might not set out initially to design for microlearning, but many learning materials developed on a larger scale (e.g., for a lesson or a whole course) can be divided into smaller parts, and those parts may be of value to some learners either used individually or in some smaller combination. The same design considerations that maximize a learning object's utility per the 5Rs similarly maximize an object's potential to be used in support of microlearning. Microlearning is dependent on granularity and providing source files facilitates the ability to create additional granularity of a learning object, as well as to customize that object. Open sharing with one of the less restrictive Creative Commons licenses can help maximize use of a learning object for microlearning purposes, as can depositing learning objects in a repository with relevant tags and other metadata applied. Additionally, items can be further promoted via social media, using tags to attract the attention of people who might be interested.

Returning once again to the example of the cookie recipe, the recipe might have originated in a whole cookbook. The cookbook, as a physical object, has costs associated with it and may not be a worthwhile purchase for a person interested in a single recipe. If shared online, in a digital format that is both open and granular, with helpful metadata, a person searching for a red velvet cookie recipe might find the one featured in that book. That person might be satisfied with the single recipe or might be interested in the whole cookbook if the recipe turned out well. They might then share and recommend the recipe to others, or possibly even the whole book. As a result, many people might learn how to make red velvet cookies.

Where OER helps extend the microlearning concept even further is by expanding the ways in which any particular object might be used. For the red velvet cookie recipe, this might mean that the cookie recipe gets reworked. The icing might be paired with a different type of cookie, or the cookie with a different type of icing. The whole cookie recipe might be paired with an entrée to create a more complete meal. It might be altered to suit specific needs, such as decorations, a gluten-free option, or different sized or shaped cookies. All of these variations might occur when different bakers encounter the recipe, and they can collectively enhance each other's future baking endeavors by sharing their revised and remixed versions of the recipe, all while providing appropriate attribution to the original recipe and the larger cookbook in which it first appeared.

A learning object may not be quite as delicious as a red velvet cookie, but it is a recipe for developing knowledge and skills. In both cases, the benefits of adhering to open design, licensing, and distribution and offering granular, editable options maximizes the likelihood that others will find and be able to make use of the item. Given the increased prevalence of microlearning as an approach to professional development and personalized learning (Shamir-Inbal & Blau, 2020; Zhang & West, 2020), as well as the incorporation of learning objects from repository platforms like Khan Academy into formal school experiences (Cargile & Harkness, 2015), interest in this area is likely to grow. Only time will tell if the microlearning trend will help further the OER agenda, and promote more widespread use of both Creative Commons licenses and repositories among educators and learning professionals as both consumers and producers of microlearning objects, and if learners will similarly find their way on this path as part of their self-directed activities.

Discussion Questions

1. What do you view as the pros and cons of sharing your microlearning objects as OER with others? In your response, address each of the 5 Rs.
2. How might sharing the microlearning objects that you have created as OER help strengthen your professional network?
3. What barriers might prevent you from sharing your microlearning objects as OER?

References

Abbasi, I. (2016). Get social: Learn to make the most of popular social networking platforms for both formal and informal learning. *Talent Development* (3), 26–28.

Amiel, T., & Soares, T. C. (2016). Identifying tensions in the use of open licenses in OER repositories. *The International Review of Research in Open and Distributed Learning*, 17(3).

Atenas, J., & Havemann, L. (2014). Questions of quality in repositories of open educational resources: A literature review. *Research in Learning Technology*, 22.

Bannan-Ritland, B., Dabbagh, N., & Murphy, K. (2002). Learning Object Systems as Constructivist Learning Environments: Related Assumptions, Theories, and Applications. In D. A. Wiley (Ed.), *The Instructional Use of Learning Objects* (pp. 61–98). Bloomington, IN: Association for Educational Communications and Technology.

Bernstein-Sierra, S. (2017). "Owning" knowledge: Looking beyond politics to find the public good. *New Directions for Higher Education, 2017*, (177), 51–62.

Bruns, A. (2008). *Blogs, Wikipedia, Second Life, and beyond: From Production to Produsage.* New York, NY: Peter Lang.

Butcher, N. (2015). *A Basic Guide to OER.* Paris, France: United Nations Educational, Scientific and Cultural Organization.

Carbaugh, B. (2020). The decline of college textbook publishing: Cengage Learning and McGraw-Hill. *The American Economist*, 1–16. https://doi.org/10.1177/0569434520936621.

Cargile, L. A., & Harkness, S. S. (2015). Flip or flop: Are math teachers using Khan Academy as envisioned by Sal Khan? *TechTrends*, 59(6), 21–28.

Chapman, J. W., Reynolds, D., & Shreeves, S. A. (2009). Repository metadata: Approaches and challenges. *Cataloging & Classification Quarterly*, 47(3–4), 309–325. doi:10.1080/01639370902735020.

Clements, K., Pawlowski, J., & Manouselis, N. (2015). Open educational resources repositories literature review – Towards a comprehensive quality approaches framework. *Computers in Human Behavior*, 51, 1098–1106.

Creative Commons. (n.d.). About CC licenses. https://creativecommons.org/about/cclicenses.

Dennen, V. P. (2016). Ownership of digital course artifacts: Who can access and use your words, images, sounds, and clicks? *Quarterly Review of Distance Education*, 17(4), 5–19.

Dennen, V. P., & Bagdy, L. M. (2019). Going open: A textbook replacement design case. *International Journal for Educational Media & Technology*, 13(2), 6–16.

Díaz, E., & Deroo, M. R. (2020). Latinxs in contention: A systemic functional linguistic analysis of 11th-grade U.S. history textbooks. *Theory & Research in Social Education*, 1–28. doi:10.1080/00933104.2020.1731637.

Dorsey, L. T., Goodrum, D. A., & Schwen, T. M. (1993). Just-in-time knowledge performance support: A test of concept. *Educational Technology*, 33(11), 21–29.

Gumb, L. (2019). An open impediment: Navigating copyright and OER publishing in the academic library. *College & Research Libraries News*, 80(4), 202–215. https://doi.org/10.5860/crln.80.4.202.

Hunt, B. D., Locklear, L., Bullard, C., & Pacheco, C. (2020). "Do you live in a teepee? Do you have running water?" The harrowing experiences of American Indians in North Carolina's urban K-12 schools. *The Urban Review*. doi:10.1007/s11256-020-00563-1.

Jones, M. (2001). Just-in-time training. *Advances in Developing Human Resources*, 3(4), 480–487.

Nash, S. (2005). Learning objects, learning object repositories, and learning theory: Preliminary best practices for online courses. *Interdisciplinary Journal of Knowledge and Learning Objects*, 1(1), 217–228.

Pittard, E. A. (2017). Gettin' a little crafty: Teachers Pay Teachers, Pinterest and neo-liberalism in new materialist feminist research. *Gender & Education*, 29(1), 28–47. doi:10.1080/09540253.2016.1197380.

Polikoff, M. S., Campbell, S. E., Rabovsky, S., Koedel, C., Le, Q. T., Hardaway, T., & Gasparian, H. (2020). The formalized processes districts use to evaluate mathematics textbooks. *Journal of Curriculum Studies*, 52(4), 451–477. doi:10.1080/00220272.2020.1747116.

Polsani, P. R. (2006). Use and abuse of reusable learning objects. *Journal of Digital Information*, 3(4).

Richards, G., McGreal, R., Hatala, M., & Friesen, N. (2002). The evolution of learning object repository technologies: Portals for on-line objects for learning. *International Journal of E-Learning & Distance Education/Revue internationale du e-learning et la formation à distance*, 17(3), 67–79.

Shamir-Inbal, T., & Blau, I. (2020). Micro-learning in designing professional development for ICT teacher leaders: The role of self-regulation and perceived learning. *Professional Development in Education*, 1–17.

Shelton, C. C., & Archambault, L. M. (2019). Who are online teacherpreneurs and what do they do? A survey of content creators on TeachersPayTeachers.com. *Journal of Research on Technology in Education*, 51(4), 398–414. doi:10.1080/15391523.2019.1666757.

Wiley, D. (n.d.). Defining the "open" in open content and open educational resources. http://opencontent.org/definition.

Wiley, D., & Hilton, J. (2018). Defining OER-enabled pedagogy. *International Review of Research in Open & Distance Learning*, 19(4), 133–147. doi:10.19173/irrodl.v19i4.3601.

Yassine, S., Kadry, S., & Sicilia, M. A. (2016). Learning Analytics and Learning Objects Repositories: Overview and Future Directions. In J. M. Spector (Ed.), *Learning, design, technology: An international compendium of theory, research, practice, policy* (pp. 1–29). Switzerland: Springer.

Zhang, J., & West, R. E. (2020). Designing microlearning instruction for professional development through a competency based approach. *TechTrends*, 64(2), 310–318.

Zschocke, T., & Beniest, J. (2011). Adapting a quality assurance framework for creating educational metadata in an agricultural learning repository. *The Electronic Library*, 29(2), 181–189.

14

RREDS

An Instructional Design Model Based on Microlearning Events and Curricular Engagement

Melissa A. Simons and Caroline M. Crawford

Introduction

Instructional design is a field that is comprehended through many different viewpoints of understanding. The evolution of an instructionally appropriate product that emphasizes information and instructional understandings is at the core of the distinctive systematic process, suggesting that instructional design can find its way back to the historic understandings of Greek philosophy's Classical period:

> As a formal discipline, Instructional Systems Design has been a long time in the making. The early contributions of thinkers such as Aristotle, Socrates and Plato regarding the cognitive basis of learning and memory was later expanded by the 13th century philosopher St. Thomas Aquinas who discussed the perception of teachings in terms of free will. Four hundred years later, John Locke advanced Aristotle's notion of human's initial state of mental blankness by proposing that almost all reason and knowledge must be gained from experience. Then, at the turn of the 20th century John Dewey presented several tenets of the philosophy of education which promoted the idea that learning occurs best when married with doing, rather than rote regurgitation of facts
>
> *(Kumar, 2007, para. 63)*

From this understanding, instructional design has advanced into an established field that represents itself as an artistic science of understanding and engagement. As the field of instructional design advances, instructional design models also advance, and theorists and practitioners rethink, not only the instructional design process, but also the informational or instructional product represented. This instructional product is appropriately represented through the naturalized analysis, design, development, implementation, and evaluative processes and procedures inherent within the conceptualization around how learners desire various user-centric methods to present the information. Further, as well as the style of engagement that supports instructional and informational engagement with the information towards addressing and attending to differentiated goals, objectives, and competencies are the undergirding need as met through the instructional design process. It has been an outstanding several decades in the enhanced development of differentiated instructional design models that lay out not only systematic design and development procedures and standards, but the depth of engagement in differentiated realms of instructional and informational encounter. Models range from Gagné's articulated Instructional Design Theory (1977) to Dick and Carey's *Systems Approach Model for Designing Instruction* (1978), which developed into Dick, Carey, and Carey's (2014) *Systematic Design of Instruction*, to Mager's work (1984) and Tripp and Bichelmayer's (1990) *Rapid Prototyping Design Model*, the first constructivist model offered by Willis (1995), to the Dorsey, Goodrum, and Schwen Model (Dorsey at al., 1997) and the Hall, Watkins, and Eller *Model of Web-Based Design for Learning* (Hall et al., 2003), leading into Crawford's *Eternal, Synergistic Design and Development Model* (2004).

More recently, instructional design models have taken an even more diverse approach towards supporting instructional and informational products, including Moore's visual approach through action mapping (2019). Further, the *Success Approximation Model* (Allen, 2018; Allen & Sites, 2012) supports an agile instructional design understanding that highlights a shift away from more traditional instructional design processes and procedures while enhancing support towards a more experienced style of internalized approaches towards instructional design. Along with differentiated styles of instructional design models that support more traditional forms of instructional and informational training events, there is also the growth of interest in microlearning events. Hug (2007) and Kerres (2007) began the discussion of microlearning as an instructional design challenge, while Liang, Cao, and Zhang (2013) began the discussion around modeling the design of microlecture understandings. More recently, Khan (2019) reframed his *learning snippets* concept towards a microlearning understanding, wherein a reenvisioning of the concept of microlearning as workforce development is exemplified, as well as attempting to support informationally appropriate venues through which to engage the end-user. Within this initial understanding around microlearning and the instructional design process, we introduce our own understanding of microlearning as an instructional and informational engagement by introducing a microlearning instructional design model, the *RREDS Microlearning Model,* based upon microlearning events, as well as curricular engagement.

RREDS Microlearning Model

The *RREDS Microlearning Model* was named as a progressive approach, suggesting the five major areas of the model as:

R = Recursive

The repetition or continuous implementations or performance executions of information or procedural understandings in new and different ways, with successive results.

R = Reflect

Knowledge, individual understanding, and conceptual frameworking.

E = Engage

Target message applying supporting materials.

D & S = Develop and Scaffold

New or revised individual understanding and conceptual frameworking and objective, competency or capability successfully met.

From a cursory level of understanding, the *RREDS Microlearning Model* components are simplistic in manner, reflecting a one-dimensional approach towards introducing information, applying the targeted information, and then remembering the new information. Yet, from a deeper undergirding of engagement and support, the model's components introduce an impressively elegant, yet curiously sophisticated understanding of the human's desire towards engagement with chunks of viably useful information. These chunks of information are framed within styles of motivational engagement that not only emphasizes individual understanding of the information within each person's own prior knowledge base and conceptual frameworking of understanding, but progresses towards working with the new information in new ways of thoughtfully embedded understanding. This thoughtful embedding of competency-based, capability-based, and objective-framed manners that offer a give and take in implicit and explicit cognitive engagement, supports leading into newly oriented or revised individual understandings of the information. Additionally, the pattern recognition inherent within the targeted engagement with the new information or instructional events enhance the applying and supporting of subject matter understanding in new ways, reflecting the opportunity towards:

- The learner creating their own pattern of understanding
- Emphasizing conceptualization of the new information through a pattern recognition engagement
- A metacognitive realm of engagement wherein the learner recognizes her or his own pattern recognition.

The *RREDS Microlearning Model* suggests a *recursive,* successive event after the learner experiences the primary instructional events embedded within the model; namely *reflect, engage, develop,* and *scaffold.* The learner can continuously revolve back into the model with an opportunity towards experiencing information in a successive manner, working through the same major model areas so as to frame, reframe, and *scaffold* the new or revised knowledge base of understandings. This *recursive* event suggests that one's individual information or knowledge base of understanding is an evolutionary and revolving process wherein the knowledge base of understandings becomes an evolution as it repetitiously re-engages back into the major *RREDS Microlearning Model* components.

This is the context through which the *RREDS Microlearning Model* was conceptualized, and through which the discussion is framed. The *RREDS Microlearning Model* as an instructional design goal is a sequential process that supports the learner's cognitive ebb and flow of information, as the learner scaffolds concepts that are multiple or singular, new, or familiar. As a result, the learner reframes her/his knowledge base level of understanding, or forms a new and meaningful concept, that influences or changes the next level of one's knowledge base of understanding. Now, what does that really mean?

The semiotic hourglass (see Figure 14.1) is a metaphoric representation of how sand, representing a learner's prior knowledge, begins to tilt the hourglass as prior knowledge funnels and mixes and then remixes through the center of the

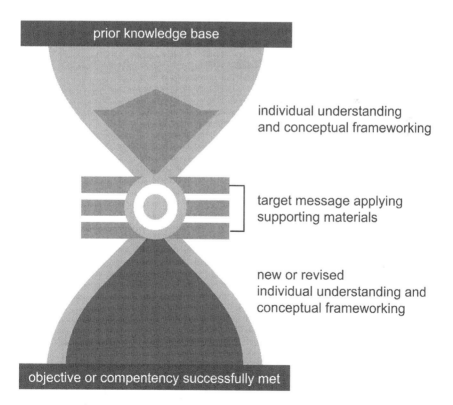

FIGURE 14.1 The RREDS Microlearning Model

hourglass. Hence, the mixing of prior knowledge and new information could reshape the learner's current thinking about the target message. As a result, the learner assimilates, analyses, and identifies the revised individual understanding supporting the microlearning objectives-framed efforts and competency level or capability level outcomes.

Thus, the reshaping of the learner's base of understanding begins as the hourglass tilts and mixes the sand as it flows into the center. The center of the hourglass includes supporting materials that reference or discuss the targeted message. During such an event the learner returns, or re-tilts, the hourglass to prior knowledge mixing the targeted message with prior knowledge to compare, analyze, or contrast the new information. The mixing of the new knowledge with the old knowledge thus causes another tilt in the hourglass remixing the new and old information, which flows between prior knowledge and the targeted message. In turn, the ebb and flow of the microlearning event's information causes potential shifts to the learner's cognitive thinking, which could potentially reshape the learner's perception while introducing new or familiar concepts.

As the learner reassembles the information between prior knowledge and new knowledge, another hourglass tilt is in the midst of occurring. Cognitively, patterns and associations begin to mix within the ebb and flow of information within the microlearning event experiential engagement. The learner awareness level increases as the knowledge base of understanding is revised into either a newly framed or reorganized conceptual framework of understanding. Thus, the mixture of new and old information intermingles. The learner adapts or revises concepts between prior knowledge, assimilated knowledge, and newly acquired knowledge understanding. The model suggests the incorporation of the target message, after which the model suggests the potential introduction of a new microlearning event. The last microlearning event applies the same action-oriented conception while working with the new instructional or informational information emphasized within the instructional event, further aligning the targeted message and the learners continuously engaged conceptual framework.

The *RREDS Microlearning Model* reshapes initial thinking around the impact of instructional events, by allowing the learner to procedurally engage with the microlearning information in new and different ways. Specifically, the learner first internally reflects upon one's own prior knowledge base, then a second experiential recognition is the engagement of the learner's initial prior knowledge as a focused activity towards distinguishing new information and beginning the process towards potentially reshaping the learner's understanding of the new instructional or informational information as well as initiation of thinking that occurs related to the subject matter. Thirdly, the learner engages in the offered additional activity, with the focus towards further solidifying the target message while analyzing and forward-leaning application of the learner's revised conceptual framework of understanding. The reinforcement of the targeted message is achieved on behalf of the learner, whether the microlearning event is directed towards objective-focused, competency-focused, or capability-focused under-standings. Additionally, a learner can choose to repetitiously re-engage back into the microlearning event, experiencing a recursively successive experience that re-engages with the information towards an evolution of subject matter under-standing at higher order levels of cognitive engagement and comprehension.

Prior Knowledge Base

Consider, that each learner's knowledge base of understanding and conceptual meaning-making ranges from novice to expert. The learner cognitively assimilates information into meaningful components, or patterns of information that implicitly forms into a knowledge base of understanding, which is eventually housed or stored in one's long-term cognitive memory. As an example, think about when a person experiences new information; the naturally occurring ebb and flow of informational understanding occurs as the learner analyzes the information and pulls from her/his own experience. From this ebb and flow of progressive understanding a pattern recognition and relation, or current and past meaningful associations, occurs. This progressive engagement with new information results in a conceptual answer. Cog-nitively, to see the example thru to the end, *A is for Apple*. Unless new information shifts and changes prior understanding, *A* will always pull from implicit cognition, presenting the information to the learner that *A is for Apple*.

Individual Understanding and Conceptual Frameworking

The *RREDS Microlearning Model* design instigates an instructionally appropriate engagement with an activity-based or scenario-based curriculum that subtly expresses and introduces the forthcoming targeted message, or focused informa-tion. Applying an activity-based introductory instructional event suggests prompting prior knowledge recognition, emphasizing the learner experiences and opportunities towards exploration or analyzation of the focused information, either individually or within a community-engaging learning environment. As the learner engages in the initiating activity, the suggested experiential response is that the learner scaffolds the targeted message's information and forms a con-ceptual frame of the targeted message, prior to actual target message engagement. As a result, the conceptual recollection builds and shapes the learner's knowledge base of understanding, supporting the advancing instructional goal of the micro-learning event.

Target Message Applying Supporting Materials

The hourglass central focus houses the primary emphasis of the microlearning event. The materials that support the target message are emphasized through a metaphoric target within the model, engaging in differentiated yet intricate labyrinth of the learner's opportunity to work with the new information or within the instructional event. The materials or associated elements within the target area depends on the curriculum and instructional events that support the prior-knowledge activity, as well as a focus upon the definitive knowledge activity.

The outcome of the target message outlines a foundational baseline of understanding where the learner recognizes a key component, or target message, used through the instructional efforts and associated materials. The consequence of a learner's ability to work with the new information, the targeted message, is towards an intense and more profound understanding of the subject matter. The targeted central delivery model structure may vary, dependent upon the specific subject matter; however, the targeted message reinforces a consistent message. Therefore, that reinforcement of a consistent message assists the learner's ebb and flow of similar or familiar information, which applies a repeat and recall methodology resulting in a formation of cognitive repetition patterns. As the learner flexes between a prior knowledge base, into forming a differentiated foundational knowledge baseline, the learner prepares for a higher order of cognitive thinking, leading into an enhanced conceptual framework of understanding around the targeted message.

New or Revised Individual Understanding and Conceptual Frameworking

Throughout the *RREDS Microlearning Model's* progressive process of procedural engagement, the learner reflects on prior knowledge, interlaces, reframes or scaffolds new knowledge, while also assimilating and gaining informational knowledge towards forming a revised conceptual framework of subject matter understanding. Thus, the learner revises individual understanding and develops an interpretation of the targeted conceptual framework. The *RREDS Microlearning Model* introduces another activity that seeks to understand if the learner clearly defines, explains, or recognizes the target message, the overarching goal of the instructional or informational focus upon the instructional design.

Metaphorically, the hourglass tilts and mixes information as the learner adopts or chooses to not adopt the information or instruction. At which time, during the learner's self-regulatory recognition or self-reflection, a differentiated conceptual framework can augment prior understandings. During the formation of a conceptual framework, consider the learner adopting or rejecting the presented information. The learner will need to decipher the perceived or actual value of information within the microlearning event. The learner must recognize that the adoption process of new information often attributes to the relevancy or value of the information, towards meeting a learner's goal as well as affirming the target message within the instructional design curriculum.

Outlining the value of the target message to the audience as embedded within the information integration process, throughout the microlearning event design, is an important yet viably integral consideration. Meaning, as the target message is presented and elucidated, an acknowledgement of the learner's thread of thought within the microlearning event, encourages further assimilation and adaptation of the new or revised conceptual framework of understanding. The adoption of the conceptual framework of understanding is the beginning, forming a solid foundational baseline for the learner to further engage in additional subject matter understandings. Meaning, as the learner receives more information about the target message, the learner can accept, reshape, revise, or expand upon their own conceptual framework throughout life or career experiences.

Objective, Competency, or Capability Successfully Met

The last aspect of the *RREDS Microlearning Model* assists in identifying the extent to which the learner's self-reflection, community engagement efforts, or microlearning experiences resulted in adoption or recognition of the targeted message. This enhances the formation of a revised conceptual framework knowledge base of understanding. The last activity subtly supports all key target message points outlined in the microlearning curriculum or supporting materials. Various delivery methods can apply during the last activity event, whether similar to the target message engagement or altogether different styles of engagement; however, the designer must know the audience and how that delivery method emphasizes the instructional design efforts and target message outcomes, before choosing how to deploy the activity.

Thus, the last activity emphasizes a crucial cognitive shift in the learner's thinking to meet the final instructional objective, competency, or capability goal. Meaning, the suggestion is that the learner experiences a cognitive change or shift as the activity progresses; as such, the learner might compare or contrast information, analyze or internally reflect upon new ideas, and openly discuss or identify ideas. The qualitative or quantitative learning analytics data during the final model activity event could potentially assist towards measuring the extent to which the targeted message objective, competency or capability level findings were successfully met during the microlearning event.

Implementation Considerations of the RREDS Microlearning Model

Recognizing that learners approach informational or instructional materials in various ways, the differentiated forms of engagement highlighted within the *RREDS Microlearning Model* implementation phase shifts, alters, modifies, and emphasizes transferences with the learner's implicit and explicit cognition, allowing the learner to experience the information using their own internalized comfortability, choice progression, and acquisition style. Therefore, the model does not force individuals or even a learning community of learners into one method of thinking. For example, providing *yes or no* lock-step scenario-based questions without an explanatory of why and how would shut down higher order thinking skills, due to the lower order design of the instructional or informational events. Additionally, the model suggests an implied single focus effort of digestible information so the learner can reflect and revisit the information as the learner progresses and seeks to recognize the target message, as a viable microlearning event that may be considered as an object with an objective-oriented, competency-based or capability-based outcome.

The redeployment, transference, and cognitive refocus exertions involving the targeted message area supports a representative outline of the targeted information, suggesting causation associated with a shift in the learner's thinking. The shift metaphorically representing a style of cognitive ebb and flow through the hourglass's fundamental separation point offers a shear stress of zero; this means that the boundary layer of prior knowledge cannot retain its viscous consistency reflective of prior knowledge solidity; instead, the fluid nature of learning and knowledge acquisition suggests that a style of osmosis slowly shifts prior knowledge understandings based upon and within newly acquired information, emphasizing a mixing, sharing, reconstituting, and reenvisioning of conceptual frameworks of understanding within each learner's implicit and explicit cognitive understandings. Targeting a metaphoric forward and backward tilting cognitive hourglass, representative of old and new knowledge as it mixes or revises the prior knowledge base, may result in a new knowledge base of understanding, resulting in the microlearning event's ultimate outcome. The shift, or Z-factor, is not one-way. Instead, the dual nature and multiple shifting understandings of cognitive informational acquisition considers that the learner may recall, relate, revise, or scaffold information into various patterns of understanding, causing other cognitive shifts rebuilding or emphasizing the conceptual framework base of understanding.

The implementation considerations (see Figure 14.2 on p. 000) of the *RREDS Microlearning Model* starts with a prior knowledge baseline within an activity-based approach, subtly supporting the target message. Next, the learner engages in the core or targeted message, reflecting upon or recalling the prior knowledge through active engagement as a prior knowledge activity. The Z-factor transpires during the prior knowledge activity engagement and the targeted message experience that then funnels into the metaphoric bottom of the hourglass, assisting the learner to incorporate new information or instructional experience through the processes of revision, description, identification, or scaffolding of prior and current knowledge that results in a revised conceptual framework of understanding around the microlearning event's target topic. The final microlearning event's activity reinforces the target message. Of importance and impact, is that the learner incorporates and combines prior, revised, and newly gained subject matter-specific knowledge that emphasizes incorporating the target message and lessons learned throughout the *RREDS Microlearning Model* effort.

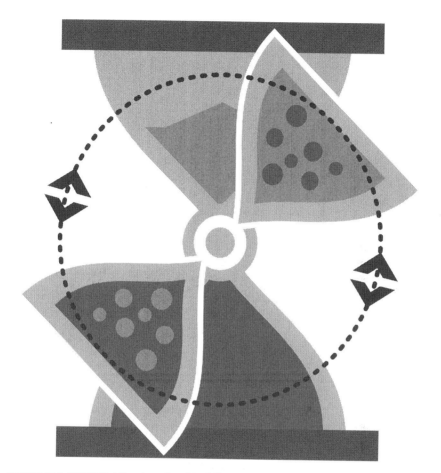

FIGURE 14.2 RREDS Microlearning Model's implementation

Underpinning Frameworks

Learning Theory Considerations

Recognizing that microlearning events are fully articulated nuggets of information that are designed as short, succinct learning opportunities, recognition around the strength of microlearning events is a forward-leaning understanding around the conception of informational and instructional learning opportunities. Additional emphasis upon objective-led, competency-focused and capability-focused microlearning products support the engagement of short-term knowledge acquisition endeavors as well as longer-term curricular training understandings. Through this chapter's discussion, the authors will not only frame an instructional design model that supports the integration of microlearning events throughout the instructional process that may be described as a time-laden engagement in the ebb and flow of learning and informational acquisition, but also view the style of microlearning within a larger training event understanding. The *RREDS Microlearning Model* develops an understanding around the instructional and informational engagement that is realized through objective-led as well as competency-focused and capability-focused microlearning engagement.

Further, an emphasis upon "priming" learning events through pre-training endeavors that are meant to support prior knowledge acquisition, knowledge checks, and remembrance of prior knowledge preceding the actual training event are framed as microlearning events, while also emphasizing after-training extension microlearning events that are longitudinal in nature. These are aspects of not only the *RREDS Microlearning Model's* prior knowledge base component, but also the extended curricular engagement that evolves around pedagogical novice, andragogy, and heutagogy. The framework undergirding this work is supported by Vygotsky's conceptual framework of understanding (Vygotsky, 1933/1966, 1934/1987, 1935, 1962, 1978, 1981), focused upon engaging in prior knowledge engagement that also supports metacognition around differentiated understanding of the prior knowledge based within rethinking and relearning new knowledge. This further re-engages with not only prior knowledge and new knowledge, but also the recognition of the community impact upon framing, reframing, and reconceptualizing knowledge within one's own professional and personalized community environment of understanding and enhanced engagement.

Bloom's *Taxonomy of the Cognitive Domain* and Anderson and Krathwohl's *Revised Taxonomy of the Cognitive Domain for the Digital Age* both offer a progressive emphasis from lower order thru higher order information engagement (Anderson, 2013; Anderson et al., 2001; Bloom et al., 1956; Crawford & Smith, 2015; Krathwohl, Bloom, & Masia, 1964). Anderson and Krathwohl's revisions to Bloom's originating *Taxonomy of the Cognitive Domain* emphasize not only the knowledge availability and attainment within today's Information Age engagement, but also the emphasis upon thought processes around initial-engagement and re-engagement of learners. With the readily available information within the Digital Age offers an emphasis upon remembering versus knowledge acquisition at the lower order thinking skills, all the way towards reconsideration of Bloom's Evaluation level that was the 1956 height of higher order thinking skills (Bloom et al., 1956). Yet, rethinking Evaluation as a lower-level higher order thinking skill, is then replaced with synthesis and Creation in Anderson and Krathwohl's revised taxonomy of the cognitive domain, that support the Digital Age focus upon readily available information while emphasizing the creation of new ways of thinking about and understanding information (Anderson, 2013; Anderson et al., 2001).

Towards consideration of metacognitive engagement, or learning about learning, the *RREDS Microlearning Model* emphasizes the newly framed individual understanding of learned information, as well as potentials around revising individual understandings and conceptual frameworking (Vygotsky, 1933/1966, 1934/1987, 1935, 1962, 1978, 1981) that supports community engagement and rethinking new knowledge and information. Additionally, Wenger's community of learning experience and learning in landscapes of practice through multiple different formats (Wenger, 1998, 2009a, 2009b, 2010; Wenger-Trayner et al., 2014; Wenger-Trayner & Wenger-Trayner, 2014, 2015) supports conceptual and cognitive checks within community-based approaches towards enhanced informational understandings. Community engagement supports and revises one's own informational and instructional learning events, towards offering a deeper understanding of new information and how this new information engages with prior information. New learning occurs, based upon the introduction of new information and instructional engagement, with a focused effort towards understanding the target message that is applying supporting material within an individual's prior understanding of information within the real world.

Additionally, conceptualizing the *RREDS Microlearning Model*, Bandura's work aligned with social learning, motivation, and self-efficacy (Bandura, 1969, 1973, 1977, 1986, 1997; Bandura & Walters, 1963). This emphasizes one's ability to develop an understanding around subject matter information through knowledge acquisition and social engagement. This supports not only motivational interest in the new information but also the conception of self-efficacy. The understanding of self-efficacy is the emphasis upon one's belief in one's ability to succeed within not only specific realms of informational engagement but also one's ability to successfully attain set goals through a sense of learner confidence.

Finally, additional understandings around Victor H. Vroom's expectancy constructs (Holdford & Lovelace-Elmore, 2001; Parsons & Goff, 1978; Vroom, 1964) support the comprehension of learning endeavors that offer motivational support towards performance engagement towards achieving desirable goals. This is impactful within the *RREDS Microlearning Model*, based upon the microlearning discernment related to the conscious choice of individuals towards re-engaging with one's prior knowledge base while introducing alternative new information through a directed message approach that has a targeted outcome towards successfully meeting objective-based, competency-based or capability-based goals. In turn, the learner can choose an opportunity to repeat the *RREDS Microlearning Model* in a recursive fashion reframing or scaffolding their new or old knowledge base of understandings resulting in revised or new objective-based, competency-based or capability-based goals. Towards supporting the concept of learning theories as understanding the framing of information, an awareness and appreciation around metaphoric representations that further support the semiotic undergirdings of signs and symbols within cultural and more personalized understandings of information is also appropriate. Not only towards framing thoughts around the representation of subject matter, but also towards framing a grasp of the *RREDS Microlearning Model*.

Metaphoric Representations

The implementation of metaphors and metaphoric cues supports each person's understanding of novel, complex, and unfamiliar information. This offers the perfect opportunity towards supporting the user's understanding through a depth of semiotic engagement. Simplistically, semiotics refers to signs and symbols that carry with it a sense of universal understanding throughout multiple cultures of awareness and encounter. Within the introduction of the *RREDS Microlearning Model* to the reader, the novel information represented throughout this model's approach to instructional and informational nuggets of impactful engagement may be a novel approach towards microlearning engagement. As such, the representation of this information through differentiated metaphoric understandings and meanings allows for semiotics to develop a situational awareness, pulling from one's cognitive framework of recognition and understanding. In turn, the user will more fully engage in the metaphoric representation of an understood symbol, towards a new and different meaning of implementation. Within this discussion, the metaphoric representation of *time* as displayed through time symbols and iconography includes the hourglass clock, the clock with a dial face that can also be reimagined through a Salvador Dali-esque Surrealist spiraling reconsideration of metaphoric symbolism.

Metaphors can be defined in innumerably different ways, directly dependent upon the realm within which metaphors are the topic of discussion. As an informational understanding, metaphors offer a representation of new or complex information within the bounds of previously understood frameworks. As suggested by Scardino and Crawford (2000), metaphors can be framed

> as integral to user interface design and an environment in which information can be presented in an understandable fashion, so as to aid the user in developing an understanding of the information being presented and to aid in the development of a mental model of understanding. Metaphors may also carry an imaginary, creative aspect to them that aid the user in the further development of information usage and understanding. Creativity is an aspect of human thinking and intelligence that directly parallels the integration of metaphors within a learning environment. The creativity emphasized through the use of metaphors towards the further understanding and integration of information is imperative towards the contextual situation that drives the human to conceptualize the information into mental models of understanding.
>
> *(p. 813–814)*

Further, Samuel Taylor Coleridge stated,

> The imagination ... that reconciling and mediatory power, which incorporating the reason in images of the sense and organizing (as it were) the flux of the senses by the permanence and self-circling energies of the reason, gave birth to a system of symbols, harmonious in themselves, and consubstantial with the truth of which they are the conductors.
>
> *(as quoted by Veale, 1995, para. 1)*

Additionally, as suggested by Crawford (2003):

> Metaphors have an impact on every portion of our environment and every day of our existence. As such, metaphor may offer a fundamental sense of comprehension and levels of reassurance that are essential requirements for the learners within an eLearning environment. ... The imagination augments the learner's level of knowledge comprehension and attainment, and promotes the advancement of higher order thinking skills due to the representations of universal comprehension that underlie the eLearning environment's organizational structure, scope and sequence. Further, the incorporation and assimilation of metaphorical cues, especially through the use of metaphorically augmented graphics, augments the information context.
>
> *(p. 78)*

Z-Factor

The Z-factor is an intriguing consideration within the *RREDS Microlearning Model*, as this term is commonly noted as suggesting the extent to which the quality of a product and the contents of a product are judged to be worthy of and deserving of additional awareness, consideration and attention. Within a microlearning event that is focused upon instructional or informational focused effort, the Z-factor is reflective of the quality of timeliness and engagement of the microlearning user, towards a depth of substantial cognitive focus, a recognition of immediate worth and worthiness associated with time, effort, and engagement, as well as the user's judgement associated with the short-term and long-term value of the microlearning event as designated by the progressive user understanding around prior knowledge base and an individual end-user's understanding and conceptual frameworking associated with the microlearning topic. The immediacy of the objective-focused, competency-focused, or capability-focused outcomes of value and worth within the user's community environment may suggest scholarly, social, cultural, or additional styles of value and worth related to the quality of the microlearning product and the immediacy of the microlearning's content as defined by subject matter viability and impactfulness within short-term as well as long-term cognitive significance as assessed, estimated, and appraised by the end-user.

Enhancing the Metaphor: Styles of Curricular Engagement

Through the *RREDS Microlearning Model's* overarching discussion and more detailed model component discussion, an understanding of the model's framework was established. Yet, from a curricular engagement consideration, exactly what does that look like? A framework through which to contemplate curricular engagement is around considerations towards the learner's prior knowledge base within the subject matter milieu. This may be delineated as *pedagogy*, as framed through the tabula rasa or subject matter novice approach, *andragogy* as framed through a level of subject matter knowledge attainment but that looks towards enhancements of the subject matter understanding and expertise through informational and instructional events, as well as *heutagogy* as framed through an acknowledgement of a strong subject matter knowledge base underpinning that delves into deeper understandings of specialization information through a self-determined selection approach towards information attainment. The learner's acquisition and conceptual understanding of new knowledge within a microlearning approach is intriguing, engaged in differentiated styles of microlearning employment and execution as a style through which people can engage with information and instruction. As such, the styles of curricular engagement are framed through the understandings of *pedagogy, andragogy,* and *heutagogy.*

Additionally, towards enhancing the time metaphoric representations as enhanced frameworks of understanding, the time metaphor engages the progressive and differentiated engagement, a time-laden engagement in the ebb and flow of learning and informational acquisition. As previously framed, the metaphoric representation of *time* as displayed through time symbols and iconography includes the hourglass clock as metaphorically representing the model. Further, through a curricular engagement discussion around *pedagogy, andragogy,* and *heutagogy,* the clock with a dial face that can also be reimagined as a framework of metaphorically conceptual understanding that emphasizes the conceptualized implementation of the *RREDS Microlearning Model* informational and instructional snippets as based within the learner's prior knowledge base, acquisition of novel and impactful knowledge, as well as style of microlearning availability, implementation, engagement, and outcomes that structure around meeting the objective, competency or capability as the focus of the microlearning event.

A somewhat Surrealist viewpoint may be appropriate towards engaging within this metaphoric representation of implementation and styles of curricular engagement, engaging the unconsciousness of the implicit and explicit cognitive mind's interworkings. The strength of highlighting implicit and explicit cognitive understandings throughout the informational and instructional learning opportunities presented as microlearning events, highlights not only the social engagement and association-based understandings embedded within implicit cognitive engagement. Yet, that explicit cognitive engagement reverberates and recognizes conceptual frameworks of understanding that are interworking with new information as well as prior attitudes, beliefs and thoughtful reflections that may be analytic in nature, towards engaging with information and instructional opportunities in new and differentiated ways.

Pedagogy

Pedagogy as a learning and cognitive understanding has traditionally been allocated to the younger learner's cognitive development. Yet, from a differentiated perspective, one may view pedagogy as a novice learner approach wherein the subject matter knowledge base is not currently sufficiently developed for a higher order thinking and understanding engagement (Anderson, 2013; Anderson et al., 2001; Bloom et al., 1956; Crawford & Smith, 2015; Krathwohl, Bloom, & Masia, 1964). As such, a pedagogical perspective towards informational and instructional relevance may be delineated as a novice learner approach wherein a viable knowledge base, a conceptual framework of understanding, has not yet been viably developed.

Within this understanding, the *RREDS Microlearning Model's* curricular engagement may be framed as a clock face wherein microlearning events are progressively presented and embedded as subsequently interactive approaches towards developing a learner's appropriate knowledge base of understanding. The progressive numerals on the clock face, traditionally offered as a continuously advancing numerical designation, instead is reframed towards a gradually advancing, step-by-step piecemeal approach towards gradually increasing the learner's understanding of the subject matter desired to acquire. The microlearning events are designated as occurring in a step-by-step manner, presenting a previously decided upon progression of microlearning events that occur one after the other. As the hands of the clock progress around the clock face's numerical designations, equally appropriate do the microlearning events systematically engage the learners in progressively systematic informational or instructional products that are progressively presented to the learner. The outcome is the learner's acquired knowledge base and conceptual framework of understanding, derived from the differentiated and progressively engaged microlearning events as metaphorically represented in Figure 14.3 (see p. 000). This figure represents a learner's lack of knowledge, controlling a progressive knowledge acquisition approach to learning.

Andragogy

Andragogy is understood as an adult learning theory, wherein Knowles (1950, 1962/1977, 1975, 1984a, 1984b) suggests this is the art and science associated with adult learning. Yet, what is adult learning? Adult learning suggests that the learner engages in a readiness to learn that may suggest prior knowledge, an initially developed conceptual framework of understanding, as well as the potential towards experiential engagement with the subject matter. Implicitly important within a discussion of andragogy and the *RREDS Microlearning Model's* curricular engagement is the prior knowledge base that emphasizes a recognition of the learner's prior knowledge and readiness to engage in the subject matter in new and different ways. Also, integrally important, is a recognition of the learner's level of subject matter understanding and suggested expertise with the subject matter, towards appropriately designating microlearning events that would be deemed prior knowledge checks and an assurance of implicit cognitive and explicit cognitive engagement with the subject matter. Upon appropriately

FIGURE 14.3 RREDS Microlearning Model's pedagogical novice metaphorical curricular engagement

designating the learner's actual subject matter understanding as designated by prior knowledge and conceptual frameworks of understanding, the learner can progressively engage in microlearning events within the *RREDS Microlearning Model's* implementation of instructional and informational microlearning events as appropriately introduced to the learner.

Within this understanding, the *RREDS Microlearning Model's* curricular engagement may be framed as differentiated clock faces, wherein each learner's quality of knowledge base and subject matter expertise, as well as conceptual framework of understanding, suggests the microlearning event's progressive points at which the learner may initiate viable microlearning events. This approach ensures the learner does not plod through mandated knowledge base microlearning events already successfully achieved and the potential negative impact upon the learner's readiness to learn as well as oriented engagement in the microlearning event learning processes, but instead that the learner may begin engagement with the initiating microlearning event that recruits and inducts the learner into the appropriately viable and engaging microlearning event. This engagement not only motivates the learner's progression forward into a depth of learning event, but also ensures the allowance for the learner to progress without a backward-leaning approach that mandates the motivationally lacking and disengaging expectations around plodding through microlearning events within which the learner has already achieved successful accomplishment of the designated microlearning event's successfully met objective, competency or capability designation. Simplistically stated, the andragogical approach to microlearning as curricular engagement embeds the expectation that the learner's prior knowledge acquisition will be buttressed and acknowledged. This means the learner may progress forward into the microlearning event that adequately addresses the learner's readiness to learn without postponing or lacking the immediacy of solicited application as a recognized accumulation of knowledge base with the subsequent forward-leaning approach that supports the motivational engagement with enhanced subject matter knowledge acquisition.

The representation of several clock faces supports the traditional offering of continuously advancing numerical designations as displayed through each clock face; however, the differentiation is that each clock face emphasizes a different time designation. The introduction of the traditional hourly time designation metaphorically represents the subject matter progression from the 12:00 time designation, progressing on an hourly rate as one progressively views the clock faces in the graphic representation available in Figure 14.4. Impactful and worthy of highlight is the shadowed area on each clock face, with the initial clock face's shadowed area designated from 12:00–1:00, the next shadowed clock area designated from 12:00–2:00, and so forth. 12:00 designates the point at which no prior knowledge is attained, 1:00 designates a small amount of prior knowledge has been attained, and the learner should begin engaging in microlearning events at the 1:00 level of subject matter progression, while another learner may have a more advanced subject matter knowledge base and conceptual framework of understanding that is designated by the 2:00 level of subject matter progression, and so on. This representation is integrally important to the learning within an andragogically appropriate curricular engagement, as the learner begins engaging with the microlearning events at the appropriate microlearning event level of subject matter engagement. Impactful to this metaphoric representation is a recognition that the shadowed area of the clock face may be represented as the learner's prior knowledge acquisition. Meaning, each clock face represents a differentiated learner's readiness to engage with the microlearning events. The learner does systematically engage in microlearning events, but the progressively systematic information or instructional products that are progressively presented to the learner are couched within an understanding and recognition that the learners should not have to successfully re-learn and re-address objective-based, competency-based and

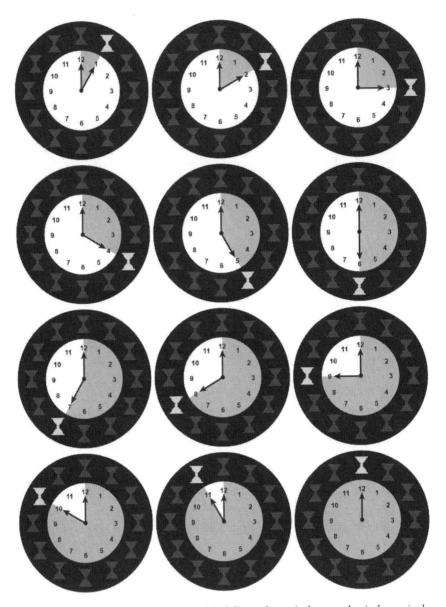

FIGURE 14.4 RREDS Microlearning Model's andragogical metaphorical curricular engagement

capability-based expectational mandates that have been previously achieved. The adult learner achieves a recognition of subject matter prior knowledge and conceptual framework of understanding, embedding motivational engagement, and readiness to learn associated with engaging in microlearning events at the appropriate progressive point in the microlearning event progression. The outcome is the learner's acquired enhanced learning and knowledge acquisition, derived from differentiated and progressively engaged microlearning events as metaphorically represented, yet the learner begins engaging with the microlearning events at the point that is most appropriate from an objective-laden, competency-based, and capability-based understanding.

Heutagogy

Heutagogy is a style of learning that was coined by Hase and Kenyon (2000, 2007, 2013), with the initiation of heutagogy as a style of learning described by Hase and Kenyon (2007) as:

> So, over a bottle of a nice crisp white wine one cold Canberra evening, Chris and I described the notion of self-determined learning that best described an extension to pedagogy and andragogy. Chris eventually came up with the term heutagogy, which is derived from the ancient Greek for 'self' with some adjustments and the 'agogy' added. Heutagogy is concerned with learner-centred learning that sees the learner as the major agent in their own learning, which occurs as a result of personal experiences
>
> *(p. 112)*

The self-determined learning approach towards a learner who has achieved not only a knowledge base and conceptual framework of understanding around a subject matter but also a depth of understanding that embraces the subject matter more fully is impressive, yet the introduction of heutagogy as a form of learning through a complexity theory approach (Hase, 2000; Hase & Kenyon, 2000) more fully comprises, supports, and articulates learning as a natural extension into intriguing forays and self-determined roads that may have not yet been traveled is an astoundingly freeing opportunity towards learning in a more Surrealist and non-traditional manner. Meaning, the learner is the central focus of the learning experience, with the learner-centric approach being the ability of the learner to choose their own guiding interests associated with the subject matter knowledge base and conceptual framework of understanding. The learner self-selects where the subject matter will guide the learning efforts and engagement, not the instructional facilitator. Through this means, the learner is developing expertise in areas of the subject matter that intrigue or call out for additional curiosity. As such, the complexity associated with higher order thinking approaches and the centric focus upon the learner's primary interest in progressive understandings around tenets of the knowledge base guide the learner's journey. This is neither curriculum-centric, instructor-centric nor competency-centric or capability-centric as an approach; instead, this is a learner-centric approach that allows freedom of choice, freedom of knowledge base extension and complexity systems that are adaptive and potentially recursive approaches at a deeper cognitive level of understanding and engagement. As quoted from Hase and Kenyon (2007):

> it had become obvious to us (and many constructivists around the globe I am sure) that people only change in response to a very clear need. This usually involves distress such as confusion, dissonance, and fear or a more positive motive such as intense desire. The satiated and the comfortable are less likely to make a behavioural change no matter what others may desire and we'll come back to this later in relation to teacher-centred approaches to learning.
>
> *(p. 112)*

This is impactful towards an understanding of the styles of curricular engagement brought forward by the *RREDS Microlearning Model*. Specifically, the microlearning approach supports and enhances the opportunity to delve into focused information or instructional events on an as desired, and as needed basis. This supports the opportunity for the learner to self-select and self-define information with which to work, on an as desired and as needed basis. The learner, with a developed and well-articulated knowledge base and conceptual framework of understanding, self-determines what information is most desirable and impactful during a specific progression of analytic engagement and the appropriately complex and embedded engagement with the information and instructional events.

Within this understanding, the *RREDS Microlearning Model's* curricular engagement may be framed as a Salvador Dali-esque approach to a Surrealist spiraling reconsideration of metaphoric symbolism. Complexity theory, as suggested by Hase and Kenyon (2000, 2007, 2013; Hase, 2000), embeds an understanding around the learner's progressive needs to enhance their understandings of subject matter that intrigues them, that may extend far beyond curriculum-centric, competency-centric, capability-centric instructor-centric and even instruction-centric guided approaches towards controlling the learner. The learner has attained a competent level of knowledge base representative towards reaching higher order thinking skills levels of attainment, with the learner expanding beyond the bounds of the traditional learning experiences and into the complex world of analysis, evaluation, synthesis, and creation of potentially new ways through which to think about and view the subject matter. As such, why are microlearning events appropriate within a heutagogical approach to learning?

A metaphoric representation of understanding this complex comprehension of the self-directed learning progression may be an appropriate lens through which to view the *RREDS Microlearning Model's* curricular engagement. The traditional face of a timepiece is reenvisioned, introducing a surreal view that is complex in nature, unknowing the next step approach within the learning journey and where it may lead the learner. The clock face is reframed as a swirl of knowledge, a swirl of subject matter opportunity towards connecting, reconnecting, and recreating knowledge through analysis, synthesis, evaluation, and the potential creation of new ways of thinking and being. The microlearning events are designated within the Surrealist clock face interface, replacing the numeric designations as microlearning events that are metaphorically designated through the hourglass iconography. The surreal representation of the microlearning events as a swirling conundrum of complexity and depth of analysis frees the learner from any progressive approach towards engaging with microlearning events, allowing the learner to pick and choose microlearning events on a self-selected and as-desired means of engagement and re-engagement with information and instructional events. The progression of the clock hands around the clock's spiraling Surrealist clock face are progressive yet non-committal in nature, rethinking the flow of ideas and information on innumerable levels of thought process, conceptual framework re-engagement and enhanced understanding, as well as a learner-defined systematic engagement with the microlearning events. The outcome is the learner's acquired enhancement of understanding around more defined and specialized areas within the larger depth and breadth of the subject matter area of expertise and focus, deriving from the differentiated understanding around the learner's self-defined and self-designated journey deeper into the subject matter understanding, engaging microlearning events as metaphorically represented in Figure 14.5 below.

Summary and Next Steps

The *RREDS Microlearning Model* is an instructional design model that is based upon the concept of microlearning events that support and engages learners at different levels of curricular engagement that includes pedagogy as novice learner, andragogy, and heutagogy. The *RREDS Microlearning Model* supports the immediacy of focused subject matter information or instructional events that occur in a progressive yet timely longitudinal approach. This style of focused attention towards achieving objectives-laden, competency-focused, or capability-focused engagement with subject matter offers the opportunity for learners to more holistically work with and develop understandings of the subject matter at differentiated levels of cognitive engagement and taxonomic understanding (Anderson, 2013; Anderson et al., 2001; Bloom et al., 1956; Crawford & Smith, 2015; Krathwohl, Bloom, & Masia, 1964). Yet, towards highlighting the metaphoric representation approach towards conceptualizing the model suggests that the time metaphor's foundational approach towards an hourglass understanding with an emphasis upon the targeted subject matter message and the application of supporting materials strengthens the learner's prior knowledge base, then the learner's individual understanding and conceptual frameworking from a forward-learning engagement. The centralized, yet focused approach towards the target message and applying supporting materials, with the *shaking up* engagement of the subject matter's microlearning target message acting as the implementation approach that lends itself towards working with the information, gives way to new or revised individual understandings and conceptual frameworking,

FIGURE 14.5 RREDS Microlearning Model's heutagogical metaphoric curricular engagement

resulting in the learner successfully meeting designated microlearning event objectives or competencies as designated.

The *RREDS Microlearning Model's* approach towards curricular engagement embraces the Z-factor approach wherein the quality of the product and the contents of the product are independently judged to be worthy and deserving of the learner's awareness, consideration, and attention. No matter whether the curricular engagement is designated as objectives-based learning events, competency-based, or capability-based learning events, the focused approach towards microlearning as curricular events embraces an immediacy and depth of packed and focused information that supports the learner's implicit and explicit cognitive understandings that occur through not only informational but also instructional learning opportunities.

Implications associated with this model embrace an approach towards a differentiated way to consider learners at different stages of subject matter engagement, no matter whether the learner is defined as a young learner or an adult learner, no matter whether the learner is defined as a novice learner or an expert learner. A forward-leaning approach towards this work emphasizes further research around the *RREDS Microlearning Model's* implementation within differentiated realms of instructional engagement.

Discussion Questions

1. How do you weigh the current value of the *RREDS Microlearning Model* within the instructional design realm?
2. As conjectured analysis, based upon the *RREDS Microlearning Model* as it is currently framed, what impact do you think the model will have on future instructional design models and curricular engagement? Please provide examples.
3. How might you differentiate the *RREDS Microlearning Model's* implementation within novice pedagogy, andragogy, and heutagogy learning endeavors?

References

Allen, M. W. (2018). The Successive Approximation Model (SAM): A Closer Look. In Dempsey, J. V. & Reiser, R. A. (Eds.). *Trends and Issues in Instructional Design and Technology*, 42–51. New York: Pearson.

Allen, M., & Sites, R. (2012). *Leaving ADDIE for SAM: An Agile Model for Developing the Best Learning Experiences*. American Society for Training and Development.

Anderson, L. (2013). *A Taxonomy for Learning, Teaching, and Assessing: A Revision of Bloom's Taxonomy of Educational Objectives*, Abridged Edition. London, UK: Pearson.

Anderson, L. W. (Ed.), Krathwohl, D. R. (Ed.), Airasian, P. W., Cruikshank, K. A., Mayer, R. E., Pintrich, *et al.* (2001). *A Taxonomy for Learning, Teaching, and Assessing: A Revision of Bloom's Taxonomy of Educational Objectives*. White Plains, NY: Longman.

Bandura, A. (1969). *Principles of Behavior Modification*. New York: Holt, Rinehart & Winston.

Bandura, A. (1973). *Aggression: A Social Learning Analysis*. Englewood Cliffs, NJ: Prentice-Hall.

Bandura, A. (1977). *Social Learning Theory*. New York: General Learning Press.

Bandura, A. (1986). *Social Foundations of Thought and Action*. Englewood Cliffs, NJ: Prentice-Hall.

Bandura, A. (1997). *Self-Efficacy: The Exercise of Control*. New York: W. H. Freeman.

Bandura, A., & Walters, R. (1963). *Social Learning and Personality Development*. New York: Holt, Rinehart & Winston.

Bloom, B. S. (Ed.), Engelhart, M. D., Furst, E. J., Hill, W. H., & Krathwohl, D. R. (1956). *Taxonomy of Educational Objectives: The Classification of Educational Goals*. Handbook 1: Cognitive Domain. New York, Toronto: Longmans, Green.

Crawford, C. M. (2003). *Integrating metaphorical cues to enhance learner conceptual frameworks: Understanding within Web-based academic coursework*. Paper presentation at the meeting of The International Conference on New Directions in the Humanities, Island of Rhodes, Greece.

Crawford, C. (2004). Non-linear instructional design model: Eternal, synergistic design and development. *British Journal of Educational Technology* 35(4), 413–420.

Crawford, C. M., & Smith, M. S. (2015). Rethinking Bloom's Taxonomy: Implicit Cognitive Vulnerability as an Impetus Towards Higher Order Thinking Skills. In J. Zing (Ed.), *Exploring Implicit Cognition: Learning, Memory, and Social-Cognitive Processes*, (pp. 86–103.) Hershey, PA: Information Science Reference (an imprint of IGI Global). doi:10.4018/978-1-4666-6599-6.ch004.

Dick, W., & Carey, L. (1978). *The Systematic Design of Instruction*. New York: Glenview, IL: Scott, Foresman and Company.

Dick, W., Carey. L., & Carey, J. O. (2014). *Systematic Design of Instruction* (8th ed.). London: Pearson.

Dorsey, L., Goodrum, D., & Schwen, T. (1997) Rapid Collaborative Prototyping as an Instructional Development Paradigm. In C. Dills & A. Romiszowski's (Eds.) *Instructional Development Paradigms*, p. 449. Englewood Cliffs, New Jersey. Educational Technology Publications.

Gagné, R. M. (1977). *The Conditions of Learning* (4th ed.). New York: Holt, Rinehart & Winston.

Hall, R. H., Watkins, S. E., & Eller, V. M. (2003). A model of web-based design for learning. In M. G. Moore & W. G. Anderson (Eds.) *Handbook of Distance Education*, 367–375. Mahwah, New Jersey: Lawrence Erlbaum Associates.

Hase, S., & Kenyon, C. (2000). From andragogy to heutagogy. Ulti-BASE In-Site.

Hase, S., & Kenyon, C. (2007). Heutagogy: A child of complexity theory. *Complicity: An international journal of complexity and education*, 4(1), pp. 111–118.

Hase, S., & Kenyon, C. (Eds.). (2013). *Self-determined learning: Heutagogy in action*. A&C Black.

Holdford, A. D. A., & Lovelace-Elmore, B. (2001). Applying the principles of human motivation to pharmaceutical education. *Journal of Pharmacy Teaching*, 8(4), 1–18.

Kerres, M. (2007). Microlearning as a challenge for instructional design. In T. Hug's (Ed.) *Didactics of Microlearning: Concepts, Discourses and Examples*, 98–109. New York: Waxmann Verlag.

Khan, B. (2019). Microlearning: Quick and meaningful snippets for training solutions. *International Journal of Research in Educational Sciences*, 2(2), 275–284. http://iafh.net/index.php/IJRES/article/view/107.

Knowles, M. S. (1950) *Informal Adult Education*. New York: Association Press.

Knowles, M. S. (1962, 1977). *A History of the Adult Education Movement in the USA*. New York: Krieger.

Knowles, M. (1975). *Self-Directed Learning*. Chicago: Follet.

Knowles, M. (1984a). *Andragogy in Action*. San Francisco: Jossey-Bass.

Knowles, M. (1984b). *The Adult Learner: A Neglected Species* (3rd ed.). Houston, TX: Gulf Publishing.

Krathwohl, D. R., Bloom, B. S., & Masia, B. B. (1964). *Taxonomy of educational objectives: The classification of educational goals*. Handbook II: The Affective Domain. New York: David McKay.

Kumar, S., (2007, July 12). Instructional Design [Blog post]. https://sunilfrench.blogspot.com/2007/07/learning-theories.html.

Liang, L., Cao, Q., & Zhang, B. (2013). Research on a micro-lecture design model through comparative case study [J]. *Open Education Research*, 1, 65–73.

Mager, R. F. (1984). *Preparing Instructional Objectives* (Revised 2nd ed.). Belmont, CA: Lake Publishing.

Moore, C. (2019). *What is action mapping?* [Blog post]. https://blog.cathy-moore.com/action-mapping-a-visual-approach-to-training-design/.

Parsons, J. E., & Goff, S. B. (1978). Achievement & motivation: Dual modalities. *Journal of Educational Psychology*, 13, 93–96.

Scardino, D. F., & Crawford, C. M. (2000). *Developing metaphorically inclusive graphics within an informative and visually engaging web site*. In Proceedings of WebNet World Conference on the WWW and Internet 2000 (pp. 813–814). San Antonio, Texas: Association for the Advancement of Computing in Education (AACE). www.learntechlib.org/primary/p/6517.

Tripp, S. D., & Bichelmayer, B. (1990) Rapid prototyping: An alternative instructional design strategy. *Educational Technology Research and Development* 38(1), 31–44.

Veale, T. (1995). Metaphor, memory and meaning: Symbolic and connectionist issues in metaphor interpretation. www.compapp.dcu.ie/~tonyv/Thesis/chapter%201.html.

Vroom, V. H. (1964). *Work and Motivation*. New York: Wiley.

Vygotsky, L. S. (1933/1966). Play and its role in the mental development of the child. *Soviet psychology*, 12(6), 62–76.

Vygotsky, L. S. (1934/1987). *Thinking and Speech*. In R. W. Rieber & A. S. Carton (Eds.), The collected works of L. S. Vygotsky, Volume 1: *Problems of General Psychology* (pp. 39–285). New York: Plenum Press.

Vygotsky, L. S. (1935). *Mental Development of Children During Education*. Moscow-Leningrad: Uchpedgiz.

Vygotsky, L. S. (1962). *Thought and Language*. Cambridge MA: MIT Press.

Vygotsky, L. S. (1978). *Mind in Society: The Development of Higher Psychological Processes*. Cambridge, MA: Harvard University Press.

Vygotsky, L. S. (1981). The Genesis of Higher Mental Functions. In J. V. Wertsch (Ed.) *The Concept of Activity in Soviet Psychology*. Armonk, NY: Sharpe.

Wenger, E. (1998). *Communities of Practice: Learning, Meaning, and Identity*. Cambridge, MA: Harvard University Press.

Wenger, E. (2009a). A Social Theory of Learning. In K. Illeris (Ed.), *Contemporary Theories of Learning: Learning Theorists … In Their Own Words*. New York, NY: Routledge.

Wenger, E. (2009b) Social learning capability: Four essays on innovation and learning in social systems. *Social Innovation, Sociedade e Trabalho*. Booklets 12 – separate supplement, MTSS/GEP & EQUALPortugal, Lisbon. https://wenger-trayner.com/resources/publications/essays-on-social-learning-capability.

Wenger, E. (2010) Communities of Practice and Social Learning Systems: The Career of a Concept. In Blackmore, C. (Ed.) *Social Learning Systems and Communities of Practice*. Springer Verlag and the Open University. https://wenger-trayner.com/wp-content/uploads/2012/01/09-10-27-CoPs-and-systems-v2.01.pdf.

Wenger-Trayner, E., & Wenger-Trayner, B. (2014December 30). Learning in landscapes of practice. https://wenger-trayner.com/resources/publications/learning-in-landscapes-of-practice.

Wenger-Trayner, E., Fenton-O'Creevy, M., Hutchison, S., Kubiak, C., & Wenger-Trayner, B. (Eds.). (2014). *Learning in Landscapes of Practice: Boundaries, Identity, and Knowledgeability in Practice-Based Learning*. London: Routledge.

Wenger-Trayner, E., & Wenger-Trayner, B. (2015, April 15). *Introduction to Communities of Practice*. https://wenger-trayner.com/introduction-to-communities-of-practice.

Willis, J. (1995). A recursive, reflective instructional design model based on constructivist interpretivist theory. *Educational Technology* 35(6), 5–23.

15

MICROLEARNING IN THE WORKPLACE OF THE FUTURE

Johnny Hamilton, Darci Hall, and Theresa Hamilton

Introduction

In the past several years, we as learning professionals have seen massive changes in the corporate learning and development space. There was a time that Learning and Development was seen as a checkbox to complete – a compliance requirement that reduced the risk to the organization. That has now changed. Learning is now seen as a strategic driver of organizational performance and personal growth. In the coming years, more companies will include a seat for learning at the executive table. Learning will earn its seat in the C-suite because it will:

- prove Return on Investment (ROI)
- deliver real-time data
- provide actionable analytics
- predict workforce trends, and more.

How will the learning profession live up to the shift from minor to crucial – and why is this change happening now? To put it simply, the world has changed. To see how this works, let's explore another shift that happened a few decades ago – a shift from delightful to expectation. When airbags were first invented, Lexus was one of the first car manufacturers to include them, but it was an optional feature. The only way to get an airbag and to have that added layer of safety was to buy a Lexus. Today, airbags come standard in all cars. Airbags went from an option that was a differentiator, a delighter, and something innovative to now being an expectation – a standard feature.

Compare that to what has happened in learning. Several decades ago, instructor-led training met everyone's expectations. Then, we delighted our learners with LCD projectors and PowerPoint presentations. Soon, those were standard expectations. Then, we evolved and delighted with e-learning, mobile access, streaming video, and microlearning. All of those have now become standard. Many in the learning industry would be fine to stay here because people have come to expect these from learning – and we can deliver it. The only problem is ... the world continues to change. Will microlearning continue to evolve and adapt to these changes?

Today, social media, entertainment, and commerce have been disrupted by technology, mobile access, and new designs. People experience, and now expect, a high degree of engagement, personalization, and ease of use when they shop, watch shows, and join social media. Companies such as Netflix, Amazon, Facebook, and Apple spend billions of dollars to design, research, and continually refine user experiences to make them exceptional. We have all become accustomed to better experiences when we shop and get entertained.

Yet, what do people experience when they learn in the workplace? Typically, it is something that is less than these "consumer-grade" experiences. Current learning often is:

- content-centric, not learner-centric
- one-size-fits-all instead of personalized
- not nearly as engaging as consumer-grade experiences
- delivered to them instead of something they seek
- prepackaged rather than collaborative.

People will disengage if their workplace learning experiences do not match or even come close to their consumer experiences. But really, is learner disengagement all that bad? What will happen if workers disengage from their learning? Here's a typical result:

1. Workers won't learn much, which leads to ...
2. Their behaviors and performance not changing substantially, which leads to ...
3. Little or no impact on the business outcomes, which leads to ...
4. A lot of wasted time, effort, and money – i.e., no ROI.

Significant upscaling and reskilling of 54 percent of the workforce will be required in the next five years. Lack of professional development continues to rank among the top three reasons why people leave companies (World Economic Forum, 2018). A lack of key skills is a serious threat to their company's growth for 8 in 10 CEOs (PwC, 2019), yet only 18 percent give employees the ability to actively develop themselves (Deloitte, 2018). If businesses aren't upskilling and keeping their best employees, they will fail or become irrelevant. It has been predicted that 50 percent of S&P 500 companies will be replaced over the next 10 years (Innosight, 2018).

As learning professionals, we need to get this right. We can do better. We need to earn that seat at the business table. So how can we be part of the solution to support our companies to not only survive, but to thrive and stay relevant in this new reality? It's not about creating more learning or completing more courses. It's about designing the right conditions for learning. It's about getting the right knowledge at the right time to increase performance that drives business outcomes. We have the knowledge, skills, and tools to begin to effect this change now. By 2025, these tools will be even more robust and powerful, and our learning designs will be fully implemented. Just imagine what our work will be like in the future. In this chapter, we will explore what microlearning could look like in 2025 in forward thinking companies.

You will meet Olivia and explore a day in her work life. Although her story is fictional, her experiences, opportunities, and the learning solutions explored are all real. Her story is separated into five parts:

1. My lifelong learning is about skills, not degrees.
2. The things all around me are learning experiences.
3. My learning adapts to me, not the other way around.
4. When my learning is tiny, it doesn't get in the way.
5. I'm pursuing my dream job.

Each section first explores Olivia's story to discover what a day in the life could be in the workplace of 2025. After every scenario, you will discover what enabling technologies and design considerations are needed to support that experience. Note, this is not to imply that many or most companies will incorporate these experiences by 2025 – but there will be some that are early adapters and will be leading the way. Finally, the chapter will explore how the Learning and Design team at Providence has been designing, prototyping, and implementing the precursors to these workplace learning solutions of the future.

It is important to note that Providence is a not-for-profit health system and as of 2020, is the ninth largest system in the United States of America with 119,000 + caregivers/employees that serve in 51 hospitals, more than 800 clinics, and provide a comprehensive range of health and social services for over 2.1 million people across the western U.S. (Providence, n.d.a). Providence started in 1856 and has a long heritage of meeting new challenges by pioneering innovative solutions (Providence, n.d.b).

Olivia's Learning in 2025: A Five-Part Story

Olivia is a learning manager for Tobias Financial, a company with 50,000 employees in four states. She is traveling to meet with the executive team to discuss workforce planning for their new acquisition in its office in San Antonio, Texas. She is a lifelong learner and actively pursues opportunities to grow.

Part 1: My Lifelong Learning is About Skills, Not Degrees

Olivia's Story: Workplace Skills

Olivia leaves her hotel at 8:00 in the morning and takes a ride share service to the new office building. Olivia has been a learning manager for six years and wants to become a learning executive. Her bachelor's degree in literature that she earned 11 years ago has very little to do with her current role or the new role that she is seeking, but that's not stopping her. She's actively seeking and completing learning experiences to prepare herself in her career development.

As Olivia rides in the car, she finishes listening to a podcast about leading with influence on her mobile device.

"That was fascinating," she tells herself with a smile. She's smiling because this is the last item on her learning pathway called "Strategic Planning." The pathway had several blogs to read, a TED Talk to watch, a downloadable worksheet to complete, a few microgames to play, and this podcast. She taps "Mark Complete" on her mobile app to indicate her progress. This pathway is the last piece to complete her overall learning plan to become a learning executive. She decides to message her manager, Steven, to share the good news.

"Hey Steven, guess what? Check out my profile – I just finished my Executive Leadership plan!" Olivia exclaims.

"That's wonderful! Are you ready to take your Executive Skills assessment?" Steven messages back.

"I sure am! I'm going to nail it. By the way, can you update your ratings of my Skills in my profile? I want to make sure all my progress is tracked," Olivia responds.

"Absolutely. Let's discuss it at our meeting you scheduled next Tuesday to talk about your career," Steven replies.

"Great. I want to share some podcasts and articles I've finished since we last talked. There's this great one from Simon Sinek that I want to talk about," Olivia shares.

"Sounds good. I'll recommend some people to connect to that know a lot about his work," Steven suggests.

Workplace Skills in 2025

As we can see from the scenario above, in 2025, the workplace has become a learning place. Every role will have skills associated with them. In addition to preparing for those new skills, workers also focus on the skills needed for particular projects and how to upskill for them. These skills are accessed at the point of need, on the fly, mostly via mobile devices. Businesses will be shifting their focus in their workforce, as shown in Table 15.1.

TABLE 15.1 Workforce shifts in businesses

From	To
Four year degrees	Skills/competencies
Organizational hierarchy	Agile teams/projects
Job descriptions	Skills required

The skills that are in high demand include creativity, collaboration, persuasion, design thinking, digital literacy, analytics/visualization. Note that many of these skills are easily transferable between roles within a business.

There is also a shift from a *Push* paradigm (where content is assigned to workers) to a *Pull* paradigm (where workers seek content when needed). As shown in Table 15.2, learning needs to be designed differently in a *Pull* paradigm.

As you can see in the right column, much of this learning is aligned to microlearning in that it is mobile, informal, and social enabled. Most learning happens within the flow of work to help improve performance, efficiency, and accuracy. Microlearning is most powerful when it is mobile-enabled and accessed at the point of need. This is not a *check the box*, compliance driven activity – it is a just-in-time learning solution. Workers are empowered to set up what is relevant to them and learn new skills to advance in their career development. This is where social and peer learning happen – learning that is self-directed and empowering.

It is important to note that *Pull* paradigm complements, but does not replace, a *Push* paradigm. For example, longer form and required e-learning modules still have an important place in the learning ecosystem. It is necessary to dive deep into new or complex content that all workers must understand (such as regulations or product/services essential to the business). However, these assets are now complemented by informal learning, which is not mandatory, and microlearning, which is much shorter and can be accessed in the flow of work to address a specific need.

Workplace Skills Now

At Providence, all of our learning traditionally has been pushed to workers and tracked through a Learning Management System (LMS). In 2019, we designed

TABLE 15.2 Comparing Push and Pull learning

Push learning	Pull learning
Mandatory content	Self-directed learning
One-size fits all	Personalized learning
Send people to training	Peer-to-peer and team learning
Required, long e-learning modules	Informal content/microlearning

and piloted Degreed, a Learning Experience Platform (LXP), that was launched across the enterprise in 2020. Workers can now take charge of their own learning, skill development, and career growth by enhancing their traditional, formal *Push* learning with a variety of informal learning that they can *Pull*. Workers are encouraged to learn, track, and share:

- articles they have read
- podcasts they have listened to
- videos they have watched
- insights they gained from group discussions.

These learning activities can be accessed anytime, anywhere, and on any connected device. This vast amount of user-generated data enables our organization to identify learning trends, behaviors, and hot topics in real time. Our learning professionals are also able to respond by designing, developing, and deploying microlearning and other experiences that address these areas in a matter of weeks – not months or years.

Reflect

- How much of your current learning that you develop is a Push paradigm and how much is a Pull paradigm?
- What skills would you define for the role you are currently in? For your previous role?

Part 2: The Things All Around Me Are Learning Experiences

Olivia's Story: Internet of Things

Olivia arrives at her destination – the office building of their latest acquisition. During her visit, the things around her provide valuable information to help her live and work better.

As Olivia walks up to the building, she checks the screen on her wrist for a quick view of a 3D map of the office building. From it, she sees where her meeting is on the second floor, as well as how to walk there and which elevator to take. Her digital assistant, Sam, gives her a notification through her wireless earbuds.

"Olivia, you are 15 minutes early to your appointment. Did you want a quick bite or check the news for a few minutes?" Sam asks in her ear while simultaneously showing a café in the office building and a top new story on her wrist screen.

Olivia taps the café on her screen. On Olivia's smart glasses, walking instructions appear on the bottom of her view.

"Sam, do they have any vegan blueberry muffins?" Olivia asks as she walks to the front entrance.

"No, they do not. However, they do have a berry protein bar that matches your fitness profile. Are you interested in that?" Sam asks.

"Forget about it," Olivia replies.

As Olivia walks through the main entrance, she walks to the reception area. A security guard looks up from his tablet and greets her.

"Hi Olivia. You're from our California office, is that right?" the security guard asks.

"Yes I am. I have a meeting with the executive team here this morning. Mind if I check out some things in the lobby for a few minutes?" Olivia asks.

"Sure. The sculpture and framed pictures are enhanced. Do you need any assistance in accessing them?" the guard asks.

"I'm good. Thank you," Olivia replies as she walks over to a painting on the wall of one of the company's founders. She pauses to take a look at it, and as she does so, several icons appear on the side of it within her smart glasses. She looks at the virtual *About* icon, the artwork springs to life and turns into a short video. As it's playing, her wrist screen vibrates, reminding her that she has five minutes to arrive at her meeting destination.

"Cancel. Show me the way," Olivia says to Sam and the interactive painting fades away while the navigation dots and arrows replace them. They guide her to the elevator, second floor, and show her turn by turn where to go for her meeting.

On her way, she passes by some cubicles and offices of some of her colleagues that she has worked with, but has never met in person. She recognizes Clark's name, from marketing, in an empty cubicle. As she looks at his smart nameplate on his desk, she sees his schedule on her wrist screen that shows he's in a meeting until 10 o'clock.

She says, "Leave a message," pauses, then says, "Hey Clark, do you want to get together for lunch today? I'm in a meeting in conference room 2."

"Message saved and sent," the smart nameplate replies.

Olivia leaves and walks to her meeting.

"Internet of Things" Learning in 2025

As is evident from the encounters Olivia has in the previous scenario, the Internet of Things (IoT) is a concept in which many everyday items, such as work badges, framed art, and nameplates are connected to the Internet and are interactive. The scenario includes four types of *things* that are described in Table 15.3 below.

5G Connection

In order to power the Internet of Things, an ultrafast connection to powerful cloud-based services is needed. Throughout most populated areas, 5G wireless connectivity is available, which is up to 100 times faster than its predecessor, 4G,

TABLE 15.3 Types of Internet of Things

Types of "Things"	Example
Scannable image/objects	The framed painting does not have any integrated electronics, but its image has been coded to launch to Augmented Reality experience – accessed through a mobile device (smartphone or tablet) or smart glass.
Passive electronics	Olivia's work badge has an embedded chip in it that is easily scannable at a distance by readers. Information encoded in the chip can include data such as personal, payment, and security. The security guard was able to not only validate that a company employee just walked in, but her company profile as well.
Active electronics	The smart nameplate incorporates active electronics such as microphone, speaker, and Wi-Fi Internet connection that accesses online services in the cloud. The device itself has very little processing power. The complex analytics and processing are performed by distributed infrastructure by one or more students.
Wearable	Olivia's smart glasses, wireless earbuds, and wrist screen are devices that are meant to be worn and add a digital layer to the real world, as well as connect to powerful interconnected online services to access real-time data such as maps, schedules, and more. Next-gen GPS provides accuracy to several inches, so location-based experiences are more detailed.

and can connect 10 times faster (known as latency). Because many IoT "things" will not have screens and/or keyboards (such as smart speakers, smart glasses, and smart nameplates), people will interact with them using their voices.

The Natural Language Recognition

Voice User Interface (VUI) technologies rely on cloud-based services in order to perform the highly complex natural language processing. Spoken words not only need to be decoded from sound waves into text, but the intent of the phrase must also be analyzed and determined. Idioms and euphemisms such as, "Forget about it," that are used in conversational speech must be inferred and understood.

Artificial Intelligence and Machine Learning

AI leverages Machine Learning and advanced algorithms to process this information and refine its algorithms in real time. The more people use natural language recognition, the more accurate and efficient it becomes. That is because Machine Learning does not require humans to manually update the code and algorithms, the computer learns by itself based on its experience.

Multiplatform Integration and Standardization

Once the intent of the spoken words has been determined, the appropriate action or response is processed. This generates a query to its associated backend integration (i.e., calendar, reference lookup, payment processing, streaming media, etc.) to serve up the requested information. All of this needs to happen seamlessly and within a fraction of a second (low latency) in order to ensure a great user experience.

Quantum Computing

To perform an ever-growing array of ever-increasing complexity of tasks, companies leverage cloud-based quantum computers within their infrastructure, which have a thousand to a million times more computing power and speed than today's supercomputers. The data that is collected is highly detailed and contains many identifiers. It is also formatted in standardized protocols that facilitates transferring between systems.

"Internet of Things" Learning Now

Today, the IoT is not widely available because the technology infrastructure still is in its infancy. It's made some headway in home automation with things such as security systems, thermostats/lighting, and voice-enabled remote controls. There has been very little development in the IoT in workplace learning. However, at Providence, we have been exploring and developing experiences that are the building blocks of IoT.

Scannable Image/Object

We have explored two ways that Augmented Reality (AR) enhances learning. In 2018, we incorporated an interactive branching scenario into a traditional classroom training. Workers scanned their notebook binder with an app on their smartphones to launch the experience.

You are able to try it out by following the directions in Figure 15.1. You can also read more about this Brandon Hall award-winning design (Brandon Hall, 2018) in the whitepaper titled, *This is What Happens When MicroLearning Meets Augmented Reality: An Augmented Reality Enhanced Whitepaper* (Providence St. Joseph Health, 2018).

In 2020, the Augmented Reality technology evolved to no longer require people to download and install an app to launch the experience. Workers could now launch it via WebXR with a simple QR code and their browser. Check it out yourself by using your mobile device's native camera software or a QR code app (if needed) to launch the experience in the poster in Figure 15.2 that was used to announce a new learning platform.

FIGURE 15.1 Augmented Reality enhanced microlearning scenario
(Hamilton, 2017)

Active Electronics

Voice activated digital assistants such as Amazon's Alexa, Apple's Siri, and Microsoft's Cortana currently can understand basic spoken requests like playing music or answering factual questions. They also provide some increasingly complex interactions, such as buying things and making reservations.

In the realm of microlearning, we began developing our own Voice User Interface (VUI) experiences using Amazon Alexa in 2017 and won an award for *Best Advance in Leadership Simulation Tool* (Brandon Hall, 2017). We started with a simple skill called *Safety Stories* in which workers use the Alexa app on their mobile device or talk to a smart speaker to request and listen to a safety story at the beginning of a meeting. Then, we developed a simulated conversation skill named *Giving Developmental Feedback* so workers can refine how they provide feedback to their team. This more closely resembles an actual conversation because workers must both speak and listen during the experience. In the realm

FIGURE 15.2 Augmented Reality enhanced educational poster (Hamilton, 2020)

of VUI, the challenge is to design and develop engaging microlearning experiences in which there is nothing to see nor touch. The whole experience is based on what you say and hear. To learn more about this design, read the whitepaper *A New Learning Design Using Alexa Voice User Interface* (Providence St. Joseph Health, 2017).

Wearables

We also use the Virgin Pulse app to track our fitness and learn healthy tips. It connects to biometric wearable devices such as Fitbit that track fitness metrics like movement and heart rate. Workers can learn what their actual behaviors are in real time and take micro actions (like taking a quick stretch break) to align their performance to their goals. They can also be prompted to try new, healthy snacks at the times when they are most likely to want them, such as the mid-afternoon. Changing behavior through targeted nudges moves microlearning to a whole new level.

Reflect

- How could augmented reality microlearning experiences be used in your workplace today?
- What wearable devices do workers in your company currently use? How might those change and be better in the near future?

Part 3: My Learning Adapts to Me, Not the Other Way Around

Olivia's Story: Adaptive Learning

Olivia joins her meeting with the executive team. As the learning manager, she has some thoughts to share as they discuss their strategic workforce plan. Olivia confidently points out a few of the outcomes produced from their adaptive learning strategy, which adapts the learners' experience in real time, based on their responses.

> "Comparing the expense to train our workers using a traditional versus an adaptive 4.0 architecture, you can see here that our costs have been reduced by over 60 percent, resulting in a savings of over $7.2 million," Olivia states, as she references a chart on a slide.
>
> "Those savings are substantial, but can you be sure our workers have the same level of learning as they did with the traditional approaches?" asks Thomas, the Chief Financial Officer.
>
> "Well, it's hard to answer that because with traditional learning designs, there's very little data we can analyze beyond who completed the courses," Olivia responds.

"That makes sense – I used to think that's all we could do in learning," Thomas replied.

"We can do a lot more. With our adaptive 4.0 system, we not only can provide personalized learning and then analyze it in real time, we can take that to the next level," explains Olivia.

"What's the next level?" asks Thomas.

"Predictive analytics, for one. I've been working with Colin to map our workers' performance metrics to the data in our adaptive learning platform. This closes the feedback loop and directly connects learning to business outcomes," Olivia says.

"And that's given Brenda and me some new abilities," says Colin, the Chief Technology Officer.

"That's right. We're also making a broad range of accurate predictions based on knowledge and performance gaps that have dramatically improved our ability to map workforce planning, and with greater efficiency. Let me show you some preliminary results …" Olivia mentions, as the rest of the executive team listens intently.

Adaptive Learning in 2025

As we can see from the previous scenario, by 2025, learning in the workplace will be highly personalized, adaptive, and predictive – these are the hallmarks of Adaptive 4.0. Several decades ago, when adaptive learning was introduced, it utilized branching scenarios and decision trees. This is Adaptive 1.0 in which workers can choose different experiences by the choices they make. Then Adaptive 2.0 emerged with simple algorithms – but although there was differentiation, it was limited because the learning pathways were already preset. Workers selected different levels, which took them on pre-determined pathways of content. In Adaptive 3.0, Artificial Intelligence has created a true personalized learning experience as the system adapts to a worker's performance in real time to provide the right level of instruction at the right time. Workers will have a different experience if they revisit the content since they will presumably answer questions differently. Finally, in Adaptive 4.0, learning performance is mapped to workplace performance. This requires a high degree of backend mapping using API (Application Protocol Interface) protocols so that the learning system can share information with other business systems that track worker performance, business output, and other metrics. For example, if a worker has a number of personal safety incidents, then a safety course may be automatically recommended.

With Adaptive 4.0, executives and frontline managers will always tie learning to business outcomes, because now it can be measured and analyzed. They will place greater emphasis and value on developing and measuring training KPIs (Key Performance Indicators) within their organization. The Chief Learning Officer

(CLO) and Chief Data Officer will have greater influence in the C-suite because they will have the data to back up their business expectations and outcomes. However, a business cannot do this lift by themselves. Rather than looking for vendors to farm out the work, smart businesses will seek out technology partners with which they can have a collaborative, productive relationship so they can thrive and adapt as the technology changes.

By 2025, workers will come to expect personalized learning as the norm, and they will be frustrated when it is not. That is because the technology all around them will be increasingly personalized – so why should their workplace learning be any different? Workers will be able to:

- master the material at their own pace
- choose their learning modalities (i.e., watch, read, practice)
- learn at their optimal level of difficulty (to stay in the flow)
- access self-remediation and reference resources.

Key benefits of personalized learning include:

- enhanced learning experiences
- improved performance and business outcomes
- reduced training times
- increased engagement/participation, especially for non-mandatory training.

Adaptive Learning Now

At Providence St. Joseph, we partnered with Fulcrum Labs, an outcomes-driven technology leader in Adaptive 3.0 learning solutions that enables companies to exceed their learning and development Key Performance Indicators (KPIs). We designed, developed, and implemented an adaptive learning pilot that recently won a Brandon Hall Award in Content Management Technology (Brandon Hall, 2019), a BIG Innovation award (Business Intelligence Group, 2020), and an American Business Association Gold award for Corporate Learning (American Business Association, 2020). Fulcrum's Adaptive 3.0 platform allows workers to choose how to engage with the content via watching, reading, and practicing, and uses Artificial Intelligence and Machine Learning to dynamically adapt a worker's learning experience in real time. In the pilot, workers had the option of enrolling in our Fulcrum adaptive learning course or taking a traditional series of short videos to learn how to use a new software platform that was being rolled out. Those that took the adaptive Fulcrum course showed a 416 percent engagement increase compared to a 70 percent increase with the traditional videos. Find out more outcomes on page 18 of the solution brief titled, *Now is the Future of Workplace Learning* (Providence St. Joseph, 2019).

Reflect

- What learning have you developed or would like to develop that leverages Adaptive 1.0 (branching), 2.0 (simple algorithms), 3.0 (AI enhanced) or 4.0 (tied to performance/outcome metrics)?
- How many vendors have you established true partnerships with (rather than a service for hire) and what has been the outcome of them?

Part 4: When My Learning is Tiny, it Doesn't Get in the Way

Olivia's Nano-Learning Story

After the meeting, Olivia checks her notifications and sees that Clark wants to get together for lunch. She walks to the elevator and her wrist screen vibrates to notify her she has a question of the day. While waiting for the elevator to arrive, she taps her screen to open it. The question pops up as she waits, "What does Code Black mean?" The doors open and by the time she gets in, she's considered her answer from the four shown. As they go up two floors to the cafeteria, she submits her answer and gets feedback that she got the answer correct and she's now third on the top score leaderboard for her team. As the doors open for her floor, she walks out with a smile.

After lunch with Clark, she decides to stay in the cafeteria for a few minutes and video chat with Steve, her manager. They talk briefly about the meeting, her visit at the new location, and the turbulent flight she had the day before.

> "Olivia, that reminds me, I saw you struggled last week with a question about safety protocols. Could you touch base with Elizabeth about it?" Steve asks her.
>
> "Sure. I wasn't familiar with the updated evacuation procedures," Olivia replies.
>
> "I know these protocols can be confusing. Elizabeth has been excellent in that area and I think she could help you out. I'll follow up with you next week to see how you're doing," Steve mentions.
>
> "Great. Thanks for the support," Olivia says with a smile.

Nano-Learning in 2025

As demonstrated by Olivia in the previous scenario, nano-learning takes micro-learning to an extreme, where it takes less than a minute to complete, but occurs on a daily basis over a period of weeks or months. Nano-learning can be defined as learning that occurs in less than a minute. Some easily relatable examples include asking a smart speaker how many tablespoons are in a pint, using your smartphone to search for directions to a restaurant, and watching a YouTube video on your tablet to learn how to make a double-sided copy on your specific printer.

Learning in such a small timeframe does not disrupt the flow of work, yet it keeps the content top of mind for workers. Olivia was able to answer a question as she was going to lunch. Responses are received, analyzed, and accessible by frontline managers in real time. This enables managers to respond quickly to areas of concern and provide any additional support needed. The key here is not just learning material, it is comprehending and retaining it. Using spaced learning is a proven methodology for organizations to ensure their workers keep what they have learned.

Many studies have shown that in as little as 30 days, up to 79 percent of knowledge is forgotten (Murre & Dros, 2015). This phenomenon is called the *forgetting curve*. This means that regardless of the design or modality of the initial learning, workers will not be able to recall a majority of what they learned when they need to a month or two later. Given this, how can a company expect performance to improve?

The forgetting curve is offset by nano-learning's spacing effect (by presenting information over spaced intervals of time) and testing affect (by providing immediate feedback after questions). Studies by Qstream (Qstream, n.d.) have shown up to 170 percent increase in retention using this methodology.

When combined with adaptive learning that is powered by Artificial Intelligence, additional questions can be suggested based on worker's real-time responses or by changing business circumstances. For example, a worker may show promise in a different area and for a different business need. The system could make a recommendation that would benefit the business by filling in a gap and the worker by providing individualized professional career growth. Conversely, if a worker is not reaching required mastery, their profile might be flagged for review to indicate a lack of fit for the current position.

In addition, the library of nano-learning experiences developed could be shared beyond workers to the extended community. Topics such as making the most effective use of preventive programs, healthy living strategies, and communicating effectively can be useful not only to workers, but to their customers and to the community at large. Further, nano-learning can be used beyond the training realm. When a topic of interest needs to be messaged or a new program/location/service is offered, nano-learning can be an effective tool.

Nano-Learning Now

In 2019, we completed two pilots of nano-learning ahead of an enterprise launch in 2020 for three of our annual compliance courses using Qstream. We exceeded our Key Performance Indicators (KPI) with a 93 percent engagement rate, an 18 percent proficiency improvement, and an average of 38 seconds spent per question. For our compliance courses, we anticipate a savings of over $20 million per year due to our new learning design because training time is reduced by over 50 percent. Workers spend less than a minute answering a question and if they get it right, they move on with their day. If they get it wrong, they have an opportunity to review relevant content. In this way, they only spend time learning what they need to learn – as opposed to spending a fixed time in a course on material they already may know and then getting assessed on it.

An additional benefit is that workers' learning performance is analyzed in real time and their managers are provided weekly actionable analytics via email and access to an online dashboard. Frontline managers know who on their team currently is performing well and who needs additional support on specific items. This empowers managers to be able to take proactive steps to improve performance and address small issues before they become large ones. Explore more details about the pilot by viewing the webinar titled, *3 Proven Ways to Impact the Future of Workplace Learning: High ROI, Data Informed Managers, Engaged Learners* (Qstream, 2020).

Reflect

- What, if any, methods do you use to track learning retention?
- What learning data do your frontline leaders have access to and how current, specific, and easy to analyze is it?

Part 5: I'm Pursuing My Dream Job

Olivia's Career/Workforce Story

Near the end of her day, Olivia gets an exciting notification about her skills profile. She calls her mother, Diane, to share the news.

"Mom! Guess what? My profile was matched at work to the role I've been dreaming of!" Olivia exclaims to her mother over the phone.

"That's amazing! But what are you talking about? What profile and what's the role?" Diane asks.

"Remember last time I visited, I showed you the scenario simulations on my phone? I was playing the role of the financial executive and I needed to solve a bunch of challenges," Olivia replies.

"Yeah, all of that stuff was way over my head. How did you know what the right answers were?" Diane asks.

"There were no real right or wrong answers. Through my responses within the different scenarios, the AI created a profile with a lot of different factors like my strategic thinking and business acumen. It's sort of like a personality test – but this related to business skills," Olivia explains.

"OK, but what does that mean?" Diane asks.

"Well, what it means is that my profile matched current high-performing and high-potential executives. That basically means that I've shown that I have the mindset and skills to be successful in a new role that just opened up," Olivia explains.

"So, does that mean you have the job? And what is it?" Diane asks excitedly.

"No, mom – I don't have the job. I still have to go through the interview process – but now *I* know and *they* know that I'm a great fit," Olivia says.

"Wow! That's fantastic. That's a far cry from when I was interviewing for my first job when I left college. We had paper resumes and letters of reference. It sounds like they already know you before they interviewed you," Diane shares.

"Right?" Olivia agreed.

Career/Workforce Learning in 2025

Olivia's work skills have changed over time. When she entered the workforce, she had studied literature, which had little to do with developing e-learning. Then she acquired managerial skills and became a learning manager. Recently she has been learning executive skills for her next career step. When she was in school, she was preparing for a single focus. However, today's K-16 education (elementary through college) focuses on preparing students for the workforce of the future, one in which they will need to adapt and change. According to the World Economic Forum (2018), 53 percent of companies need to reskill and upskill their current workforce to meet the changing demands of the workplace, and that trend is only expected to increase. In light of these data, many schools have shifted to develop students' skills and mindsets (such as critical thinking, problem-solving, and collaboration) to do *anything*, rather than a particular *something* such as engineering. Instead of just acquiring a college degree about the *hard* skills in their area of expertise, students create a profile of their skills that are soft or transferable across jobs.

In the business sector, companies are also shifting toward identifying a profile of transferable skills that are reflective of their high potential (HiPo) employees, which then can be matched to profiles of current and prospective employees. To capture this profile, companies develop game-based simulations that are aligned to their organization's work activities. These simulations can be taken over a period of time in short, episodic intervals (microlearning) in which workers generate demonstrated performance data. Doing so is more reliable and valid than traditional methods of data collection such as focus groups, interviews, and surveys. Because the simulations are powered by Artificial Intelligence and are accessed on any device via the cloud, they are better than using work samples to create a worker profile because deploying and analyzing simulations can be accomplished at a scale and speed unimaginable a few years ago. Using the behavioral people analytics from these simulations, companies are able to drive business results with a data-driven approach in new ways, such as:

- Identifying current state behavioral capabilities, such as strategic thinking within the organization, function, department, team, or individual within a matter of days
- Providing custom tailored learning and development opportunities support for workers based on their capabilities profile

- Identifying areas of excellence and gaps across the global enterprise and measure worker development by real-time trending data
- Increasing retention by identifying at-risk turnover populations by mindset.

Career/Workforce Learning Now

At Providence, we have been piloting a simulation for clinical executives to generate and validate the usefulness of a new category of people analytic data. Using the Recurrence Gamulation® platform, we co-developed simulations based on current, real-world situations that our clinical executives face, such as reducing costs. This will enable us to gain behavioral insights from these contextual work samples. We will then match their profiles to other performance metrics to establish a correlation, as well as identify areas of excellence and gaps. After the pilot, we plan to deploy it to all of our key executives, as well as expand the skills and competencies assessed. We will also begin leveraging this data to move, promote, and acquire employees with deeper insight.

Reflect

- What percentage of your current workforce do you think will need to reskill and/or upskill within the next five years?
- How valuable would it be to your organization if you could match profiles of current and prospective employees to those of your high potential/high performing workers?

Other Considerations

Olivia's story has explored how the future of microlearning will be influenced by the Internet of Things, adaptive learning, workforce placement, worker skills, and nano-learning. However, there are some other issues that are worth considering when exploring the future of microlearning.

Privacy Issues

When you learn things in an informal or social learning setting using a workplace tool, your activity is being tracked. This can benefit you as you can document the learning progress you are making toward your career goals. It can also uncover some unconsidered issues including:

- What actions can/should be taken if an algorithm predicts your behavior/performance will become problematic?

- What and how much can you opt out of in terms of your learning/work behavior that is being tracked?
- As backend systems are integrated, what information of yours can be shared between them?

Is Learning Paid Work Time?

As microlearning becomes more ubiquitous, informal, and a part of daily work life, the lines will become blurred between what is formal and informal training. Traditionally, training time was easy to discern because workers enroll in an in-person or online course that had a defined, set time associated with it. You were either working or you were learning – you did not do both concurrently. Companies typically designate a set number of hours per year allowed for paid training – anything above that is not compensated.

However, as described in this chapter, many microlearning experiences in the future blur, if not erase the line between formal and informal learning, which raises a number of interesting questions, such as:

- How do you compensate workers when their learning lasts less than one minute?
- Is reading an article or sharing an insight in a group discussion compensated?
- Do you get compensated for using your own device if you are using it for workplace learning?

Integrating Microlearning into a Learning Ecosystem

How does learning happen in the workplace? Workers are doing formal learning outside the flow of work – and this happens typically on a monthly, quarterly, or annual basis. In between those formal events, workers are doing informal learning, in the flow of work, every day, week, and month (Degreed + Harvard Business Publishing, 2019), as shown in Figure 15.3.

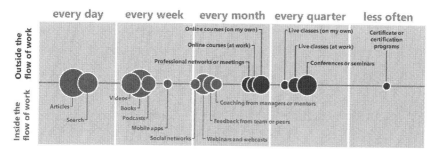

FIGURE 15.3 How workers learn in and outside the flow of work (Degreed + Harvard Business Publishing, 2019)

This is not either formal *or* informal learning: this is the power of *and*. This is balancing formal *and* informal learning. We are bringing learning into the flow of work and life. Learning is about having a robust ecosystem in which all of these activities are included.

Beyond the format of a learning asset, another important distinction to consider in a learning ecosystem is the intent of each asset. For example, when workers read an article, they may be doing so to seek knowledge, assess their understanding, see how to apply their skills, or sharpen their understanding of a topic. The SAASS framework (Hamilton and Hamilton, 2020) describes how learning ecosystems can provide self-directed learning opportunities to:

- Seek (acquire knowledge)
- Assess (determine understanding)
- Apply (practice skills)
- Sharpen (refine skills)
- Soar (track progress).

Rapid Technological Advances

We are living in a time of rapid technological advances. Gordon Moore, the cofounder of Intel, famously predicted in 1965 that the number of transistors on integrated circuits doubles approximately every two years (Schaller, 1997). That prediction, known as Moore's Law, continues to stand the test of time through 2020 – not only for microprocessors, but for a computational power as well (operations per second). As it relates to microlearning, this phenomenon means that devices will continue to become smaller and more powerful, opening the door for the Internet of Things, which support learning experiences beyond traditional computers and mobile devices.

However, in some areas of technology, the *rate* of change is increasing. In these cases, the growth rate is not linear – it is exponential. Consider the progress in human flight, the cost of sequencing the human genome DNA, or the total number of computers in the world. In each of these cases, the changes that have recently occurred in a short amount of time (one to five years) can equal the total amount of change attained until that point. This is the power of disruptive technologies and we can expect more of these to occur as the pace of innovation speeds up.

Some areas that show promise in the near future include:

- brain-computer links
- smart clothing
- nano-technology
- ubiquitous worldwide Internet.

The Dawn of the 4th Industrial Revolution

We are all familiar with the Industrial Revolution. It happened when the steam engine changed the world and brought an age of mechanization in the 1700s. That was actually the first revolution. The second revolution centered on mass production in the mid 1800s and was driven by electricity and fossil fuels. The third revolution happened in the mid 1900s and brought automated production, which was supported by electronics and information technologies.

Today, we are at the dawn of the fourth Industrial Revolution. New technologies such as Artificial Intelligence, big data, cloud computing, and how they connect Internet of Things and other physical systems are changing the world we live in. This is uncharted territory and we will experience many advances and innovations previously in the realm of fantasy and science fiction.

Summary

Imagine what will happen when you are able to implement one or multiple approaches explored in this chapter to architect and implement your own learning. Although many of the tools and technologies are new, the fundamentals of learning and design have not changed. Our core knowledge set of instructional design is still valid and essential.

However, the world is changing. Our authoring tools and people's expectations of what a good digital experience is are vastly different and will continue to evolve. Are you going to change to keep up with the world? You can choose to either get in the game now to stay relevant and thrive or you can choose to keep doing what you're doing and watch as other companies pass you by. In business, there *will be* winners and losers. Continuing to do learning in traditional ways may have been a safe approach until now – but not anymore. To be successful in the new world of business, we need to lean in to better, not safer. The point is, when it comes to innovation in learning – it doesn't matter *how* you get in the game, it matters *that* you get in the game.

Claim your seat at the table. In this new learning landscape, how can you get in the game to stay relevant and thrive? Here are a few ideas:

- Reach out to a new network and start a discussion
  - LinkedIn Group: The Future of Workplace Learning
  - LinkedIn Group: Microlearning with Augmented and Virtual Reality
  - Medium: The Future of Workplace Learning
- Explore and experiment with some of the solutions explored in this chapter
- Launch a pilot project
- Act now.

This last point is the most important. Do something in the next 24 hours – even if it is small, just do something. Then build on that momentum and do the next step.

Share your experiences with your network and reach out to us. We cannot wait to see what you build.

References

American Business Association (2020). Product management and new product awards. https://stevieawards.com/aba/product-management-new-product-awards.

Brandon Hall (2017). Best advance in leadership simulation. www.brandonhall.com/excellenceawards/excellence-technology.php?year=2017#BestAdvanceinLeadershipSimulationTools.

Brandon Hall (2018). Best approach to innovation. www.brandonhall.com/excellenceawards/excellence-learning.php?year=2018#BestApproachtoHCMInnovation.

Brandon Hall (2019). Best advance in content management technology. www.brandonhall.com/excellenceawards/excellence-technology.php?year=2019#BestAdvanceinContentManagementTechnology.

Business Intelligence Group. (2020). BIG innovation award. https://www.bintelligence.com/big-innovation-awards.

Degreed + Harvard Business Publishing. (2019). Learning alone doesn't drive business forward. Skills do. https://get.degreed.com/how-the-workforce-learns-report-2019.

Deloitte (2018). 2018 global human capital trends. https://www2.deloitte.com/content/dam/Deloitte/at/Documents/human-capital/at-2018-deloitte-human-capital-trends.pdf.

Hamilton, J. (n.d.). The future of workplace learning. LinkedIn. www.linkedin.com/groups/10495140/.

Hamilton, J. (n.d.). Microlearning with augmented and virtual reality. LinkedIn. www.linkedin.com/groups/13574716/.

Hamilton, J. (n.d.). The future of workplace learning. Medium. https://medium.com/the-future-of-workplace-learning.

Hamilton, J. (2017). What were you thinking? [Augmented reality enhanced image]. Providence St. Joseph Health. https://projects-jh.s3-us-west-2.amazonaws.com/zaps/WhatWereYouThinking/What+Were+You+Thinking.png.

Hamilton J. (2020). Providence Rise Poster Toucan [Augmented reality enhanced image]. Providence St. Joseph Health. https://projects-jh.s3-us-west-2.amazonaws.com/zaps/Curious/ProvidenceRisePosterToucan.pdf.

Hamilton, J. & Hamilton, T. A. (2020, April 9). Learning experience platforms promise a "full sandwich" of learning. Medium. https://medium.com/the-future-of-workplace-learning/learning-experience-platforms-promise-a-full-sandwich-of-learning-78453ed3edbe.

Innosight (2018). 2018 corporate longevity forecast: Creative destruction is accelerating. www.innosight.com/wp-content/uploads/2017/11/Innosight-Corporate-Longevity-2018.pdf.

Murre, J. M., & Dros, J. (2015). Replication and analysis of Ebbinghaus' forgetting curve. *PloS one*, 10(7), e0120644.

Providence St. Joseph Health (n.d.a). How we began. www.providence.org/about/our-heritage.

Providence St. Joseph Health (n.d.b). The future of health for all. www.providence.org/about.

Providence St. Joseph Health (2017). A new learning design using Alexa voice user interface. https://s3.amazonaws.com/articles-jh/VoiceEnabledLearningDesign/A+New+Learning+Design+Using+Alexa+Voice+User+Interface.pdf.

Providence St. Joseph Health (2018). This is what happens when microlearning meets augmented reality: An augmented reality enhanced whitepaper. https://s3.amazonaws.com/articles-jh/MicroLearningMeetsAugmentedReality/Whitepaper-+This+is+What+Happens+When+MicroLearning+Meets+Augmented+Reality.pdf.

Providence St. Joseph Health. (2019). Now is the future of workplace learning. https://articles-jh.s3.amazonaws.com/FutureOfLearning/Solution+Brief-+Now+is+the+Future+of+Workplace+Learning.pdf.

PwC (2019). PWC 22nd annual global CEO survey. www.pwc.com/gx/en/ceo-survey/2019/report/pwc-22nd-annual-global-ceo-survey.pdf.

Qstream (n.d.). Knowledge retention and behavior change that impacts outcomes. https://qstream.com/brain-science.

Qstream (2020). 3 proven ways to impact the future of workplace learning: High ROI, data informed managers, engaged learners. https://qstream.com/library-items/3-proven-ways-to-impact-the-future-of-workplace-learning/.

Schaller, R. R. (1997). Moore's law: Past, present and future. *IEEE Spectrum*, 34(6), 52–59.

World Economic Forum (2018). The future of jobs report. http://www3.weforum.org/docs/WEF_Future_of_Jobs_2018.pdf.

INDEX

Page numbers in italics refer to figures. Page numbers in bold refer to tables.